Carl,
Wishing you the very best of success and selling.

The Selling Chronicles

*My Journey from Caveman to
Modern Day Selling Professional*

Steven Lewit

This publication is designed to provide accurate and authoritative information in regard to the subject matter covered. It is sold with the understanding that the publisher is not engaged in rendering legal, accounting or other professional services. If legal advice or other expert assistance is required, the services of a competent professional should be sought.

CEO, Wealth Financial Group: Steve Lewit
Editor: Lynette M. Smith
Design and Production: The Martin Group
Production Consultant: Dan Seidman, Sales Autopsy

© 2009 Steve Lewit

Published by Wealth Financial Group

All rights reserved. The text of this publication, or any part thereof, may not be reproduced in any manner whatsoever without written permission from the publisher.

Printed in the United States of America

Lewit, Steve
   The Selling Chronicles / Steve Lewit
ISBN - 10: 0-9821483-0-5
ISBN - 13: 978-0-9821483-0-3

© 2009 Steven Lewit. All rights reserved.
This book or any part thereof may not be reproduced, stored in a retrieval system, or transmitted, in any form or by any means, electronic, mechanical, photocopying, recording, or otherwise, without the prior written consent of the author.

For my beloved Jessica

Table of Contents

Introduction 1
For All the Chickens on Earth 7

Section I: The Chronicles 9
Chronicle #1: Who Am I? 11
Chronicle #2: I Am Caveman Selling Machine Professional 21
Chronicle #3: I Am My Own Worst Enemy 39
Chronicle #4: I Don't Respect Human Intelligence 53
Chronicle #5: I Am a *Yes Man* 71
Chronicle #6: I Learn to be a *No Man* Salesperson 81
Chronicle #7: I Don't Walk in My Prospect's Shoes 93
Chronicle #8: I Am Fearless, or So I Think 113
Chronicle #9: I Can't See I'm Getting Exactly What I Want 131
Chronicle #10: I Don't Know That the World Works in Reverse . 151
Chronicle #11: I Guarantee Myself Failure 169
Chronicle #12: I Don't Understand My Role
  as a Sales Professional 179
Chronicle #13: I Am Linked to a System
  That Guarantees Loss of Control 197
Chronicle #14: I Don't Know How to Use My Intuition 215
Chronicle #15: I Close Like a Champ But Lose Like a Chump .. 237

The Selling Chronicles

Section II: The Modern Day Selling Structure 241

Structure Chronicle #16: The *Must List* 243

Structure Chronicle #17: Developing Your *Reality Based*
  Chain of Events 249

Structure Chronicle #18: Linking Your *Reality Chain*
  with the *Must List* 261

Structure Chronicle #19: Establishing Priority:
  Uncovering My Baggage from the Past ... 269

Structure Chronicle #20: The Power of Reality 273

Structure Chronicle #21: Where Do You Go From Here? 285

Section III: My 21st Century Selling Vocabulary 289

Introduction

When it comes to selling, I live in a different world than other sales professionals. My world doesn't look the same, behave the same, or work the same as the world of a traditionally trained salesperson, the world I call "caveman selling." I don't go for the close, I don't chase, I don't do warm-up, I don't do dog-and-pony shows, I don't do tie-downs, I don't do trial closes, I don't probe, I don't get excited, I don't manipulate, I don't try to get prospects to go in any certain direction, I don't aim for the win, I don't look super professional, I don't know all the answers, and, to the best of my ability, I try to do nothing that traditional salespeople do. Yet, I close sales—a lot of sales—and I would say, having met and coached hundreds of sales professionals, that I am more efficient and have more fun doing it.

My selling world is a mystery filled with change and unpredictability. When with a prospect, I never know exactly what, when, or why things will happen. Yet, within the course of exploring that mystery, sales are made: special kinds of sales, where they seem to fall out of the sky into my hands, just like that—no fuss, no muss, no chasing, no nothing. Simple! Easy! Mystifying! But only mystifying until you understand how my world works. Then it is not mystifying at all. It is just the way it is. This book is about unscrambling the confusion and inadequacy of traditional selling systems, learning a new language, a new way of being in your selling career, and entering into a mysterious world from which all sales effortlessly result, by themselves, dropping like fruit into your lap. The process and content of this book will go against everything you have ever been taught about our fine profession. It will test your mettle. It will test your willingness to stay open minded, reconsider things around you, look at yourself through new eyes, and explore aspects of yourself that you may not really like. It will bring you to a new reality—one that will be sobering, refreshing, challenging and energizing, all packaged in a whole lot of pleasure and enjoyment.

You will especially enjoy reading *The Selling Chronicles* if you carry within yourself, as I did, a huge amount of disappointment with the "same old, same old" of traditional sales trainings—filled with false promise, out of touch with modern societal trends of thinking and relationship, energy draining, and falling short of adding any dimension to your life except money, and, in most cases, not even enough of that.

The Selling Chronicles is divided into three sections: Section I—The Chronicles, Section II—The Modern Day Selling Structure, and Section III—The 21st Century Selling Vocabulary.

Section I. In this section of the Chronicles I share the critical conversations I had with the person who introduced me to this type of selling. My goal is to give you a history and candid insight into my thoughts and reactions to what he was saying and teaching. You may, of course, have a whole different set of reactions. All I'm hoping is that, whatever your response, it is as meaningful to you as it was to me.

Section II. The Modern Day Selling Structure section will give you the basic tools to redefine your selling and capture the vast amount of sales wealth that you are now missing. It will show you, step by step, how to deprogram yourself from the negative influences of traditional selling and

Introduction

then build a meaningful selling methodology that will improve not only your sales but also the quality of your life.

Section III. The Vocabulary and Definitions are a compilation of references that you will see throughout the book. These will act as a guide to your new language, kind of like a Berlitz dictionary that you would use when visiting a foreign country. This section will serve as a quick refresher and reminder of the lessons given, to use whenever you're thinking about your selling, planning a sales meeting, or debriefing yourself about a meeting you've just had.

Although I am pretty blunt about a lot of traditional selling techniques in this book, and although I may sound very unforgiving about the things that salespeople think and do, please know that I have the deepest respect for anyone who has ever seriously attempted to learn this profession. Selling is not easy, and it requires a deep commitment to self and family. It challenges people to their very core. No matter how you sell, as long as it's with integrity, you should be proud of yourself; and I, for one, stand side by side with you, despite my often sarcastic or uncomplimentary comments.

At worst, I hope you like reading *The Selling Chronicles*. At best, I hope it somehow enables you to go further in your career. At super best, I hope that *The Selling Chronicles* teachings will motivate you to help other professionals negotiate through this mysterious world where sales are made with ease and enjoyment. There's nothing like being in a sales meeting with nothing to do and nothing to gain; relaxing into a healthy, adult–to–adult conversation with a prospect; never getting any stalls or "think about its;" never having to worry about how I'm doing or what I should say next; never having to pull memorized lines out of a book on closing or a book on handling objections; never going for the close, yet closing more often and with greater ease than most sales professionals in the world today. These are feelings and experiences that few sales professionals ever have, or even believe are possible. Yet, they are possible, very possible. And that possibility is contained in the lessons that follow.

The Selling Chronicles is not just another selling method. It is not a gimmick that will be in fashion today and out of fashion tomorrow. It is built with the flexibility to change with every prospect, with every situation, and with every generation. It cuts to the core of human interaction, human communication, and human shortcomings. It is designed to develop a core set of values and principles from which selling takes on a new paradigm based on an elevated sense of consciousness and human awareness. In actuality, *Selling* has more to do with communication, purpose, and motivation than it does with selling. It sees sales as the result of a chain of events in which the sale is a mere outcome, like the sprouting of a seed when it is properly watered.

Moreover, *The Selling Chronicles* defines wealth from sales as more than just money. It is about quality of life, energy, family time, rest time, peace of mind, fun, excitement, self-esteem and the many other qualities that weave into the fabric of our lives, especially those that money can't buy. Having said that, I believe that *Selling* will make you richer; that is, more financially secure, but that is not the only goal. If it accomplishes only that, I would be rather disappointed, but at least satisfied that it did accomplish something.

While traditional salespeople want to win and believe that selling is all about winning, *The Selling Chronicles* takes the opposite view: that it is all about your willingness to lose, rather than your desire to win, that makes sales flower. Indeed, much of *The Selling Chronicles* is based on a simple observation that the world doesn't work as we believe it to work, but works in reverse from the way we see it. And, although that observation is simple once you see it, very few people can see that reality through the maze of selling fog perpetrated by the teachings gleaned from a selling

Introduction

consciousness developed over a hundred years ago. Traditional salespeople simply haven't got it yet. Just as you can't force the plant out of the seed, you can't force a sale out of a prospect.

I don't think anyone will argue that we live in a world where power and force are admired and nurtured; and well they should be. Power and force are important components to self-sustenance and protection. The question, however, is what *kind* of power and what *kind* of force? The power and force generated by *The Selling Chronicles* precipitates action that is founded in fundamental values such as kindness, respect, and appreciation. Yet it is not some airy-fairy notion that lacks the elements of doing business and gaining profit. It does those things, but does them for the benefit of all involved, a win-win of the highest order.

On a closing note, I want you to know that the value of *The Selling Chronicles* rests not in its words, but within your willingness to be open-minded and look favorably upon change. *The Selling Chronicles* is just a guide, much like the white lines on a highway or street lights on a city block. There really is nothing to learn in this book. What is really to be learned lies within your reaction and consideration of what is being presented. This book is not really about selling. This book is really all about you, not from my point of view, but from yours. It would be my greatest pleasure to see you learning about you, and enjoying you more than you have ever enjoyed you in your life.

Here's to good reading and great discoveries.

—Steve Lewit

# The Selling Chronicles

For All the Chickens on Earth

Once upon a time an eagle egg rolled, during a storm, out of its nest, down a big hill, and found itself nestled amongst a flock of chickens. The chickens, not knowing any better, sat on the egg, hatched it, and took care of the baby eagle.

Over the years, as the eagle grew up, he did all the same things that chickens do, pecking on the ground, playing in the chicken coop, snuggling at sleep time with other chickens, even clucking like a chicken. For all intents and purpose, the eagle was a very happy chicken.

One day, the now older eagle looked up into the sky and saw this magnificent bird circling in the air. When he inquired from his more senior chicken friends as to what the bird was, they told him it was an eagle, the king of the skies. Then, for a long time he gazed up into the sky, longingly appreciating the beauty, the strength, the freedom, and the confidence of the king of the skies.

Years passed and the same event happened over and over again, until our earthbound eagle became very old. He never stopped watching and dreaming about the eagles he saw crisscrossing the sky. He never stopped, right until the day he died.

Section I
The Chronicles

Chronicle #1
Who Am I?

I am a sales professional, a very good one—among the tops in my field, financial services.

But, it wasn't always that way. At one time I was just a good salesperson, getting by, but never being able to take it to the next level, to the top, to the fulfillment of my selling dreams. No matter how hard I worked, no matter what I did, no matter what book or trainer I went to, I would only rise to that certain level, my level, and no higher. It was like I was destined to stay there, no matter what I did or who I did it with. Frustrating? Disappointing? Discouraging? You bet, especially in face of my firm belief that we each have the power to create our own destiny and to reach the highest of potentials.

The recurring question in my mind, announcing itself after each lost sale, over each dry period, consistently drumming itself deeper into my consciousness seemed fair and simple: What on earth am I doing wrong? Yet as simple and fair as that question was, it had no suitable answer. In fact, like a germ, it brought up a host of other seemingly fair and simple questions: If I make my own destiny, why am I making this one? Why can't I get to where I want to go? Why can't I find a better way? *Is there* a better way? Is this really the best I can do? These had no suitable answers either. I was infested with selling doubt and questions, with no inoculation in sight. Then I met *him*. Then things changed. Completely!

I want to tell you what happened, what changed, what I went through, and how my destiny recreated itself far better, exponentially better, than it had ever been. I want to tell you that story. Why? Because on one level I'm proud of it and I want to write about it, share it; and on another level, a much more important level, I have this circling thought that maybe, just maybe, it will mean something to you, change your destiny, and bring you all the amazing things it has brought me.

The Background Story

I am good at what I do, but I want to get better. To improve, to get better, to change my destiny, I diligently study my craft. I spend considerable time sharpening my selling skills—learning how to recognize buying signals, when to use *tie-downs, trial closes*, methods of getting people to say *yes*, how to answer all the standard objections, and, most importantly, when and how to *close*. In fact, I spend a lot of time learning how to *close* because I know that you can't be a good salesperson unless you are a good *closer*. At least, I thought I knew that.

I also work hard at developing a thick skin so I can handle rejection, stay positive, and remain enthusiastic. I read all the latest books, attend sales seminars and, of course, listen intently to my fellow salespeople who are themselves great closers, to hear their wisdom and see how I can duplicate their greatness. I want to be great, just like them.

I have a lot of energy. At the beginning of each day I pull myself up from the frustrations and disappointments of the day before. I am ready to "go get 'em" when the sun peeps over the horizon. However, at the end of the day, behind the mask of success and enthusiasm that I ritually wear, I am really tired—tired of rejection, tired of getting "think about its," tired of not knowing why people aren't buying, tired of losing sales, tired of the pressure I feel in sales meetings, tired of prospecting, and tired of chasing. Oh, God, am I tired of chasing. I am also tired of feeling jerked around by my prospects, losing control of sales meetings, being treated like a salesperson, and knowing, deep inside, that my self-esteem is under constant attack and suffering badly. The truth is, although I make good money, I'm really hurting.

The Secret I Keep
But I won't admit to myself, or anybody else, how tired I really am and how I really feel. I simply bury my reality in superhuman effort. I have learned the gospel of "hard"—work hard, play hard, push hard. I am hard nosed! So hard, in fact, that I have convinced myself that I don't even have the tired and frustrated feelings I feel. After all, winners in sales don't have these feelings, and I am a winner. I know I am. I just know it! I am! I'm telling you. No kidding! This is my secret.

I often ask myself if the *reality* I present to the world is totally opposite to the *reality* that is boiling within me: Who really cares? And, even if it were true and someone did care, what could be done about it anyway? Selling is selling, and it's all part of the game. I'm no wimp, remember? I'm hard nosed. So I just suck it up, push it behind me, look the other way, grit my teeth, and wait patiently for the rising sun.

I do, however, like to feel that I'm making some progress. So, to continue to pull myself higher, I read a lot and attend sales lectures and seminars. After each seminar I attack the next week of selling like a gladiator, loaded with energy, relishing every meeting, pushing ahead, totally renewed in my craft.

By the end of the week, more bewildered than ever, I am back to my old self. I discover all too quickly that my newborn energy is tapped from a shallow well; here today, gone tomorrow. I want to be like that seminar leader: adrenalin in human flesh; great; knowing all the answers; fast! Man, if only I could be like him. Uh … what was his name again?

My Ability to Rebound

Running out of energy is no problem for me, because even though I am hard nosed and relentless in my craft, I know I can be harder and still more relentless. At least, that's what they tell me I can be. So, I knuckle down and, as if doing sit ups, push and push to become better, stronger, and harder. I am told I need to work smarter, longer, more efficiently; to study more, and attend more workshops. They tell me I need to pound the rock. And I do. While I pound like hell, my results are not much better: the same closing ratio, the same stalls, the same objections, and, oh, yes, the same feelings. So, I work harder still. In fact, I am convinced that my destiny is to work harder and harder until I either give up and accept my level of achievement (or non achievement) or else become the superstar I want to be. Wow, superstar! Super … star! I like that. I wonder if that means I can work more hours than ever, see even less of my family, make more money, have less satisfaction, and less fun? No one's ever really talked to me about anything like that. Hmm … I'll just ignore that passing thought, even though it sounds like the truth.

Sometimes I take a deep breath and ask myself why I keep getting the same results, no matter what I try, no matter how hard I work, and no matter what I learn. Sure, to be honest, I do make some gains here and there. But, my selling as a whole is pretty much in a rut that I can't climb out of. It is a mystery that I can't solve. Every new sales idea, method, and technique sounds different and better to me; but when I use them, they lead me to the same place, the same results, and the same frustrations. It's like buying a new hammer, with a new and improved head, and still hitting my fingers instead of the nail. New tools, same results—ouch!

So, I ask myself, what's the deal? Is it just me, or are other professionals experiencing what I am? And what about those guys who are on top? Do they have these feelings? Do they have *any* feelings? How about the folks who are just getting by, or not getting by at all? What on earth are they going through?

I'm not sure I really want to know. Handling what I'm going through is certainly challenging enough for me.

The Meeting

Then I meet *him*. He tells me that I'm working way too hard. I'm running around like a chicken without a head, and that, when it comes to selling, I've got it all backwards. *All* backwards! Not a little backwards, or somewhat backwards, but *all* backwards. Everything! Every … thing! My whole bag of selling tools and tricks. Flat out … ass backwards. Period!

So I'm kind of skeptical, but I ask him a few questions, innocent questions. And what does he do? He comes down on me like a ton of bricks. Without a blink he says, "Look, I'll answer your questions, but I want to make this one thing very clear: I can't help you."

I think I know where this is going, and it does, as he continues, "Only *you* can help you. That's the first thing I've got to get across to you if you want to learn anything, if you want to be better, if you want to have a higher quality of life, close more sales, have more fun. Don't rely on me. Don't rely on anybody. It's all up to you. It's your bag. No excuses. If it doesn't get it done, *you* didn't do it. It's no one else's responsibility to take care of you. You've got to grow up."

Now I think that's a pretty bold statement for this guy to make. It takes me by surprise, but it tweaks my interest: first, because I know that he's tops in his field; second, because he looks like he's too relaxed and having too much fun to be tops in his field; and third, well, you know, hope springs eternal—maybe he really does know something that I don't know. I ask him to tell me more.

The Selling Chronicles

> **Selling Paradigm**
> Paradigm is a fancy word representing a set of theories, opinions, and beliefs you are locked into. It's also a word that salespeople should never use with prospects.

"If you could step outside yourself, you would see that you are locked into a *selling paradigm* that is, to you, *reality*. But, it really isn't! You think you are a modern day selling professional. But you're not! You believe that you are using modern day selling techniques. But you're not! You trust that the new ideas and tools you use are new. But they aren't!"

New Is Not New at All

He continues, without letting up, without so much as a blink, "You get the same results because, under the *illusion* of newness, you keep doing the same thing over and over again. You don't believe you are doing the same things, but you are. How else could you be getting the same results? You can't see that all the books, conferences, workshops and coaches that you tap into draw from the same single core selling philosophy—it's all about *closing*. Right?"

I nod my head and start to say, "But—"

He interrupts. "Look, you're getting advice and training from the same cookbook, using the same recipes, just with a different cover and different spices. To make matters worse, it is a selling cookbook, a selling philosophy, developed over a hundred years ago, redressed for modern consumption, to be sold to salespeople in the world who are just like you."

Very quickly, I say, "But it works!"

Even more quickly, he says, "It works. Of course it works! If you use a dull saw to saw down a tree it will work. It just won't work well. **You're using selling tools that are created from a knowledge base developed for a world from the past, an environment from the past, and thinking from the past.** You have, without knowing it, bought into old-time selling, the selling of the 30s, 40s and 50s. The paradigm you believe in is mired, reinforced, and proselytized by the consciousness of millions of other salespeople like you, and it blinds you to the truth. You know the three monkeys—Hear No Evil, See No Evil, Speak No Evil—well, that's you. You can't hear, see, or speak reality. You can't see that your tools are old and dull edged. And, you cannot fathom the possibility that you have been sold a bill of goods about selling, convinced to read an old book with a new cover, and convinced further to believe that it is a new story. You are dead wrong! You won't like this and I know I'm not being very nice here, but you are, Steve, the easiest sale out there."

He's right. I don't like that. He's also right that I'm the easiest sale out there! This guy is upsetting me, really upsetting me. I've worked a long time to get where I am. Yeah, I know I'm not where I want to be, but I'm getting there. I am. So what's backwards about that? These are proven techniques I am using, not old, dull tools. I have reality shoved in my face every day at every sales meeting. I can't avoid it. I know what's going on because I'm living it. I'm not sure what his game is, but I think I'll move on to someone more helpful.

Before I can take a step away, he adds, "Now, Steve, here's what you're thinking. You're saying to yourself that you worked hard and a long time to get where you are; that you are headed in the right direction; that you are in touch with reality, probably because it hits you in the nose everyday; and that you a pretty savvy about what is happening; and that I'm the last person on earth who you think can help you change your destiny. Am I wrong about that?"

Reluctantly, I shake my head slightly and say, "No, you're right."

The Little Voice That Is

"Now, here's what's really happening. There's a little voice inside of you that agrees with everything I'm saying; a voice that is just a whisper, telling you there is a better way; that you can have more fun, be happier, close more sales; that these tools *are* old and you've heard the same things said over and over again; that people don't respond the way that you would like them to; that you lose control of your sales meetings; that your self-esteem could be higher. And you won't listen to that whisper because, if you do, you will need to change; give up a lot of stuff; rearrange your ego; move into the unknown; get frightened; and face your fears. And part of you, a big part of you, would like your world to stay just as it is and doesn't want to rock the boat, even though there are big leaks in the hull. Did I get that wrong about what's really going on inside you?"

I mumble, "No, no, that's what's going on."

"So, Steve, where do we go from here?"

I turn inside to think. His words are challenging and comforting. They're challenging because this is stuff that no one talks about, real feelings about our business. They're comforting because he is actually talking about them, putting them right on the table for everyone to see, not hiding them. I have a choice to make—walk away and keep doing what I'm doing, or keep talking, seeing what he has to say, taking a leap into the unknown. The word "unknown" kind of hits me over the head. The unknown! That means I won't know ahead of time what will happen. I won't know where I'm going. I won't know anything about anything, it's the unknown. I try to ignore the queasy feeling that the unknown brings to me. Actually, I prefer not to think about it at all; it's too big and, well, too unknown. On the other hand, hmm, if you don't put your hand into the candy jar to pull something out, you won't get any new candy. New candy or old candy? I think a long time and take a deep breath: New candy it is. I begin to hear the whisper inside me about what is really happening in my selling life. It's just a little whisper. Has it been there all the time?

"You tell me," I say. "Where *do* we go from here?"

Chronicle #1

Where Does Steve Go from Here?

Time to Get Up

He asks, "Steve, what do the words *wake up* mean to you?"

"Easy," I say, thinking that that was a very simple question, "*Wake up* means not to be asleep; to be alive, alert, and aware of what's going on."

> **Wake Up**
> The process of becoming aware. Sometimes you will need an alarm clock or a wake-up call. In selling, it's not making sales over and over again, until one day the bell rings (usually when you go to the bank to make a withdrawal instead of a deposit).

"That's right." And then, looking quite serious, he says, "The challenge you face is that you think you are awake in your selling. And, because you think you're awake, you will defend your wakefulness 'til the cows come home. But the truth is that you are not awake. You are out of touch, asleep at the wheel, on auto pilot, and selling like a programmed robot. That's the biggest hurdle I have in talking to salespeople. They fight, fight, fight; defend, defend, defend; in all kinds of ways. They tell me how great they are; how sharp they are; how many sales they have closed; how they have grown; how they are the apple of the eye of their buddies. But there's one thing they can't tell me. They can't tell me about the little whisper that says there's something wrong, that they could be happier; spend more time with their kids; not worry as much; have less stress; be healthier; work out more; play more golf; travel more. Either they can't hear that whisper, or they don't want to. Either way, the problem is that they will never know how asleep they are until they wake up. If we work together, that's what you will have to do, wake up. And, no matter how many times I might knock you over the head, in the end, you can only do that by yourself."

I could certainly understand what he was saying. I've heard that little whisper many times before, but just ignored it. When I talk with other salespeople, especially the more successful ones, they always tell me how great they are doing; what's terrific in their careers; how well they *closed* this one, and how they got that one. They always tell me, kind of like my friends who buy a lot of stocks, about all the winners; all the successes; all the triumphs. Now that I'm talking about it, it's quite amazing how well everyone is doing. But, then there's that little whisper that something is really not right, that things could be better, considerably better; just a little voice, easily pushed away as a passing thought, or a distant hope, or an impossible dream.

"Well," I say, trying emphatically, to separate myself from those other salespeople who will defend themselves, "I am pretty *awake*, but I am game to do better."

He laughs and softly says, "We'll see!"

Chronicle #2
I Am a Caveman Selling Machine Professional

He says, "You are a selling machine, a caveman selling machine."

"No, I'm not. I've learned my craft and I sell like a professional."

"You're right. You are a caveman selling machine professional."

"Okay, what do you mean?"

"Think about it. You're always on the hunt, like a caveman, for the sale, for the kill. You use caveman selling tools and caveman selling tactics. **Your caveman headset wants to lead all your prospects, like sheep, to their ultimate fate: your sale.** To get the sale, you manhandle people—tie them down, get them to say *yes,* leap over and through their objections. And you bring fire to your meetings by trying to light them up with your unending enthusiasm. When you're with a prospect, you have one goal: *Close* the sale. Every technique you have learned is created for one reason and one reason only: to get one step closer to the *close*. Your focus, like the caveman out to get his woman, is single minded, intense, and well practiced: to *close* the sale. You will do

Caveman Salesperson
An eagle-eyed *Homo sapiens* who's looking for hot prospects. This species is specifically trained to do whatever it takes to prey on other *Homo sapiens* in order to make money.

whatever it takes to gain this end. Nothing will get in your way. Sounds like a caveman to me."

Indignant, I say, "Excuse me, but what's wrong with trying to *close* a sale? Let me put this together for you: salesperson—*close* the sale. They go hand in hand. Like you said earlier, one thing comes with the other. If you're going to be a salesperson, you've got to *close* the sale. Caveman, shmaveman, makes no difference to me. You've still got to go for the *close*. How about that, our first meeting and we're in trouble already."

"Steve, I'm not surprised. *Closing* is at the heart of your selling sleep and at the core of your selling nightmare. Even in your sleep, your selling dreams are about *closing*. And that dream is acted out time and time again in your everyday selling. You are awake, but awake in a dream. Let's go a little further and you tell me if what I say rings any bells for you, okay?"

"Yeah, sure. Don't feel any pressure to hold back."

A Wolf in Sheep's Clothing

"Not only are you a caveman selling professional, but you are a very cunning caveman selling professional. You cloak your caveman aggressiveness and overt desire to win by putting on a friendly air and the pretense of immense knowledge and wisdom. You create an aura that you are smarter than the people you are trying to sell to, and you know, better than they do, what is good for them. You then put on great presentations and talk nicely with your prospects, making them think you have their best interests at heart. Some of you actually convince yourselves that you really do have the clients' best interests at heart. It isn't true at all. **At heart is one thought and one thought only: closing the sale.** You *are* a wolf in sheep's clothing."

"Well," I respond, "of course I am nice to people. And let me tell you, I do have their best interests at heart. And you're right, I kind of am a wolf in sheep's clothing. Look, if I don't sell, they won't buy. I've been down that road before, being just a nice guy, and I'll tell you where that got me: nowhere! Absolutely nowhere!"

He asks, "If you have their best interests at heart, then why do you care if they buy or don't buy? They will do what's best for them."

I respond quickly and sarcastically, "Right, like people really know what's good for them. That's what selling is about. Otherwise, most people won't do anything, even if it's good for them. That's human nature. I have to move them through the system to get them to buy. I have to show them what would be better for them. I have to get them excited, press their hot buttons, and fix their troubles. I have to make sure they make a decision, or they won't. That's my job. That's what I am trained to do. That's what sales is all about. That's what *closing* is all about."

He listens carefully. I think I scored some points. Of course, I want him to know that I am not defending myself like he said I would, but just telling him the way it is; reporting the facts, so to speak. Selling is a tough profession, which you would think he already knows. So what's up with that?

Best Practices, Caveman Style

Then he says, "Okay, let's hold that thought for a little bit and take a closer look at what you are saying. In one way, shape or form, caveman selling incorporates these steps:
- Always be closing.
- Get them to say "yes."
- Find hot buttons and use tie-downs.
- Use trial closes to see where they are.
- Always be positive and enthusiastic.
- An objection is the beginning of the sale.
- Show how the features and benefits of your product can solve their problem.

Does that sound about right?"

"Right."

"Now, where did all these ideas come from?"

Hesitant, I say, "I'm not sure exactly where they came from, but I can tell you this: They are tried and true and have been used successfully by millions of salespeople for a very long time."

"Good," he says, not hesitating at all. "From the beginning of your selling career, you have had these selling techniques and the concept of *closing* drummed into your head. But, think about it. They have been taught and used so often, by so many people, and with so much passion, that you don't connect with the fact that they were originally built for the world that existed in the early 1900s. Now, think about that. Back then, people did not think, respond, feel and behave the way they do today. Prior to the personal freedom breakout of the 1960s and 1970s, people looked to government, schools, churches, doctors, and other professionals as a child would look to a parent. There was no sense of co-creativity, partnership, mutuality, self-determination, freedom to express feelings, synergy, reciprocity, equality, and respect. If you went to a doctor, doctor knew best; if you went to school, teacher knew best; if you went to church or synagogue, the priest or rabbi knew best. People took advice and authority as the gospel. They worked for companies for 20, 30, 40 years, trusting that the company would take care of them in return. They looked to the government to solve their problems, as if the government were some kind of authority on problem solving. That is what the world was like back then."

I Put Myself in the Center of the World

"The core methodology of today's selling beliefs evolved in that historical environment," he continues. "If people looked to everyone else to tell them what is best for them, then it would be natural for selling to adopt an attitude of knowing what is best for people too. If people did not know how to work through effective decisions, then it became the task of the salesperson to make decisions for them. And with the taking of decision-making responsibility on the part of the salesperson came the need to control and manipulate people in order to move them closer to the ultimate end, the *close* of the sale. **Over time, closing became the name of the game.** After all, if you couldn't *close*, you couldn't collect a check. The environment of the early 1900s bred a salesperson whose pride and self-esteem rested on his *closing ratio*. And his *closing ratio* rested on his ability to maneuver his prospect into a disempowered position whereby the sales professional could *close* the sale and do it, of course, in his mind, in the best interests of his prospect.

> **Closing Ratio**
> A number in which many salespeople take great pride. The most important element upon which you can build and maintain a big ego.

"From that point on, the idea of *closing* gained momentum as every sales guru, teacher, book, mentor, manager, team leader, business and co-worker developed new and more sophisticated *closing* techniques. In the 60s, a vast group *closing consciousness* seemed to develop a life of its own, a reality of its own, regardless of the society to which it was addressed. *Closing* soon moved from the beginning and end all of selling, to become the *God of Selling*. Every aspect of the world of selling was, and still is, infused with one ultimate consciousness, one goal: to *close* the sale. I hope this doesn't insult you, but when it comes to selling, *closing* is the god you worship."

> **The God of Selling**
> That from which everything in selling comes; in this case, especially, the concept of closing, a sub-god to the God of Selling itself.

He looks at me closely. I think to see how I am going to respond. And I do respond, though with a little irritation, "Sure things have changed. But if you don't *close*, what on earth can you do to make a sale? Anyway, the newer sales techniques say that if you do the right things, the *close* will take care of itself. That's really where I'm headed. Not quite sure how to get there yet, but that's where I'm headed."

A Fallacy Revealed

He replies very slowly, with a sarcastic edge. "Really? Sounds terrific! Selling with no *close*. And what makes you think that these so called newer techniques are really new?"

"Well, they're new to me. I have never heard them before."

"Okay, let's go with that a little bit. Suppose new cars came out this year and the company advertised that they were totally different from anything they had ever produced in the past. Being interested in a new car, you go down to the car store. And there it is, magnificent, the nicest car you have ever seen; new colors, new tail lights, new grills, new tires, everything new. You get excited and open the hood, fantastic. You can't even see the motor. Everything is computerized and neatly covered. It looks clean, efficient, technologically superior. So you buy one. Then one day, you have to get it fixed. You watch as the mechanic opens the hood and removes the engine covering. And there it is, the engine, the real thing. And it's the same old engine that you had ten years ago. No changes. Nothing. How would you feel?"

"Duped."

> **Close or Closing**
> Closing is an annoying process that "pisses off" your prospect while you try to get what you want.

"Steve, if you look under the hood and take off the covering, you will find that all selling today, no matter the promise, is about manipulating people so that you can get to an end result that you want, making a sale. Whether it's a formal *closing* technique, an informal *closing* technique, or a *no-close closing* technique, the core idea hasn't changed; the salesperson's job is to make the sale, to *close*. Now, what you don't understand is that *closing* really upsets people. They see it coming and they don't want any part of it."

I am the Product of an Old System

"Here's the problem," he says. "You, like all other caveman sellers, still carry deep within you, in your core thought processes, ideas and concepts that were developed and more suitable for a time 80 years ago. Whether you know it or not, admit it or not, or articulate it or not, these key thoughts, taken directly from that time period that no longer exists, continually percolate and drive much of your thinking and selling, including the caveman selling steps we talked about just a few minutes ago. At the end of the day, you see them as your responsibility as a professional salesperson. And, of course, you want to be as responsible as possible. So, here is what these might sound like in your world view:

- Because you are a professional and know your field, it's your responsibility to solve people's problems for them.
- Since your profession is sales, it's your responsibility to drive hard, influence, and maneuver people to get your sale.
- Because you want to be seen as strong and invulnerable, it's your responsibility to keep your feelings to yourself.
- Since people really don't want to hear the truth, it's your responsibility to dance around it, to somehow walk a crooked line instead of a straight one, so as not to upset them.
- Since people do not like change, are indecisive, and therefore won't buy of their own volition, it's your responsibility to insist on decisions for them.
- Because you are a salesperson, it's your responsibility to deal with whatever your prospects throw at you.

"Throughout the 60s, 70s, 80s, and all the way up to today, these ideas remain powerful metaphors that drive the traditional selling process. For certain they have been, over time, softened, shaped, colored, transformed, and reworded. But to no different end, as virtually every salesperson today still enters into his or her sales meetings with one overall desire—to save people from themselves, manipulate their thought process, hide their own feelings, mistrust their prospects and, of course, *close* the sale."

My Caveman Selling System

He takes a deep breath, holds it for a moment, and then exhales deeply. Then he takes another moment, seeming to organize his thoughts. Then he says, "Look, you go into sales meetings with hope and a positive attitude.

"You have trained yourself to believe that almost everyone can be sold, especially since they will ultimately catch your enthusiasm and excitement about the product you are selling. In that meeting, a meeting which is the result of your hard work as a prospecting machine, pounding the phones and the pavement, club in hand, looking for your next kill, you diligently follow the selling system prescribed by your tribal predecessors:

- Warm-Up
- Data Gathering
- Presentation
- Tie-Downs/Trial Closes
- Handling Objections
- Closing

Everything is built for the final scene, the end of the drama, the *close*. Deep down, no matter what new technique you have studied, you know your number one goal is to *close, close* again, and to *close* again after that. Over and over again during the meeting you hear the ancient wisdom coursing through your head…. *is this a closing opportunity; should I close now or wait; which close should I use; did I miss a chance to close; can I close on the first call or will I need a second; should I try a trial close now; how many times did I try closing already; did I close hard enough and often enough?* Steve, is this making any sense to you?"

Chronicle #2

I must say that he has my attention. Even in the stuff I have read about selling systems that have no *close*, the *close* is still the objective. Now I'm the one taking a deep breath, saying after exhaling, "This time I have to agree with you. No matter how I try to focus on just helping people, in the back of my mind, ticking away like a time bomb, is the question of how to get to *close* the sale, when to *close* the sale, if the sale will *close*, or how can I make the sale *close*. It's like someone implanted a transmitter in my head. Must be the *closing* coach, or, uh, hmm, the *closing* god. Or better yet, the God of Selling itself."

He laughs. It's the first time I've really heard him laugh. It's full, right from the gut. Real. It makes me laugh too. His laugh turns inward, but his body is still moving up and down to its rhythm. And then it is done.

When Sales Go South, I Do Too

"Steve, because you are so good at what you do, because you work so hard, and because you follow this tribal selling dance so diligently, you are surprised when things begin to go wrong during the sales meeting. 'Hey,' you say to yourself, 'this meeting feels like it is going south. What on earth went wrong?' **You feel ambushed by objections, uncertainty, questions, and declining enthusiasm,** all of which you never saw coming. In the heat of the battle, you quietly mumble, 'Why can't they see how good my stuff is? I thought they were about to make a 'yes' decision. How come they are hung up on such a small technical feature? They were excited a few minutes ago, and now they look depressed. It just got awfully quiet in here. I wonder what's the matter? Boy, after the work I've done, they're now telling me someone else needs to review it. Why can't they just be straight with me?' Does that sound familiar?"

"Unfortunately, it does."

"Then you are lost. You feel the pressure caused by your prospect's objections and stalls, and sense that your respective roles have just reversed—you were initially in control, putting the pressure on your prospect, making certain he was headed down the right path, and now, suddenly, he is in control, putting pressure on you, going down the path he wants to go. Then, as you look into your ancestral caveman selling manual, you can't find a suitable solution to getting control back. So you respond by putting pressure on the prospect, the natural thing to do. And he responds with more stalls and objections to you, also the natural thing to do. Then, along with the sale slipping into oblivion, you feel your self-confidence and self-esteem slipping into oblivion with it. Numbed by yet another lost possibility, you then use your caveman strength and unflagging willingness not to give up, and go in search of your next battle, the next *close*, and probably, unfortunately, the next lost sale."

> **Pump Session**
> A process by which salespeople are pumped up, like balloons or tires, so they can do better at selling. Usually a lot of hot air is used. Known for momentary pain relief for selling failure.

His words bring back memories of my office's sales meetings, or maybe I should call them "pump sessions"—week after week, the "go get 'em, tiger" messages; the ritual speeches; the ceremonial cheers; the custom of setting new goals. Even when my companions were fired, I remember it too felt ritualistic, as if to send me a message about my future if I don't get it done. And how about the conventions, how we stood and cheered after each speech. How we got excited with each new sales idea. And then, how we couldn't wait to get home and back to business, fired up, pumped up, alert, ready, and hungry for our next sale, our next kill. Is he right? Is that group hysteria the same hysteria that cavemen experienced when they danced beneath the stars and a shining full moon, getting ready for the next battle? Am I the product of that, a caveman dressed in modern clothing?

The little voice in me provides a quiet answer, "Yes." But this time I don't ignore it.

Chronicle #2

Where Does Steve Go from Here?

Past, Present and Future

He takes a pad of paper and draws a straight, horizontal line across it. Then he marks the center of the line and writes the word *present* above it. On the left he puts the word *past,* and on the right he puts the word *future.* Then he says, "Look, you and your prospect are here, in the present." He draws an outline of two people. That's where everything happens. The past, well, it is gone, just a memory. And the future, it has yet to come, just a hope. But, memories of the past impact the present moment; while expectations of the future impact the same present moment.

> **Push of the Past**
> Past experiences, usually negative, that push you in the present moment and affect everything you do in a sales meeting. Note: Your prospect is doing the same thing.

"Think of it this way. You're standing here in the present with a prospect. The past is pushing on both of you. Mostly the negative things from the past, the things you don't like, the bad experiences you had, especially the ones you'd prefer not to remember and try to erase from your memory. Without either one of you knowing it, those past experiences color everything each of you does and says. Everything! Nothing either of you says or does in the present moment is exempt from the influences of the past.

"Now, let's go to the future. The future consists of your hopes, your dreams, and your fears—mostly the fear of losing something, like the fear

> **Pull of the Future**
> Hopes, dreams, and fears that pull at you in the present moment. These condition and impact all your actions and decisions in sales meetings. Note: Your prospect is doing the same thing.

of losing a sale. The future impacts you and your prospect in the present moment and feels like a pull. It is pulling you forward. And, depending on how each of you interprets the future, the pull of the future, in the present moment, will be different. But it too will affect everything both of you say and do in the present.

"So, there the two of you are, each in your own worlds, *pushed from the past, pulled by the future*, and not even aware of what's happening to each of you. What a picture! You see, no one's aware of that, of the forces working on you and your prospect in a sales meeting. Yet, those forces will dictate—if left to their own volition, if not considered and harnessed—how the meeting will flow. You see, that's the beginning of understanding what being asleep is all about, not seeing what is right in front of you in the present moment."

Selling Is Stimulating, but in the Wrong Way

"Now Steve, every time you say something, it either stimulates something from the past or something from the future in both you and in your prospect. Now he reacts to what you said, not even understanding why he reacted that way. When he reacts, that stimulates something of yours from the past, or the future, or both. Then you react. Being asleep, you have no idea that you are reacting at all. Then he reacts. Then you react.

> **Knee-Jerk Party**
> Typical communication method between salesperson and prospect whereby one person reacts to the other without really knowing why. Often makes the knees sore.

And so it goes, each of you reacting to the other. I call this a *knee-jerk party*, each person knee-jerking to the other. What a picture! And you call this communication. So, how does the present moment between you and your prospect look now?"

It takes me a few minutes to sift through this picture of me and the prospect sitting there, me knee-jerking to him, and him knee-jerking to me, and both of us being pulled from the future or pushed from the past, not knowing why or how or even that it is happening. Not a pretty picture. Sort of like Keystone Cops, Abbott and Costello or a Laurel and Hardy act. Although I try not to, I dig deep to find a suitable defense. Ah, I've got one.

"Well," I say, "that's not a pretty picture. But that's why I've trained myself to be a good salesperson, so I know what to say and when to say it. So I don't just react."

"Okay, that's a good point. And there *is* a part of you that is not reacting. So, let's take a closer look at that part. Okay?"

I'm getting a little leery about this *okay* thing. Every time I say "okay," he comes up with another great and challenging point. But that's the whole point, I guess.

"Sure, Okay with me."

"It's like this. The two of you are sitting there having a *knee-jerk party*. But in your mind, it isn't that way at all. For whatever your prospect says or does, you have a pat answer, an answer that you have learned from your caveman friends. So, in that sense, you are not reacting. In that sense—and this won't sound very complimentary, either—you're acting like a robot. You've been programmed and now you execute the program, so you're not in a reactive mode, you're in a programmed mode. So, we need to look at the program and how it works. Right?"

He doesn't wait for my answer, which would have been "Right," anyway.

I am Pulled in Two Directions at Once

"That program is fixed in time and space. It was developed, as I've been talking about, to fit a different world, a different kind of people, a different prospect. And, more importantly, that program can't adjust to the moment–to-moment changes that you and your prospect undergo from the *push of the past* and *the pull of the future*. And since memories and expectations are in a constant state of change, every present moment is different from the next present moment. Everything is in a constant state of change. Nothing stays the same. Not one of your prospects is the same in one moment as he or she is in the next. And what are you doing? You are either *knee-jerking* or giving your programmed response, neither of which has anything to do with the reality of you or your prospect in the present moment.

"And you see, Steve, that's what the caveman mentality is all about. Just to charge mechanically through things to get his way. Today, we would say that person is hard nosed or tough. It would be more accurate say that he is asleep, dead, empty of life. Here's the deal: **Things that don't change are dead.** Your sales system, which doesn't address change over lifetimes and change in each moment, is pretty dead. Prospects are more apt to buy (and salespeople will be less apt to force a sale) at sales meetings that are full of life. Unlike the caveman's trying to force round pegs into square holes, meetings that are full of life just evolve, are exciting, non-combative, mutually satisfying—the best buying atmosphere you could have."

"This is all pretty philosophical. Can you give me a real life, concrete example?"

"Sure. Today, for example, some of your prospects may have lived through the attitudes developed during the depression, war years, drug years, and industrial years. They may have experienced flower children, Gen Xs, Gen Ys, yuppies, and multiculturalism. Likewise, you may have lived through the same time periods, but had totally different experiences.

Now, you sit with a prospect and say innocently, 'Sir, how can I earn your business today?' The prospect immediately remembers another salesperson who asked the same question and how this salesperson took advantage of him. Layered on that thought are memories of Mom and Dad telling him never to trust a salesperson and layered onto that thought is a TV exposé he saw as a child, showing how, let's say, communism is taking over the United States, and you remind him of a picture of a communist he saw years ago in a newscast. So you ask an innocent question and your prospect gives a totally defensive answer: 'No way in the world, I just want information about your blah, blah, blah.' Being prepared, you use a programmed response to build excitement and enthusiasm. So you excitedly and enthusiastically do a presentation of the feature and benefits of your product. When the prospect says, 'Thank you, I'll give you a call,' you don't know what happened.

In meetings like that you and your prospect are like two ships passing in the night. In this example, the prospect's answer was loaded with distrust. That issue was never addressed and stayed simmering below the surface because your selling program was not built to address it. Furthermore, if the prospect somehow shifted again, maybe because he had an argument with his wife last night, the program will not address that either. Just as cavemen are programmed to go for the kill no matter what, caveman selling tactics are designed to program you to approach and sell each person, regardless of the circumstances or situation, in exactly the same way as you are headed for the close. In other words, these are mechanical programs which are the outgrowth of a mechanistic culture that ultimately have formed *mechanical salespeople*. They are simply inappropriate for today's world."

I Am the Square Peg in the Round Hole

I think I'm beginning to understand. When I'm with a prospect I do have a set of stock answers, stock *tie-downs*, stock *trial closes*, stock *closes*, stock phrases and stock *presentations*. They never change. I remember spending

> **Mechanical Salesperson**
> An old-school salesperson who believes that a square peg fits any size hole. Akin to a bull in a china closet, or believing that if you walk a straight line in a world that is changing, you will get where you want to go.

hours memorizing from a book that was one *close* after the other—the cash register *close*; the Ben Franklin *close*; the impending disaster *close*; the doorknob *close*; the hold the pen *close*; the assumptive *close*; the I must have done something wrong *close*; the silence *close*. If one didn't work with a prospect, I'd move to another, and then another after that. Now that I think about it, *closing* like that is like shooting a shotgun of selling pellets, hoping that one will hit its mark. Somewhere in the background I could hear General Custer yelling "Charge!" And like a good soldier—or, should I say, like a good caveman—I would charge at my prospect with whatever I had.

He continues, "Steve." Then, more emphatically, "Steve! Snap out of it. Where are you, what are you thinking?"

"Oh, I was just deep in thought, thinking that this might make some sense. Just some of it, mind you. Not all of it. Just some of it! I think. Like I'm a square peg in a round hole, or something like that."

"Steve, if you could recognize change, you would realize that because of that change, in every moment of time you must change the way you sell. You would handle each prospect's changing emotions and thinking independently, differently, probably never in the same way. You would see that the personality of today's prospect is quite different from the personality of prospects from years past, and the personality of the prospect of today will be quite different from the personalities of prospects in the future. You would think realis-

> **Aware**
> The state of knowing what is really happening with you, your prospect, the communication between you and your prospect, and the process of your meeting. Aware is the opposite of asleep, a disposition in which many salespeople find themselves far too often.

tically and logically. You would *awaken* from your sleep and say to yourself something like, 'Why on earth am I using the same core selling techniques that people used in 1930? If the world has changed, and it has, I would think that selling would change, and it hasn't. Cars are different, architecture is different, materials are different, clothing is different, dialogue is different, teaching methods are different, exercise methods are different, and nutrition is different. So why is selling still the same: *Close, close, close*? It doesn't make sense!'

Give Up Selling? Are You Kidding?

Once you wake up, even a little bit, to this simple fact, that you need to question the soundness of the core concept of your selling—the idea of focusing on *closing* the sale—you will have come a long way. You will then have opened a door that will, over time, allow you to see just how bizarre the idea of *closing* is, especially for the world in which we live. You will see that although caveman tactics produces sales, it produces them at a great expense in many dimensions of your life—financial, physical, emotional, and spiritual. You will see that the concept of *closing* the sale, like everything else from the past, needs to change, big time. Actually, if you really wish to grow beyond your caveman style, it needs to be eliminated totally, today, immediately, right now!"

I swallowed hard. "So you're asking me to give up the very thing from which I have made all my sales, my ability to *close*?"

"No, worse than that. I am asking you, if you can find it in yourself, to never even try to make a sale ever again. Let me repeat that: **I am asking you to never try to make a sale ever again!** And what I know is that if we eliminate your desire to *close* a sale, that's a giant step to eliminating your desire to sell the prospect so you can get a sale. That's what I'm really asking. No more trying to make a sale, no more selling! **Can you handle that idea?**"

"I can handle the idea. I just don't know if I can put it into practice. How can I possibly do better and close more sales by giving up all my ideas and the drive I have to make sales? That doesn't make any sense to me. Actually, it sounds like a lot of hooey. But, it also sounds interesting enough to keep me playing. I guess I need to know what I replace my caveman selling with and how that is going to help me do better."

"Fair enough. The game continues."

Chronicle #3
I Am My Own Worst Enemy

The ideas he presented during our last conversation are still circling in my mind. I find the whole idea of my giving up *closing* and my desire and drive to make a sale very challenging, to say the least. A part of me feels like he is full of it. Another part of me feels like there is something to what he has to say. So, in my head I've got this ongoing conflict of thoughts, trying to determine if I'm just wasting my time and putting myself behind some unknown eight ball, or if I'm really on to something rather important that will empower my jump to a new level.

By the way, being the serial experimenter I am, in my last few sales meetings I tried to approach my prospects without the idea of closing or of making the sale. Needless to say, I couldn't do it. Furthermore, I felt like an idiot. So, I just went back to what I always did. Of course I got the same results, the same frustrations and the same disappointments.

I'm Willing to Try ... But!
Trying something new and failing at it is not something new for me. Why only last year I took a few golf lessons, the result of which, in my mind, was a new swing and breaking 80. I hit the course with a Tiger-Woods-

like confidence and approached the first tee with a strut suitable only for #1 in the world. "Today," I said to myself, "is the beginning of the new, higher level of my game." By the third hole I was so far over par—and my old scores—that an oxygen tank would have been helpful. By hole number four, I had not only given up on everything that I'd learned, but I'd decided to give myself a new lesson and self-correct what the pro had messed up. By number nine, I felt like an embarrassed idiot, just as I later felt when I tried to use my mentor's stuff in my new selling experiments.

At the beginning of this meeting I shared all that with him. This was his reply:

"Steve, I appreciate your trying to implement some of the things we have been talking about. But, right now, you don't have enough knowledge power behind you to make your break from your caveman habits. All we've talked about is just one big impractical concept that may sound a little appetizing to you, but which you cannot implement. How about we agree that you will hold off any major implementation until you've heard most of the story? Then we can implement, piece by piece, and build your power base. Okay?"

That makes a lot of sense to me and I quickly agree. I really didn't like feeling like an idiot.

The Sales Meeting Exploded

"Let's break a sales call down into its simplest elements. Now, you believe that a typical sales call has two players, two components—you and your prospect. What you don't see is that a typical sales call really has three components—you, your prospect, and the communication that flows between you, usually in the form of words, data, diagrams, body language, dress, and eye contact. In business and in life in general, it is through these different types of communication, the third component, that you connect to your prospect and your prospect connects to you. It is this third component, the piece that forms the connection between you and your prospect, that gets mishandled and manhandled in a sales meeting. This mishandling comes about because neither you nor your prospect can comprehend clearly just what each of you is communicating to the other. Although you appear to be talking and connected with each other, for the most part, you are not."

"If you enter a sales call with the overriding idea that you want to *close* a sale, at some point during the sales call your prospect will feel a subtle (or not so subtle) push or pull designed by you to move him in the direction that you want him to go—closer to the *close*. That's what the caveman attitude is like: If they won't go where I want them to go on their own volition, I'll just figure out how to push or pull them there. At some point, usually rather early in the meeting, you will say something that pushes one of your prospect's *knee-jerk* reaction buttons, and he will then push yours, beginning a *knee-jerk* party. At that point, both of you are thinking that the other is just not getting it, not listening. The fact is, neither of you are getting it because there is no communication taking place; you are absolutely disconnected from each other; walking and talking in your sleep.

The Selling Barrier

> **The Selling Barrier**
> A structure manually created by you and your prospect when using caveman selling techniques. Often used for a great game of hide-n-seek, whereby neither person really understands nor speaks truthfully to the other.

"So, what happened next? Once your prospect feels that push or pull, he will immediately feel that you are not in an honest and respectful communication with him. In some way, he will feel something negative—manipulated, disrespected, pressured; soon he will feel mistrust, discomfort, fear, a double message, or that you are dishonest or insensitive. At a more emotional level, he will feel that his personal space and feelings have been violated. These thoughts and feelings, as small and subtle as they may be, send every prospect into a defensive mode. They know that there is something that they don't like or that isn't right about their meeting with you, and their dukes go up. And, along with their dukes going up, they begin to erect a barrier, a selling barrier, which gets increasingly larger and denser the more you work them over. Steve, have you ever felt a kind of barrier between you and your prospects?"

Without hesitation I answer a resounding, "Yes."

> **Stalls and Objections**
> Elements within the Selling Barrier that are defensive tactics used by prospects to get information without making a decision. Often seen as a hurdle that needs to be jumped over, as if in a race. Typically creates panic and fear in the salesperson.

I choose not to tell him the whole truth, that when I step through the door for a meeting with a prospect, I often feel that they are on the defensive before I even start talking; that the *barrier* is already there and it just gets worse when I try and manipulate the direction of the meeting. It's really strange, but I can feel it right away. It's like they are waiting for something to happen that they think is going to happen and have already prepared to defend themselves. It's not that they are not courteous or friendly; they are. It's just that they are very apprehensive, like waiting for the hammer to fall. And they see me as the hammer. So, they are in a defensive mode right from the start. That's why *warm up* is so important, to get them out of that mode.

There's More Than Meets the Eye in a Sales Call

So I decide to tell him this. "Yeah, I agree. That's one of the better things I do at the beginning of the meeting—*warm up*. I'm really good at that."

As the words leave my lips I realize that he's not going to agree. So I'm not surprised when he says with some excitement, "*Warm up*! Now that's

Chronicle #3

> **Warm Up**
> The idea that people are somehow not warm already and need to be warmed up (like food in the microwave). Denies the fact if people are that cold they are probably dead.

an interesting concept. *Warm up*. Actually—and I'm not going to be nice here again—*warm up* is almost worthless. Plus, it gives you the false sense of security that you have taken the *selling barrier* down. I'll get to that in a little bit. For now, let's stay focused on the communication. Okay?"

I say, "Okay" while I am wondering how he can possibly dislike *warm up*. It's *warm up* man, *warm up*. That's almost as holy a grail as *closing*. What on earth could possibly be the problem with being friendly, trying to break down *barriers* right at the beginning of a meeting. That's one he *is* going to lose. *Warm up*. I'll just tuck that one in the back of my mind and be ready when he brings it up again.

"So," he continues, "here you are with your prospect, the first two components of your meeting, then the communication between you, the third component. And now, with the construction of a *sales barrier*, you have four components to the meeting. That's a much more complex meeting, which, in your caveman thinking, you have the responsibility to unravel. Looking at it that way, your responsibility level to solve the puzzle, with the building of a *sales barrier*, just went up 33%."

"So," I say, trying to stop my head from spinning around, "what you're saying is that there's more going on than meets the eye. Is that right?"

"Exactly! In fact, there is much, *much* more going on than meets the eye. Mostly because your eyes don't see, your ears don't hear, and your words don't speak the right things. Remember the three monkeys?"

"The three monkeys? Yes, I remember them. I'm starting to feel like they are all sitting on my back. Get it? Monkeys on my back?"

He doesn't laugh. In fact, he doesn't even smile. In fact, he just continues as if I didn't say a word.

I'm a Person Too

"Steve, we've been talking about your prospect and his experience. But what about you? You are not immune to what is happening either. You have your own set of thoughts and feelings. The moment you feel that *sales barrier*, the first thought that runs through your head is that, in some way, you are losing the sale. Think about it: As soon as any difficulty comes up in a sales call, your thinking immediately jumps to the worst thing that could happen to you, losing the sale. **Losing the sale is the worst fear of any salesperson.** It is your core fear—another sale is biting the dust. Panic, either minor or major, erupts. With the intensity of a man about to lose his life, with your caveman fire ignited to protect yourself from disaster, the only alternative you have is to dig deeply into your bag of selling tricks to try and hunt harder—not for your prospect's sake, but for yours. You see, Steve, you will, under all circumstances, do just about anything to avoid feeling the pain of not being able to *close* or of losing the sale. You absolutely, unconditionally, always want to get rid of this, your deepest selling fear, as quickly and as decisively as possible.

> **Fear**
> The root of all your selling problems, issues, hopes, concerns, fantasies, and disturbances. Typically hidden by a severe case of false bravado to the extent that the salesperson believes it is nonexistent. (see *Denial*.)

"So, you drive harder with the stuff you've learned. And, of course, the prospect feels your drive and immediately, in self defense, reinforces the *selling barrier* that you are trying to overcome, which of course causes a *knee-jerk* reaction from you, and then his reaction to your reaction. All the while, the *selling barrier* is growing as large and as strong as a wooly mammoth."

I'm Stuck Like a Chipmunk

"It is a never ending cycle that ultimately ends in a stall that comes in the form of 'I need to think about it.' Then you're off to the caveman *chase*, trying to corner your prospect and move him or her out of the 'think about it' mode. 'Just what is it you need to think about?' you ask, innocently. Or, 'What will change between now and a week from now that will make any difference?' Or, 'Thinking about it is usually a sign that I didn't explain something correctly. What might that be?' Then it's calling, follow-up letters, answering machines, more stalls, and more chasing. You, at this point, have lost all control of the sales meeting, which in turn, makes you feel disempowered and ineffective. At the end of the day, you're exhausted and you don't know what went wrong. So, like a diligent tribal warrior, you go back and study your tools of warfare, only to have a similar thing happen at the next meeting, and the meeting after that."

The Signs Are All Around Me

"Steve, the signs are all around you, but you don't want see them. Because when you make sales, you think you're on the right path and just need to better learn how to hunt and kill. You are blind to the disturbing nature of the conversations you are having; the divisiveness of your method; how you really feel, and the false sense of 'helping others' when indeed, your only real desire is to help yourself. You sense the *selling barrier* that is between you and your sale, and your *knee-jerk* reaction is to dig deeper into a toolbox built for a different time and place so that you work harder at your sale. When it is all said and done, you have a mess on your hands, an unhappy prospect, a lost sale, **and no clue as to why.**

"Steve, you can't control what your prospect does. But, you can control what you do. Or, at least, you would like to think that you can control what you do. Pre-programmed actions, or *knee-jerk* reactions, are beyond your control. They almost happen by themselves. You don't have the power to stop them or alter

> **Chase**
> A college-like effort to catch what you want. Often the result of teasing by the prospect, who appears irresistible to you.

them. That's why they are called *knee-jerk* or pre-programmed. Think about it: If you can't control yourself, and your prospect can't control himself, how successful can that meeting be? You are your own worst enemy because of your inability to control yourself, your inability to handle your emotions, your inability to see the *push of the past* and the *pull of the future* in proper perspective, and your inability to see how all this compounds your difficulties at every sales meeting. You see, you worry about *closing* while ignoring the most critical factor in your sales meetings, you!"

"Me? I'm the problem? Is that what you're saying?" The words come out with a little bit of an edge. I have always seen myself as a very nice person and a person who knows what he is doing. Now my prospects, well, they're another story. I'm not sure he realizes how difficult prospects can be and how hard you have to work with them to make a sale. How can I be the problem? He's got that backwards. I'm really the solution, not the problem.

"Yes," he replies, "that's what I'm saying. Really pisses you off, doesn't it? Offends you. Puts you in the center of the storm. Right?"

Abruptly, "Right!"

"Can you control anything about your prospect?"

"No, I can't. Not really. Actually, not at all."

"Now tell me candidly, how you are at controlling you; not only in selling situations, but in other aspects of your life—dealing with your spouse; getting angry at the guy that cuts you off; getting upset because you have to wait for your food; annoyed at your children because they won't do what you tell them; frustrated with your assistant because he misses an appointment in you calendar. Tell me candidly, I mean really candidly, on a scale of 1 to 10, 1 being out of control, 10 being in full control, where would you put yourself?

"I'd say about 7."

"And, you won't like this at all, but I'd say the truth is about 2, especially when it comes to selling. You are out of control and cannot see or don't want to see through your programmed, mechanical, knee-jerk, pushed and pulled reactions to each event that confronts you in an ever-changing world. Now, we have a different opinion. I see you differently than you see yourself. Interesting, isn't it? Okay, suppose you're right. Then we have to get your personal control center from a 7 to a 9 or 10. But, suppose I'm right, we have to get your personal control center from a 2 to a 9 or 10. If we can accomplish either, your selling will improve. So, let's leave 'who's right' on the table and agree that there is some work to do. Okay?"

"Okay," I say. "What's next?"

Where Does Steve Go from Here?

The Denial Story

"Steve," he begins, "Let me see how you relate to this simple story."

> Two children are playing together. After a while the playing gets rougher as one child starts chasing the other while batting him over the head with a broom. I walk into the room and grab both kids by the collar to stop the ruckus.
>
> The kid with the broom starts screaming at me, "What are you doing? Leave me alone! What are you doing?" and tries to pull away from me while kicking and screaming as hard and loud as he can.
>
> When I get him to quiet down a little, I say to him, "You're asking me what I'm doing. Now I'm asking you what on earth you are doing? All I can see is that you're beating your friend here over the head with a broom."
>
> The child looks at me indignantly. "Well, of course I am, some

friend he is, he keeps telling me what to do. Screaming at me how I should do things. He never stops!"

"Telling you what to do? What is he telling you to do?"

"Yeah, telling me what to do. He just keeps yelling at me, 'Stop, don't hit me again. Stop, don't hit me again!'"

We laugh together. He asks, "Now, Steve, what do *you* make of that story?"

"I think the little kid with the broom has a problem."

Denial
An unconscious defense mechanism used to reduce anxiety by denying thoughts, feelings, or facts that are consciously intolerable. Otherwise known as the elephant in the room.

"Yes he does, it's called *denial*. He can't see that what he is doing causes the response that he is getting from his friend. And in that *denial* he takes himself out of the picture, puts his friend in the center, and interprets his friend's remarks from a point of view that is exactly opposite of what is really happening. That's what *denial* does.

"When we see things, but don't recognize them, or recognize them but don't want to admit them, that is a big part of being asleep, out of touch with *reality*. **Waking *up* means stepping out of denial.** Stepping out of *denial* means that, instead of creating *knee-jerk* or programmed reactions to your own and your prospect's words and emotions, you are able to identify the appropriate action for each situation. And, as each interaction between you and your prospect is different, changing, what is appropriate in each moment will be changing too.

"Let me put it another way Steve, and let's focus on you, because you are the only one you can control. Imagine that you own a boomerang and you decide to toss it out in the field. So, you reach back and hurl it as hard as you can and off it goes. And then you forget about it. A few moments later, that boomerang whacks you in the behind and you're stunned.

Chronicle #3

'What the heck was that? Geez, a boomerang just kicked me in the butt! Who the hell would throw a boomerang while there are people out here in the field? Geez, some people are so damned inconsiderate. That really upsets me. Damn, that hurts!'"

No One Likes Being Woken Up—Especially Me!

"You see, if you could step out of denial and see that you're the one throwing the boomerang, you have two choices, to either not throw it, or get out of the way after you throw it. Likewise when you are sitting with you prospect. He's like a boomerang helper. If you throw something at him from your *denial,* he's going either boomerang it back to you (you won't see it coming) or let it boomerang by itself back to you (and you won't see that coming, either). Now if your prospect throws something at you from his perspective of *denial,* and you are *awake,* you won't boomerang it back to him (if you do, he'll get really upset) or—and this is a great thing to do—you can step aside and let whatever he threw at you come back of its own accord and kick *him* in the behind. Now imagine that: He gets hit with his own boomerang and he sees you as an innocent bystander, having nothing to do with it. And when he gets hit with that boomerang, it may be enough to *wake him up* to buy what he really needs to buy to fix his problem. You see, people will buy if they are *awake* and out of *denial.* They will want to fix their problems and rid themselves of emotions associated with their problems. Most of the time, you just have to get out of the way."

"So, in that case, I wouldn't have to do any *closes* of any kind?"

"None at all. Not necessary. Once your client wakes up, he'll take care of himself. The problem is that **if *you* try and wake him up, he'll get all upset with you.** Let me ask you this: If you decide to wake up a friend, or your children, or your wife from a nap, how do they treat you when you are waking them up?"

"They don't like it."

"Right, so why put yourself in that position? Now if they wake themselves up, even if they are an hour late for an appointment, they won't get angry at you, they'll be angry at themselves. And if they are hurt bad enough, let's say they lose a job because they didn't get to a job interview on time, then they will decide to buy a good alarm clock. They won't have to be *closed* at all, because they have awakened from their denial and started to take care of themselves in an appropriate way."

"But, how can I get myself out of denial when I am in denial and I don't know I am in denial? I deny my denial."

"Steve, you're starting to sound like Yogi Berra! But, that's the question of the day. That's why I say I can't help you. I don't want to wake you up. But if you want to wake up, get out of denial, see yourself, your family, your kids, and your prospects clearly, for whom they really are, for what they really can do, then you have to see yourself that way first; and only you can make that decision. I'll just keep doing my little dance here and you can do whatever you want."

There's No Denying My Denial

"So," he continues, "The first step in getting out of *denial* is to admit that you might be in *denial*. That's a big, big step. Just keep looking. Step back every time you can and look at yourself. Sit back for a few moments with an open mind, putting aside your failures and successes, your ideas about selling, your core beliefs about *closing*, and consider that there may be another paradigm, another viewpoint, another path, another system, that will deliver more sales, more peace of mind, greater self-esteem, and superior relationships.

"Getting out of denial is not easy. It requires you to allow yourself to blow up many, if not all, of the things that you believe about yourself and about selling. Every fiber in your being will fight against change of

Chronicle #3

> **Conscious**
> Alive in the moment. Not mechanical. Non-reactive. Not pre-digested. Not knee jerk. Not robotic. Not predetermined. In other words, a state in which you have very little experience in your selling.

this kind. To blow up like this, you have to take a step into the *unknown*. You have to let all the thoughts and beliefs that have become old friends and the foundation of who you are and about your selling life evaporate. You must go against a stream of archaic selling unconsciousness, a mountain of closing frenzy that has been nurtured and promoted by selling professionals throughout history. **You must balk at the idea that people need to be sold or otherwise they won't buy.** You have to come to see that your core selling beliefs are akin to the caveman myths that 'women can't think,' that 'the man rules the household,' that 'you have to fight for what you want,' or that 'winning is everything.' You have to diligently confront your ego, why you do things, what are your true motivations. You need to *waken* yourself to the same alertness level as that of a lion on the hunt, and then harness that alertness to see that denial because it's your greatest enemy. It blinds you from the truth about yourself. You must move into a state of being really conscious about your selling and what you are really doing. You must take the first step and develop the willingness to blow up your

> **Unconscious**
> The opposite of conscious. Remember what it was like to be in college?

current selling paradigm, to explode the myth that you are living in, and to step into the unknown. That is what our conversations are really all about."

I am kind of stunned into silence. I feel like mashed potatoes. There's a part of me that wants to whack him over the head, just like the little kid in the story, with a broom.

I like—and I don't like—what I'm hearing. I feel like I've just been nudged out of my comfort zone, not by him, but by me. He just said his piece and I listened, didn't walk away, so it must have meant something to me. I find all this very tiring; makes me feel like taking a nap. Well, maybe I'm waking up from a nap. I don't know. But, what I do know is that I want to hear more.

Chronicle #4
I Don't Respect Human Intelligence

When we meet this time I feel more prepared. Now, I'd like to say that I'm more prepared to be open-minded or to work harder at seeing through the *denial* that I can't see or something like that. But, to be honest, I am really prepared to be more defensive. That's right, defensive, just the kind of defensiveness that he said I would ultimately fall victim too. Well, victim I am, defensive I will be.

My change of heart did not come easily. I've given what he has said a lot of thought. I mean a *lot* of thought. It's not that his point of view has no merit. That would be unfair. But his point of view, in my mind, is divisive in that it undermines everything I have done and furthermore does not acknowledge that there is any good in all the work that I've diligently completed over the years. It's one thing to say that I need improvement on this or that. But it's quite another to say that I need to throw out the baby with the bathwater, including the perspective I have of myself, denial or no denial: Just throw me and my caveman selling system out.

Not only that, but let's say I throw it all out and what he has to offer is not really any good. What about that? Then I'm left between a rock and a hard place. I will have undermined the selling system that, at least, has given me some results, and I will not have a new system to replace it. Talk about being in a bad place. How bad is that?

And just let me add one more thing while I'm on a roll. This guy kind of scares me. Not a bad scary; but just scary, if you know what I mean. He seems to have a point of view about everything I say that makes me question my point of view about everything I say. There's no foothold I can find that makes me feel comfortable. None! It's like I put my foot down here and he shows me another angle and I'm off balance. So, then I put my foot down there and he shows me yet another point of view and I'm off balance again. So, not only am I a caveman, I'm an off-balanced caveman. I'm thinking that the caveman I know is better than the *reality* person I don't know.

At one time in my life I thought I wanted to be an Aikido master. Aikido is a martial art form where you don't confront your enemy or use your power directly at him, as in a kick or a punch. Instead, you align your power with your combatant and, by doing so, take it from them. So, for example, if you came at me, let's say to push me or knife me, I would start to move in the same direction you are moving. Soon we would be moving together. Once I have aligned myself with your energy, I can then begin to turn you where I want you to go, or use your energy to flip you or keep you off balance. If you've ever seen a movie with Steven Seagal, a Master of Aikido, you know what I'm talking about. Well, this guy is like the Steven Seagal of selling. I feel like he can flip me, toss me around, get me off balance, and do whatever he wants in relation to what I'm thinking, feeling, or saying. The strange thing is, you can't see it coming. All of a sudden you're on your back saying to yourself, "How on earth did I get here?"

He Shows Up, and So Do I
Well, here he comes, a pleasant smile on his face as usual. It's not that he has one of these smiling, shiny faces all the time, because he doesn't. He

Chronicle #4

is actually quite serious. Despite his challenging remarks, he is a friendly sort of dude, and I did promise him I'd do my best, so I will. But, at the same time, I'm not just going to lie down and say "Okay, right, I agree" to him without saying my piece, defensive or not.

"Steve, good to see you. I was thinking on my way over that you might not show up for our appointment. I wonder why I was thinking that? Any ideas?"

I can't believe that he's opened the door for me to say my piece. "Sure," I say. "You've only asked me if I'd be willing to throw out the baby with the bathwater, and I'm the baby and all the work I've done is the bathwater. That's a bit challenging, and I don't even know if your stuff really works!"

"Well said." His voice is actually very gentle and appreciative. "Perhaps we should give it a rest. Continue some time in the future. You've been doing what you are doing for years. Waiting a little longer certainly won't make much of a difference. If the dust settles a little, you might even decide that this is more trouble than it's worth and keep going in the direction you are going now. Does that make better sense for you?"

"No, that doesn't make any sense to me." I am again a little irritated. "If there's a better way, a so-called more modern way to sell, where I and my prospects will do better, where my life will be easier, where my sales volume will be higher, I want to know about it. I can always keep doing what I'm doing."

Now I've said it. I can see the baby and the bathwater headed right for the drain. It's like he created this vacuum and I was sucked into it. Am I really willing to do this? I guess I am. I can hear the bath water gently gurgling away.

After a moment, I add, "We were talking about *denial*. Okay, I'm in denial. There's lots of stuff about me that I either don't tell, won't tell or don't see, I'm sure. Talk to me more about how that impacts me and my prospect at a sales meeting."

"Oh yes, *denial*. That's quite a topic. Kind of like trying to understand the inner meaning of alphabet soup. Okay, let's start here. Since you live in *denial,* you can't have any idea of how little you respect your prospect's intelligence. You think you have respect for your prospect's intelligence, but you don't. That's *denial* in action."

Who Knows What's Good for Whom?

"Look, at the foundation of your caveman selling system is the idea that people really don't know what is good for them, that buyers are liars; prospects will never talk straight with you; they're poor decision makers; and they don't know how, or won't make, a buying decision unless they are somehow prodded, manipulated, or demanded to do so. While your experience is that prospects actually do behave this way, your *denial* does not allow you to see that it is a self-fulfilling prophecy, where you play the role as both the instigator and the solution.

> **Self-Fulfilling Prophecy**
> Something you bring upon yourself by what you do. In selling, it's stalls, objections, *think about its*, and virtually every other negative thing that happens to you in a selling situation. The common remedy to the Self-Fulfilling Prophecy is to blame someone else as the cause of your troubles. Creates a temporary feel-good moment that instantly dissipates when the problem soon reappears.

"Let's take a closer look at how this works. Remember, in your system and thinking, your main goal is to *close* the sale. In an effort to control the interview and reach your goal, **you will push, pull, or manipulate your prospects** to move in a specific direction that they are, in all likelihood, resistant to travel. They want to tell you how well they're doing and you try and punch holes in their thinking and show them how many mistakes they are making. They want you to know how good the product is that they are currently using and you want to show them how it is not the right one for them. They want to go left and you want them to go right. Why? Because if you can get them to go right, in your mind, you think that you are getting closer to the *close*, closer to the sale.

"Steve, have you ever gotten lost with the family in the car?"

"Once in a while, when we've gone on vacation."

"Okay. Put yourself back in the driver's seat, your wife next to you, and your kids in the back seat. You're driving to your vacation destination. Suddenly it hits you, you're lost. What do you do? Hit the next gas station for directions? No! Of course not! You have the situation in hand. You're in charge. Even an hour later, with a chorus of pleas to stop ringing in your ears, do you stop? No! The right road is just around the next bend. And on you go—unrealistic, stubborn, ashamed, whatever. You think you're getting closer to your vacation destination, but you're not. That's the same thing that happens when you try and take your prospect to your *close*. You have directions, but they are the wrong directions. You think you need to go this way or that to get to the *close*, but you don't ask. That's *denial*. It is also *disrespect*!

"Does that make sense to you?"

Every Action Has an Equal and Opposite Reaction

"Sure," I say. "I'm always looking for the opening to lead the prospect to the *close*. That's the role of *hot buttons, tie-downs, trial closes,* and getting people excited about what I do."

He stands up and puts his hand on my shoulder. Then, out of the blue, he gives me a slight push. Of course, I push back to keep my balance. Then he pulls me towards him, and I respond by pulling back, again, to keep my balance.

Then he says, "See how you pushed back? Even when I pushed you ever so slightly, you pushed back. And when I pulled you, ever so slightly, what did you do? Pulled back! Right? Now, put yourself in your prospect's shoes. He wants to go left and you want him to go right. So you push or pull, ever so slightly, but it is nonetheless a push or pull. Once the prospect experiences the discomfort or pressure from your actions, even a little bit, he or she will always move in self-protection, to get back to balance, to comfort, by pushing or pulling back. In the selling world, your prospect does that by erecting the *selling barrier* we talked about earlier.

"**Steve, you need to understand that your prospects have been conditioned by hundreds of other cavemen salespeople who have the same closing mindset you do.** All your prospects, no matter how nice and friendly you are, carry with them an expectation that you will, sooner or later, go for the *close* and that is your singular interest and focus. Even if the sales call starts nicely during your ancient technique of *warm up*, your prospect will soon see through your disguise and realize you are no different from anyone else who has ever tried to sell them.

"The selling barrier that your prospect then erects is filled with his best defense, lies, stalls, objections, non-decisions and misdirections. All prospects feel that these moves create a protective shield to fend against your core desire to *close*. Seen clearly, the *sales barrier* is just a superficial barrier of protection created as a reaction to you yourself. It is an effect, a layering, a wall that is created by you through your prospect. Once erected, it prevents you from communicating with your prospect in a way that he or she would really like; and in a way that you would like as well—with mutual ease, truthfulness, trust, and respect."

"Okay," I say, "but how does that connect with my not having respect for human intelligence?"

Is the Doctor In? And Who Is the Doctor, Anyway?

"Now, Steve, please ask yourself *this* question: Why is it that you feel it is your responsibility to move your client, if he won't go there himself, in one direction or another? How would you answer that?

Chronicle #4

"Because a prospect has his own way of looking at things. And if I let him go his way, he will probably get really confused, or just go around in circles, or won't see what I see. After all, I am the professional. Hey, if someone goes to the doctor, the doctor doesn't let them ramble away and tell him, the doctor, what to do. He steps in and says I see this, I see that and here's the medication you need to take to get better. So, I'm the doctor and my prospect is the patient. That's the way it works."

"Doc," he says. "That's good, very good. And that's just the point. You think that you are still living in an era where people go to doctors, lawyers, accountants, banks, and other professionals, and look up to them as a child would look up to a parent and say, 'Tell me my problems and give me the answers,' or, better yet, 'Fix me, please fix me!'

"Modern doctors take a very different approach. Sure, they have different fixes for different ailments. But before they make any recommendations, they are going to spend a long time with you exploring your pain, letting you take the lead about what hurts and where it hurts. And then, when it comes to recommending a medicine, they will consult with you about their experience using one type versus another; the benefits and drawbacks. They will give you the options and then you will make the decision. It becomes a *co-creative* effort rather than a *hierarchical effort,* i.e., parent to child.

"When you take the position that you can tell your prospect what is wrong with him or her, give him the cure for what is wrong, and that you know better what is good for him, better than he knows for himself, the *selling barrier* will continue to deepen. In fact, by your taking a hierarchical posture, your prospect, at some point, will actually see you in a hierarchical role, see you as his parent and begin, unknowingly, to treat you just that way, like a parent, rather than a professional. Think about it in relation to the *push of the past* that impacts the present moment with your prospect. You say something to him, and it reminds him of conversations he had with Mom or Dad."

Is That Mom or Dad I Hear in the Background?

"For example, you say to your prospect that based on your experience you know that it would be good for him to buy your planning services. It reminds him of conversations with Dad that went something like this: 'Now son, you listen here. Dad knows best and you need to work harder in school.' Then your prospect talks to you exactly like he would talk to Dad, defensive and rebellious. In this same way, everything you say to your prospect will be filtered through old memories; likewise, everything he says to you will be filtered through your old memories. In either case, the *selling barrier* will deepen and thicken as each of your responses becomes more loaded with stuff from the past. Steve, I've been rattling on. Do you see what's happening here?"

"Actually, I think I do. I want to *close*. My prospect takes a direction which I think is moving away from an opportunity to make a sale. I push or pull him in another direction. At the same time, I take the attitude that I know what is good for him, like a doctor, and that he should listen to me. This pushes all kinds of buttons in him from the past. That, combined with my push or pull ignites his energy to build the *sales barrier*. I respond with my own stuff and it ignites his energy even more. We keep doing this dance until he balks; you didn't say that, but I believe that's what will happen. And, to top it all off—you didn't say this either—since I am in *denial* I can't see that a good deal of the *sales barrier* is a result of what I bring to the table in terms of my attitude and how I approach my prospect. So, how did I do?"

I am very proud of myself. I also believe that I'm starting to get what he's talking about.

"Steve, I bow down to you." He gets up and bows like he's on stage. "That was right on. So, now the question is: Why do you adopt this hierarchically superior attitude of knowledge in the first place?"

"Yeah, that's a good question."

Chronicle #4

> **Disrespect**
> Result of the salesperson's belief that he knows more than his prospect and has superhuman powers that can solve the prospect's problems. Often a parent-child type of thinking.

"Think about how you were brought up. Chances are that it was in a hierarchical setting, where Mom and Dad were the rulers of the household, always telling you what to do, rather than a co-creative setting, a setting where everyone participated equally and decisions were made in the household as a single unit or team. Is that right?"

"Right. Mom and Dad were pretty conventional."

"So, when you take the position that you know what is better for someone than they know for themselves, you are really expressing your belief that your prospect is half empty rather than half full. You see him in his limitation because you don't believe that his knowledge and experience over the years of his life will serve him well. There is no room for *co-creativity* because, in your mind, he can't create. In your mind he doesn't know enough, is not aware enough, cannot decide enough, does not change enough, and doesn't understand enough. You, of course, are there to bail him out. How lucky can he be—you become the Dad and your prospect becomes the child? And that, my friend, **is what *disrespect* is all about**—devaluing the knowledge and ability that each person has about how to best manage his or her life. You see, no one respected what you brought to the table as you grew up, and you are passing that same *disrespect* along to your prospects."

My Opinions Didn't Count

"So, let me get this straight," I say. "No one really valued my opinion as I was growing up. I agree with that. Our family wasn't very high on family discussion. It was more like, 'Steve, do it because I told you to do it.' So somewhere inside me I want to do the same thing with my prospects, that they should do things because I told them too. Then, when they don't, I have to push or pull them so I can get to the *close*, which is the object of my meetings all the time. When they feel that push or pull, they hide behind the *sales barrier*, and I get my standard stalls and objections like, "You know Steve, I just need a little time to mull this over. How about you give me a call in two weeks or so?" Then it's onto the chase. I get the exact opposite results from what I want or expect."

I can see it clearly in my mind, my taking the position of authority over my prospect. I *am* the professional and he is just a lowly prospect. I, as a pro, should know what's best, and he, as a prospect, should listen to me. Then I have the thought, 'Well, I do know what's best and he *should* listen to me. That *is* the reality of most situations. My prospects *do* look to me as an expert in my field. Yet, if I outwardly accept the position of authority they so generously endow upon me, they get turned off because I remind them of their own disrespected history as well.

"So I *disrespect* them, which reminds them of being disrespected themselves, which causes them to disrespect me, which causes me to disrespect them even more. It's a vicious cycle. How do I get out of it?"

"Now that is a great question. Let's take a look."

Where Does Steve Go from Here?

Everything Has a Charge

As we are talking, he takes out another piece of paper, and this time he draws a triangle. In the center he draws a circle and inside the circle he puts the word "INFORMATION." Then, on the peak of the triangle he writes the word "NEUTRAL." On the lower left corner, he writes the words "NEGATIVE CHARGE." And on the lower right corner of the triangle, he writes the words "POSITIVE CHARGE."

Then he says, "Take a look at this triangle. It will tell you a lot about how people really behave and what you should be looking for when you sit with

Chronicle #4

a prospect. Once you know how people work, then it becomes a much easier task to align yourself with them and create a different and more productive atmosphere than you find at your traditional caveman sales calls.

"Let's begin with information. Information reaches your brain by way of your physical senses: seeing, hearing, touching, smelling, and tasting. When you are with a prospect, most information flows via seeing and hearing. That information is processed by the brain. What the brain does is essentially break that information into little bits of data, electrical charges, which give you an intellectual understanding of the data. It then zips that data to different parts of your body. During the zip, your body has a chemical reaction to the particular kind of charge being zipped, which creates a feeling in you, either a positive or a negative emotional feeling about the intellectual data. It is very important that you understand this. All information, all data, all intellectual understanding created in your brain through your senses is neutral. It carries in itself no emotional charge. It's only when your body processes the intellectual data packs that an emotion, either positive or negative, is created."

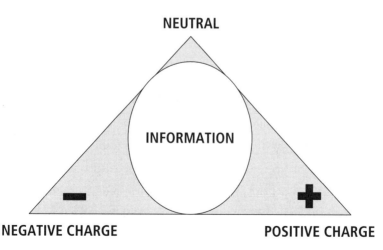

He pauses a moment, as if to say, "Do you understand how important this is?" I am quiet, probably not recognizing the level of importance he is trying to convey. But it is interesting. **Information and data are neutral.** In themselves they have no meaning, no value base, like good or bad, or better or worse or anything like that. It is just information. Interesting!

The pause continues a few more moments and he sees that I am not inclined to say anything. He continues. "So let me give you an example. Suppose you say to your prospect that your product is guaranteed. When that information is gathered and chewed on by his brain it has no more meaning than exactly that, that your product is guaranteed. It is neither a good or bad thing at this point; it has neither a negative or positive charge. But, a few moments later, he says, 'That's great.' Boom! The data suddenly has a positive emotional charge. It makes him feel good, or safe, or more confident, or whatever, and he says, 'That's great.' But, it's only great to him. The fact that your product is guaranteed is, in itself, not great. It is only great in his eyes when he becomes emotionally connected to it.

"Okay, let's take another example. You say to your prospect, 'It would help me if I asked you some questions about your current finances.' It's just an inquiry. It is just intellectual data to his brain. But, suppose he replies, 'How dare you ask me that? That's very personal information.' Wouldn't you be surprised? Sure! Who would expect that innocent data question to attach itself to such a negative emotional charge?"

Emotional Charges Create Value and Desire

"So, it is the prospect's *emotional charges* which reveal to you the value he or she places on the intellectual information or data you are processing between the two of you. Here, let me give you another example. Your prospect says to you, 'I don't believe in paying fees to have my money managed.' You take that as a negative, especially because you have heard it before from other prospects, and you have lost other deals because of it. When you hear those words, 'I don't believe in paying fees to have my money managed,' instead of treating it like the data it is, a fact, it becomes

Chronicle #4

Emotional Charges
The positive or negative emotions you and your prospect attaches to data or knowledge (which is always neutral). All sales are the result of a prospect's desire to change an emotional charge he or she is experiencing. All lost sales are the result of a lack of sufficient emotional energy to motivate change.

negatively emotionally charged in you. Why? Because the zipping little electrical charges somehow make you afraid you are going to lose the sale; a bad thing is about to happen to you; or at least, that's what you think. So, what do you do? You react defensively by telling your prospect all the great things you do when you manage money.

"But, here's the danger. You are responding in a vacuum. **You don't really know which type of charge is burning in your prospect.** You think you do, because you have such a big reaction to it, but you really don't. Had you held back from defending your position, asked some good clarifying questions, who knows what he might have said? Perhaps that he doesn't believe in paying fees because he never feels he gets his money's worth; or that he really enjoys being involved in managing his money; or that he would consider paying your fees if he got to know you better, because there is something about you he likes. So, your negative charge causes a response that is, in all likelihood, disconnected from reality. The fact is, most of your caveman responses are very much off base in this way. They are just you, impulsively acting out, being pushed or pulled by your emotional charges."

I have this picture in my mind of all these little electrical charges zipping through my brain and then creating these chemical reactions, each one turning into a little, or big, earthquake, my emotions. My thoughts carry me back to a meeting I had a few weeks ago where my prospect suddenly, after three meetings with him, said that he was going to stay with his current financial advisor. I could see the little electrical spark when he told me and how it zipped somewhere into my gut and how I started to get quite a bit angry inside. It was like a little Mount Vesuvius beginning to explode inside me. And of course, I couldn't hide my disappointment and anger and said the wrong thing to him, and then he said the wrong thing to me, and we got at each other pretty good. So there I was, acting out, just like one of my little kids. Me, a grown man, or at least, a *supposedly* grown man. Hmm! I'd better think about that.

Uh-Oh, I Need to Share My Emotions

As if reading my mind, he goes on. "Let's take this a step further. You may know from your own experiences that emotions carry a great amount of energy, either positive or negative. Now some emotions carry enough of a charge that they will drive you into action, like the emotion of anger for example. Can you relate to that?"

"More than you know." My response is very self conscious. I hope he doesn't see it.

"Okay, so when your brain gets information that makes you believe that you are getting closer to the *close,* you get excited and when you hear information that makes you think you are losing the sale, those little electrical impulses create chemical reactions that cause you to panic. Likewise, your prospects are going through a similar experience. They panic when they feel like you are pushing them, and they get excited when they like what you have to say.

The question is, what is each of you willing to tell the other about anything that happens during the sales meeting? And the answer is ...¿"

He stops talking and waits for me to fill in the answer.

I dutifully start talking. "And the answer is ... well, I certainly don't want my prospect to know that I just went into a state of panic or depression, or that I'm getting upset; and I'm sure he doesn't want me to know that he's upset about his problems, or what I'm saying, or his boss, or whatever. Especially if my prospect is a guy. I mean guys don't sit there and spill out their emotions to each other, at least not the ones they can keep under cover."

"And there you have one of the biggest secrets to modern day selling failure. No one wants to talk about their emotions. No one! Either they don't feel it's anyone else's business, they think they won't be understood, or they feel that the revelation of their emotions will somehow make other people see them as weak. So, you and your prospect sit there talking to each other, and all the talk stays on the brain level, the intellectual level, and none of it addresses the little earthquakes or volcanoes erupting inside. Yet, it is the energy of those little earthquakes or volcanoes that will drive your prospect into action, either to buy or not buy from you."

Every Decision is Emotionally Charged

"Let me put it this way. In working towards a decision, you need to peel below the surface and help your prospect discover his or her emotional bias, the *emotional charge* associated with his intellectually constructed problem. If there is no emotion connected to your prospects problem, he just won't change He won't have the inner energy to make a move. **He won't be motivated to do business.** That's where all the *think about its* and *nos* come from. On the other hand, if his problem is associated with a deep negative emotion, he will have a lot of desire to change, to get rid of that negative emotion and replace it with something that feels a lot better to him. That's where *yes,* the motivation to buy, comes from.

"Now, Steve, think about this. Isn't it true that most of your caveman counterparts are great at giving presentations and are super data givers, great presenters of information, and that they are really surprised when their prospects don't see it their way and balk at buying, especially since they've been so logical, so reasonable, and they know more about their prospects' problems and needs than their prospects know about their own problems and needs? What you don't see is that a stall at the end of your sales meeting has very little to do with the reasonableness of the data and has a lot to do with the fact that your prospect has not developed enough of a positive or negative *emotional charge* or bias about his problem and your solution."

I Want to Take Care of My Prospect's Emotional Charges

"Is that why you say that I don't respect people's intelligence, because I don't connect to the emotional side of their issues?"

"Exactly. If you see that your prospect is, in some way, incapable of taking care of himself, you will step in and try and take care of him, to control his *emotional charges*. Actually, as a caveman selling professional, you believe that you can actually create emotions within your prospects. You say to yourself, 'If I get excited, so will he. If I'm enthusiastic, he will be, too.' And in fact, for a short time he may catch your excitement or enthusiasm, but it is not sustainable because it does not have a solid basis within your prospect's emotional framework. It is not firmly rooted in his positive emotional charges. So your prospect gets excited and soon, without warning, deflates like a balloon that just had a hole punched in it; you see, artificial positive emotional charges will soon turn into negative emotional charges because there is not enough inner energy to sustain them. Sound familiar?"

"Yes, it sounds familiar."

"Once you peek below the surface you will see that information creates emotional drives in your prospect and your prospect is moved to buy, not buy, or give you a stall for a variety of emotionally charged reasons. Buy decisions come from the prospect's seeing your product as improving his emotional life, satisfying some desire, or getting rid of an emotion he doesn't want. No-buy decisions come for just the opposite reasons. **No emotion, no purchase!** Period! Stalls are no-buy decisions in disguise. They are just a nice way of saying *no* where your prospect relieves his negative emotions associated with disappointing you or hurting your feelings. If you understood how information creates emotional reactions and really wanted to develop high-quality, trusted, and

Chronicle #4

> **Surface Issue**
> Any problem, issue, or concern your prospect willingly tells you about early on in the sales call.

mutually respectful relationships with your prospects and clients, then instead of trying to inflame excitement or fear within your prospects, you could help them connect to their own emotions, to discover their own excitement or fear, and then help them relieve or satisfy whatever it is that is a priority to them. You see Steve, that's what respect really is, honoring other people for who and what they are."

I never thought of it that way. Never! I always felt that I needed to create an emotion within people; that I needed to take control, take the lead; that they were somehow incapable of being able to hear and feel within themselves what is good, right, or better for them. It became my job to do it for them, to become them, and to make decisions for them. That's a lot of work for me!

The Interdependent Sales Meeting

"Steve, you need to decide what kind of sales meeting you want to have, helping people become dependent on you, or leading them to have a better grasp of themselves via their own minds and emotions. In caveman selling, most prospect decisions are neither valued nor respected, unless they are decisions that the salesperson wants to hear. Otherwise they quickly are interpreted as a problem, a hurdle, a challenge, an objection, or a thing that keeps you from winning, which, as a caveman salesperson, you can't handle. Then, your reaction, to satisfy your emotional needs, is to take out your club of old-fashioned selling techniques and batter them over the head to get what you want.

"Once you admit to yourself that you really are not very respectful of your prospects, you will be on the road to selling recovery. You have to know that, although you treat your prospects nicely, talk to them nicely, are courteous to them and all that, deep down, you don't really respect them. You have to begin to see that your prospects' view of the world is quite different from yours and that their view is not a flawed view. You must stop thinking that you have some mysterious or great power to corral and funnel people into the direction that you want them to go, saying it is for their benefit while it is really for yours, and then expecting them to like and respect you. The idea circulating through your head, that you are getting your prospects to do something good for themselves that they wouldn't otherwise do, has to go. It is a disrespectful idea that dishonors and devalues the inherent intelligence of your prospects and derails them from taking responsibility for their own decisions and their own lives. In that way there is interdependence rather than disrespect. *Disrespect* is a subtle and dangerous put down, and every prospect you meet with feels it somewhere during their meeting with you. *Disrespect* **is the single greatest failing in the history of selling.**

> **Interdependent Sales Meeting**
> A sales meeting where there is mutual respect between salesperson and prospect. Requires the unusual and rare ability to see others as human beings who are capable adults.

"Here's a story that might help make the point.

> A priest observed a woman sitting in church with her head bowed in her hand.
>
> The priest left and came back a couple of hours later and she was still there.
>
> The priest decided that this must be a person who was deeply troubled and could use some help, which was his job. So he approached the woman and said, "Is there anything I can do to help you?"
>
> She raised her head and looked at the priest. "Father, I appreciate that, but no thank you. I've been getting all the help that I could possibly need. Until you interrupted!"

Chronicle #5
I Am a Yes Man

"So, Steve," he says as he puts his hand on my shoulder, "what do you think about all this stuff about *emotional charges?*"

> **Yes Man**
> Salespeople who focus on getting yeses during their sales meetings because it makes them feel better and they think that they are getting nearer to the close (see *Yes*). Also a form of a selling exercise whereby the prospect's head nods up and down often enough to create a pattern that will continue when it comes time for the close.

"I tell you, the way I see it is that it's pretty subtle stuff, but not the stuff I'm used to paying much attention to. I mean, I don't want to do psychotherapy with my prospects. Look, if you can get people to agree with you, to admit what they like or what they don't like, I'm not sure you have to know the deep emotional drives that move them. It's simpler than that, at least to me. You can't say it this way when you're talking to a prospect, but it boils down to 'Do you like this, yes or no?' 'Do you like that, yes or no?' 'Would you agree with that, yes or no?' And so on. If I can get to their *yeses*, than I can get to the *close* and my sale."

"Interesting," he says thoughtfully. "Did you ever get a lot of *yeses* and then when you went for the *close*, got a *no?*"

The Selling Chronicles

> **Probing**
> A selling game akin to "Where's Waldo?" Uses the process of poking clients with questions in hope of finding their hot buttons or tender spots. A tool also used by cowboys when they're herding cattle.

"Of course, prospects are prone to not telling the truth. You know, the old 'buyers are liars' deal. I don't believe that you can get around that. Prospects like to hide the truth, or just not talk about it. So, you have to keep *probing* in order to find out what they are really interested in. That's how you find their *hot buttons*, and then you can take it from there; work on their excitement through their *hot buttons* and *close* the sale."

"I see. *Probe*, get them to say *yes*, find their *hot buttons*, get them excited, and then *close*. Is that it?"

"I'm afraid it's that simple."

"Hmm. It is simple. But let me ask you a question in your example. Who's doing all the work when you sit down with a prospect, you or your prospect?"

> **No**
> A two letter word that ignites a salesperson's greatest selling fear: losing the sale. If the salesperson was spoiled as a child, this word especially rubs the wrong way. Most salespeople run from the word "no."

"Hey, I am. It's my job. I am the salesperson trying to sell something. You know, there's no free lunch. I don't see any problem with that."

"No problem. I was just thinking what *emotional charge* you have for getting the word *yes* from your prospects. Got any ideas?"

"Sure. I don't know about you, but I'd rather get a *yes* than a *no* when I get responses from a prospect. Hey, if he says *yes,* I know I'm on the right track. If I get a *no,* I have nowhere to head, I don't have a direction. Anyway, I don't like *no's*. Reminds me of my college days when I would get turned down asking for a date. Man, there were times I couldn't pick up the phone to make a call to a girl because I didn't want to get a *no*. I know we salespeople are supposed to learn how to handle rejection, and we do, but I don't think anyone really likes it. So why look for it? At the end of the day I'm digging for gold. Now, I know I'm not going to get gold in every shovel, but that's just part of digging. I don't go looking for rocks and dirt, for rejection—I want the gold, the *yes*."

"Are you still open minded? Because you sound pretty set about all this."

"Yes, I'm open minded. And I think I understand the role of *emotional charges*. Look, I'm obviously charged about not getting the word *no*. But I don't see any other way."

"Fair enough. Sounds like we have to talk about *yes* and *no*. Okay?"

"Okay!"

Yes
A word old-school selling professionals try to elicit from their prospects at all times and in all ways; considered to have a rare kind of magic attached to it.

"Let's get directly to the point. Caveman sales professionals are trained to get as many *yeses* as they can before they try to *close*; likewise, almost all caveman sales professionals can't stand the word *no*. *No* brings out their worst fear, losing the sale, and that is what they would like to avoid at all costs, feeling like they are going to lose the sale; that thought is just too painful. So, there's that pull of the hope of *yes* in the future and the push of bad feelings about *no* from the past."

The Hot-Button Game
"Now, let's take a broader view. What you don't realize, Steve, is that **you and your prospect go through life either desiring to move towards something you want, or desiring to move away from something you don't want.** Depending on the depth and power of the *emotional charge*, you will either move slowly, quickly, or hurdle mountains to get what you want or to avoid what you don't want. In the same way, your prospect will move with greater or less conviction, depending on the level and type of *emotional charge* he has. If you remain unaware of the *emotional*

charges working within you and your prospects during a sales meeting, how they push or pull each of you, it will cause all kinds of communication difficulties and levels of mistrust for both of you.

> **Hot Button**
> A mysterious hidden button that you have to find and push in order to make a sale. Somehow makes the prospect's temperature rise until he or she is hot (probably to trot).

"Steve, as you just said, caveman selling is built around the premise that you have to find a prospect's *hot button*. Old-time *hot buttons* were the aspects of your product that the prospect could get excited about—so much so, that he or she couldn't resist buying it. The idea was for you to get really enthusiastic; and that if you did, with sufficient energy, your prospect would catch your enthusiasm. You treat enthusiasm as if it were a cold or the flu: If you put enough germs of enthusiasm out there, your prospect would catch it too. The idea was to get enough *yeses*, getting them to say *yes* over and over again, and therefore so enthusiastically, that, at the end of the sales meeting, having said *yes* so many times, the prospect would have no other choice but to say *yes* and buy your product. While you want to look at this as a method of making a sale, which more than too often doesn't work, I look at this as *disrespect* at its highest. How on earth can you claim respect when you treat your prospects like they're little puppy dogs, where repeated training will get the results that you desire? 'Roll over, Mr. Prospect. 'Sit and stay, Mrs. Prospect.' 'Give a paw, Mr. and Mrs. Prospect.' 'C'mon now, just say *yes* and *yes* again to show how much you like what I'm saying.' Steve, did you ever imagine seeing your prospects like little puppy dogs?"

Once again I am really annoyed. I do not treat my prospects like little puppy dogs. Yet, I do believe that if I get them to say *yes* often enough that they will buy from me. I'd rather call it subliminal messaging. So I decide to tell him that, "I wouldn't say I treat them like little puppy dogs.

Chronicle #5

I am a much nicer person than that. I would call it subliminal messaging, so they get used to agreeing with me, something they would not normally do with a salesperson."

"Ah," he says. "Subliminal messaging or doggy training in modern dress, built especially for humans. Call it what you want, but it would be hard to convince me that training people so that you can get a sale is very respectful."

"Well, when you put it that way...."

"Remember our goal: We want to get to *reality*. We want to get to what is really happening. We want to see clearly. We want to make excellent decisions. And we want to co-create a win-win meeting. How can we do that if we coach our words in some feel good way, trying to get prospects to say something they don't mean, or get a temporary rise out of them, a thoughtless moment of agreement?"

I'm humbled. "We can't."

"No, it's impossible. Of course, your prospects are not puppy dogs, and although they may say *yes* over and over again, when it comes to the close, all too often, you get a *no*, or even more often, a *think about it*."

My Ego Speaks

"Now, layered on top of this drama of getting to a *yes,* is your own desire to avoid getting a *no*. Like most other people, you don't want to be denied what you want. You don't want to see your hopes dashed on the rocks. You don't want to feel or experience the very negative *emotional charge* of rejection. You never liked getting *no* when you were a kid, or in school, or with friends, or in a million other situations, and you don't like it now. The health of your selling ego has become almost totally dependent on getting that *yes, closing* the sale, getting what you

> **Mantra**
> Something you repeat over and over again until you come to believe in it, e.g., you should always be closing.

want and satisfying your cravings. So, for you, being a *yes man* is not only an ancient sales technique, but it is also a way you can get to feel good about yourself, feel good about your craft, and feel good about what you think you are doing for people. Your selling, as much as you may think it's about your prospect, is all about you; and you can't see that simple fact through your denial. That's what being a *yes man* is all about.

"And it goes even further than that. Soon, **you become totally dependent on your prospects for your emotional welfare.** You look upon each prospect like you would look upon your mother or father, as someone who will take care of your emotional needs by giving you what you want. And, if you don't get what you want, you will, like a child, find all kinds of ways—different strategies, different phrases, different closing techniques, different tie-downs—and pound away until you either get what you want or get sent to your room for a time out, which, of course, comes in sales in the form of a *stall* or *think about it*.

"Steve, once you've become a *yes man,* you take a giant step towards becoming emotionally dependent on your prospects, which leads to another giant step towards selling failure. **Prospect dependency leads to instant loss of control of every sales meeting.** Loss of control of sales meetings leads to selling insecurity, loss of confidence, and, ultimately, loss of self-esteem. Once control is lost with a prospect and the prospect takes command of the sales meeting, you are put in a defensive mode, in a corner, where you lose your selling power, and fall victim to your prospect's manipulations. Loss of control is instant role reversal in your selling. While you are trying to get to *yes*, your prospect is trying to get to *maybe*, and, more often than not, that is how the meeting ends. Just as *yes* is the mantra of old-time selling, *maybe* or *think about*

> **Prospect Dependency**
> When you look for help from the prospect in order to satisfy some personal emotional need, e.g., being liked, satisfying your ego, being a friend, or being appreciated.

it is the mantra of old-time buying. As good as you are at your *yes* mantra, you find that your prospect is even better at his *stall* mantras. It is an old story of cat and mouse, played out millions of times a day. Unfortunately, whereas you believe you are the cat and your prospect is the mouse, the roles turn out to be just the opposite. Now why on earth would you want to live that way?"

This time, he's hit me pretty hard. I have no defense. I have no rationalization. I hate to say this, but he's right. Why I hate to say this I'm not sure. Maybe it's the caveman "I've got to be right" emotion in me. Maybe it's just that I've worked so hard and now I'm getting a whole different point of view that actually makes some sense. It reminds me of when I was a teenager, wearing dirty bellbottom trousers and a ripped shirt, sporting shoulder-length hair, and smoking what you shouldn't be smoking. My parents suggested—or I should say threatened—that I go see a psychiatrist. So I did. When we began talking, he asked me why I wore a dirty trousers, a ripped shirt, and long hair, and smoked stuff I shouldn't smoke. I said to him, "Sir, that's what I'm here to find out."

Returning from this teenage memory, I turned and said to him, "You know, I'm starting to believe I'm not sure about why I do anything I do. And, even though you're not my shrink, I'd sure like to find out."

Where Does Steve Go from Here?

Yes, I Want to Hear "No"

"Steve ," he says, "you just need to become a *no man* salesperson. That's all there is to it!"

"Is that all there is to it? It's easy, huh? So, do I have to get down on my hands and knees to hear the rest?"

"Just having some fun at your expense," he says, with a friendly smile that diffuses any frustration I had with him.

> **No Man Salesperson**
> A salesperson who has reversed his or her natural desire to get to "yes." It is akin to turning down a date with someone to whom you are really attracted.

"Okay. Let's get to it. A *no man* salesperson is a salesperson who has very little, if any, *emotional charge* to get a *yes*. He is actually disinterested in trying to *close* a sale or to try and get, or force, any positive feedback from his prospect at all. It's not that a *no man* doesn't want to make sales; it's that he doesn't try to make sales. It's kind of like going in two different directions at the same time. I want to make a sale, but I don't want to try to make a sale, if that makes any better sense to you. If anything, a *no man* tries to discourage his prospects from buying. He tries to get them to say *no* instead of trying to get them to say *yes*. He works hard at discouraging prospecst from buying his product; he works hard at trying to find all the reasons why his prospects won't or shouldn't buy; he works hard at trying to send his prospects to his competition, telling his prospects how good they are; he works hard at pushing prospects away from him rather than latching on to them and never letting them out of his selling grasp. That's what a *no man* is, a salesperson who has given up his caveman style and now works 180 degrees differently from how he used to work.

"Steve, when you become a *no man* salesperson, you will find that you have become a very powerful salesperson. You will carry an air of independence; a sense that you are not in need of any money, or of making a sale; a feeling that you are content, easy, and absolutely out for your prospect's well being. As a *no man* salesperson, you will find that instead of chasing your prospects, your prospects will chase you. You will find that the more you try to get your prospect to go somewhere else, work with someone else, or discourage them from buying your product, the more your prospects will come fighting back to buy your product, whether you like it or not."

Chronicle #5

It's the Old Takeaway

"The old takeaway," I say. "Kind of like dating in college. The more you ran after the girls, the more they ran away. When you played it cool, not showing them any interest, or even being a bit sarcastic, they'd come flocking. Like that, right?"

"Well, you'll love this answer: In a sense, yes; but in a greater sense, no. Yes, because it works similar to a takeaway; no, because it is based on a much bigger and more important sense of relationship, trust and honesty. *No man* selling really puts your prospect first. It requires you to be gut honest about your prospect's wants, needs, experiences, and data; about the interactions and expectations of each other; and about yourself, for better or worse. *No man* selling makes the selling process a true win-win game.

"Interestingly enough, if I asked you today, you would say that the way you sell is a win-win game. In fact, I believe that you've already said that to me. But what you don't realize is that this is just a rationalization, a defense, a denial. In fact, all your caveman selling cohorts believe that when they make a sale they win (because they made a sale), and their prospects win because they are doing something that they really need to do (even if they don't understand the importance of what was just sold to them). While you are high-fiving your victory, your newly ordained clients are wondering just what happened to them and if they did the right thing. The truth is that you and your selling buddies adopt such an attitude of kindness and helpfulness, and it is so convincing, it almost obliterates the little winning twinkle in your eye that really tells the whole truth. *No man* selling, while it doesn't eliminate the good feeling of doing business, does eliminate both the twinkle and the insincerity from which it comes.

"Steve, the power of *no man* selling originates in the respectful understanding that people have sufficient knowledge to do what is right for them and they will make good decisions based on that knowledge—if given a chance. To be given a chance, your prospects need the freedom to go through their process of learning and working through their *emotional charges*. Unlike the caveman salesperson who is trying to control the whole process to get the result *he* wants, the *no man* salesperson gains control by trying not to control the process and is willing to accept any decision—let me emphasize that, *any* decision—the prospect makes."

"All right, let me see if I've got this. You think I should give up trying to get *yeses,* send my prospects to my competition, and try and figure out ways and reasons why they shouldn't buy my product. And by doing that, you're telling me that I will get more sales, have a better life, and never have to chase after them. And this is not a joke of some kind?"

"Actually, it is not a joke. And Steve, it even gets a lot better than what you've said. A lot better. Let me ask you this: Is there anything that I have said so far that that little whisper inside of you hasn't agreed with? Anything at all?"

"If I listen to the little whisper, nothing. If I listen to what's screaming in my head, there's an awful lot that doesn't make much sense right now. To be really candid, I can't fathom being a *no man* salesperson."

"Ah, we are making progress. So let's turn to that."

Chronicle #6
I Learn to Be a No Man Salesperson

"At our last meeting we talked about how the word *no* scares the daylights out of you. It carries too much of a negative *emotional charge* and you would prefer, obviously, not to deal with it. At the same time, your prospects, many of whom, having had numerous meetings with other caveman selling people, know that *yes* is the only word that you want to hear from them. They know that your happiness is dependent on them giving you a *yes*, especially when you go for the *close*. They know, by knowing your selling hopes and desires, that you have given up your independence and become dependent upon them for your emotional as well as financial support. In short, your prospects know your agenda the moment they enter a meeting with you. Better yet, your prospects have a pre-formulated game plan for you, and it is not the game plan you want.

> **Hope**
> A state of mind that causes you to chase after the prospect. Often confused with goals. It is a thing that springs eternal. Good for love, bad for selling.

"Steve, your prospects' game plan is simple and effective. It is designed not to hurt your feelings, to get as much information as they can from you, and, along the way, to avoid making any decisions or showing any

> **Think About It**
> The natural result of a lousy selling system.

inclination to buy. Your prospects accomplish this by maintaining a *think about it* mindset, by being *think about it* prospects. ***Think about it,*** in all its shapes and forms, is a safe haven for your prospects, a place where they can get all their information, make no commitment, and avoid hurting your feelings by leaving the door of *hope* opened so that a *yes* may come sometime in the future. While you are selling your prospects a product, your prospects are selling you *hope*. And you would rather have *hope* than a *no*. You cannot fathom that you would be better off with the *no* than with *hope*.

"By avoiding *no* and buying *hope*, chasing *hope* for sometime in the future, you are constantly drained of your selling energy. And, since *hope* springs eternal, you have an endless stream of it. You never run dry of *hope*. But **you will, sooner or later, run dry of the energy chasing clients requires in order to get them to buy.** In caveman selling, *hope* creates chasing; chasing causes you to lose control; being out of control drains valuable energy; energy drain causes exhaustion and disappointment; exhaustion and disappointment causes low self-esteem—all this often, all too often, resulting in those magic words, *I quit!*"

He's laid out a pretty good argument. But, I'm not buying all of it. So I lay out a pretty good argument back.

I Drive to Win, and So Do My Prospects

"Okay, no one likes to get a *think about it*, and we all know that is what the prospect is going to say, anytime he wants to avoid making a decision. In my thinking, that's what *tie-downs, trial closes, closes,* and getting people to *yes* is all about, getting them out of the idea that they need to think about anything. So, they have a game plan, and I have a game plan. It becomes a matter of who executes better."

"Well," he says, "think about what you just said to me. You have a game

Chronicle #6

plan, they have a game plan, and whoever executes better wins. You see, that's the caveman competitive sports guy coming out in you. You see yourself in a battle with your prospects. They see you in a battle with them. Each of you has your weapons that you have used successfully in the past and, to the best of each of your abilities, you use them during each and every meeting to get what you want. You are pitting strength against brute strength, his spear against your club, each trying to find the other's weaknesses, banging heads, making up, pretending friendship. What each of you want to do is win the battle. And, you repeat that battle with every prospect, and they with every salesperson, every day. I get tired just thinking about it.

"Now, if you insist on looking at selling as a combat game, the question would be, how do you get your prospect out of his or her game plan, wouldn't it?"

"That's exactly right!"

"Good. Now, what I'm suggesting here is that you becoming a *no man* salesperson will do just that and, at the same time, infuse you with energy rather than having it robbed from you. Look, you adopt the strategy of pushing prospects away from you instead of trying to draw them to you. Pretty soon, your prospects will realize that you are not cut out of the same mold as every other salesperson they have met. They never feel the manipulative push or pull from you to get what you want. Once your prospects feel that, just that one thing, they will know that their game plan is in trouble. They will know that you are not buying the *hope* that they're selling, because they will feel your independence, your non-reliance on them for emotional or financial support. They won't feel any need to erect the protective *sales barrier* and hide behind it. They will be able to relax in the meeting; and, once relaxed, once they've let their guard down, they will share much more confidential information about their real wants, desires, feelings and, most important, their *emotional charges*."

I Doubt What I Thought Was Right

My mind is spinning, and I ask myself if I will ever come out on top in these discussions. I am again off balance. Why do I need to come out on top? I know, it's because I'm so darned competitive. Maybe I think I'm in a battle with him as well as with my prospects. Maybe I *am* a caveman, and a dumb caveman at that. Wake up in the morning, kiss my wife and kids goodbye, and off to the wars, to do the battle, to hunt and kill, to make sales. Come home, my wife says, "So, how was your day, honey?" She is really asking, "What did you kill today, honey?" I know it; she knows it. She shares my caveman existence with me and neither of us really sees it. Is that denial? Is that being asleep? Is this waking up? And, if it is, a part of me does not want any part of it. It is very disturbing, to say the least, every time he points out a new idea or a new thought or a new concept that puts a doubt in my mind about things I have done or considered "right" my whole selling life.

"Uh, could you give me an example of that?"

"Sure, here's what a *yes man* sales meeting might sound like as compared to the *no man* meeting:

Prospect:	I am interested in your annuities. Could you give me some of the details on how those work?
	The prospect is fishing for information, his single greatest priority and game plan.
Steve *Yes Man*:	That's great. Annuities happen to be a terrific product. In fact, they are one of the best products we have for safe money and are delivering great results. Let me show you how and why ....
	You see a sale and you get all excited. You try to create additional enthusiasm or excitement in your prospect.
Prospect:	Well, all that's very interesting, but the annuity you just

Chronicle #6

	mentioned doesn't compare to your competition's. *He is making up a story just to get you defensive and share even more information.*
Steve Yes Man:	Oh, let me show you some data that will prove otherwise. Can you see how great it will be to have this annuity combined with the outstanding rating of the company and the bonus working for you? *You, now in a defensive mode, are scrambling as you feel a loss of control of the meeting. You try more enthusiasm combined with more information.*
Prospect:	Actually, that does sound interesting, but I'm not sure an annuity is really what fits my need. *He is hiding from you and only giving you bits of information. That is how he builds his protective selling barrier.*
Steve Yes Man:	No problem! Look, there are lots of different types of annuities. I'm sure we can find one that will work right for you. Let me give you an idea of the choices available. Then we can pick the one that works for you. Okay? *You give more information and try a tie-down. He nods his head up and down.*
Prospect:	That's just great. I didn't know there were so many possibilities. I really appreciate all that information. You've been so helpful. Let me mull this over and see what fits and I'll get back to you in a week or two. *The prospect has gotten all the information he wants and now is dismissing you and ending the meeting. This is the final phase of his game plan.*
Steve Yes Man:	Okay. But just what is it exactly that you will be mulling over?

The Selling Chronicles

	You have learned that this is a good way to handle this objection.
Prospect:	Oh, there are a lot of considerations here and I just need some time. I never make a quick decision.
	He has handled this sales angle a million times before.
Steve *Yes Man*:	Is there something I didn't do a good job of explaining?
	You learned this one, too, from your caveman friends.
Prospect:	No, you did a great job. I just need to see how the pieces fit. So let's talk in a week or two and we'll take it from there.
	The prospect feels the panic in you and relaxes. He is in total control.
Steve *Yes Man*:	Great. How about I call you in a week just to see where you are at.
	You are totally on the chase and out of control.
Prospect:	That would be great. Thanks for taking the time to meet with me.
	Success! He has gotten his information without making any commitments.
Steve *Yes Man*:	Thank you. It was really nice meeting you. Just give me a call if you have any questions.
	Failure! You have given all his information and gotten a stall.

Steve, this scenario gets repeated over and over again, millions of times each hour, in one form or another, by salespeople and prospects all over the earth. Is this ringing any bells for you?"

"Actually, I feel like a big alarm clock is going off in my head. What would a *no man* salesperson sound like?"

Where Does Steve Go from Here?

A Different, Albeit Challenging, Perspective

"Steve, that's a good question. Let me give you a different way of thinking and being. Let's see how you take to this example:

Chronicle #6

Prospect: I am interested in annuities, could you give me some ideas on how those work?

He is fishing for information, his single greatest priority and game plan.

Steve No Man: That's interesting and I appreciate that. Although annuities are very good, they are certainly not for everyone. Could you tell me a little more about your interest in them?

Instead of getting excited and moving towards the prospect by giving him a whole bunch of information, you actually take a few steps backwards, bypassing your prospect's demand for information and, at the same time, warning him that your product is not for everyone, something he never would expect you to say. Essentially, you are telling your prospect that you are not going to jump in and do a "dog and pony" show for him and that there is a good chance he may say "no" at the end of the sales meeting—exactly the opposite of what your prospect expects you to say

Prospect: Well, I don't know all that much about them, but I hear that annuities can be a safe place for money, and I like that. You see, our current portfolio is losing money, and I'm really not happy with that.

He is beginning to share the elements of his problem instead of making up a story to get more information. In the meantime, you have said nothing about your product.

Steve No Man: There's some interesting data I would like to share with you. Before I do that, could you tell me some more specifics about your losing money? To be really candid, there are different ways to solve the problem of losing money, and I want to determine if you're better off here or if you might be better off with a different financial professional.

You take greater control of the meeting by reinforcing your no man attitude as you suggest that the competition may have a better solution. Furthermore, you puzzle your prospect, who is now convinced that you are not a very good salesperson and don't do what salespeople are supposed to do. You still haven't revealed anything about your product.

Prospect: Actually, the whole thing has become a big problem for me, and I'm getting a lot of pressure from my wife to fix it. It seems that this roller coaster market is really upsetting her, which, of course, then upsets me. So, I think it might be time to make a change.

He can no longer hide from you because he is getting a big negative emotional charge. He is now driven to relieve himself of something he doesn't like, to get rid of it, a natural human reaction. With his focus on relieving his pressure and upset, he has little reserve energy to spend in erecting a selling barrier. The negative emotional charge, coupled with the absence of any selling threat from you, causes your prospect to lose his balance, and to lose focus of gathering information, his primary game plan. In fact, every time he gives you an opening to sell, you, instead of clutching at him, keep distancing yourself from him. He quickly sees you as a non-threat; and, since he doesn't get any information from you, he begins to chase you. Since chasing you is not his game plan, it causes him to lose further control of the meeting.

Steve *No Man*: Well, when you went to your current advisor, he or she gave you a game plan to fix this problem. Did you happen to bring the printout with you so I can see just what

Chronicle #6

	was suggested?
	You continue to distance yourself by reinforcing the idea that the current advisor created a plan to fix the problem. The prospect is now totally confused and has no idea what you are up to. He expects you to bash his current advisor, but you're making it sound like he's got the job done. Because of our customer's desire to relieve himself of his negative emotional charge, however, he is determined to continue, happily, to dialogue with you.
Prospect:	No, I haven't talked to my advisor about this and I don't have a fix-it plan from him. That's why I'm here today!
	The prospect now sees that you are being absolutely candid with him. He cannot dismiss you, because he still has his emotional charge and he doesn't know if you can help him or not; after all, you have yet to tell him about your product.
Steve *No Man*:	Oh, I see. Well, maybe this meeting is premature and you should go back to your advisor and see what he has to offer. After all, you've been with him for some time. He may have exactly what you are looking for. Do you think we should reschedule?
	Now, you are trying to end the meeting instead of the prospect. It is total role reversal.
Prospect:	Look, I don't have much confidence in my advisor. He hasn't called me in a year and, well, I don't think he can get the job done right now. All I really know is that I still need a solution. You're here now, so let's see what we can accomplish.
	He now finds himself beginning to beg you to stay and for you to tell him how you can solve his problem. The roles continue to be reversed.

Steve *No Man*:	Again, I don't know if I am the right one for you, but suppose I am, and I could help you out; then we'd have to take money away from you current advisor. How do you think that would work out?
	Now you are asking about the prospect's decision process and willingness to sever an important relationship.
Prospect:	Well, if it were the right solution I would deal with him. After all, it is my money!
	He moves to the edge of a cliff.
Steve *No Man*:	You would? Won't you need to think about it or review it with someone else?
	You stay cool and back away again, this time by bringing up possible stalls before your prospect does.
Prospect:	No! I'm the one. Either it will be right for me or not, that's the bottom line. You give me the right solution and I'll take it from there.
	He steps off the cliff.
Steve *No Man*:	You mean you would give me a direct "no" or "yes," and that would be the end of it.
	You set his expectation and present the "no" side first.
Prospect:	Of course. I don't have time to waste.
	Now he is speaking to you "man to man," honestly and candidly. He has become a real prospect.
Steve *No Man*:	I guess I could live with that. You know what? If it's okay with you, I'll be real candid too. If I think I can't help you, I'll just tell you straight out. Fair enough?
	You move back yet one more time to solidify your position and control.
Prospect:	Fair enough.
	Success! Because he has demonstrated a drive to solve his prob-

Chronicle #6

	lem and a motivation to do business, he will finally get the information he wants.
Steve *No Man*:	Great! Let me share with you that data I thought would be important for you and show you how it will get the pressure off your relationship, and, at the same time, give you a more suitable financial direction.
	Success! You present your material knowing that you have knocked out the competition and will get a firm decision at the end of the meeting process.

Steve, do you see how both you and your prospect win in this example?"

They Work, I Relax, We Both Win

I am amazed at what just happened and the possibilities of it. *No man* selling creates a whole different atmosphere. It takes all the work that I have to do and puts it directly in the lap of the prospect. Being notoriously lazy and trying to find all the angles for less work, more money, I kind of like that—sit back, give nothing away, sell the competition, and relax until he finds the emotional charge he wants to get rid of and tells me what it is. Sweet!

Finally I answer his question. "Yeah, it's got to be a win-win because I'm not trying to sell anything and he won't buy unless he has this inner drive to get rid of his *emotional charges*. I win, he wins. Did I get that right?"

"Yes, you did. Bravo! But, let me elaborate. You win because you relax into the conversation, don't expend any energy being manipulative, tell the truth about the potential fit of your product, how the competition might stack up, what might be the right steps for him to take, and what kind of decisions he will make at the end of the meeting. Most important, you bring up all the potential pitfalls to a decision and sale before your prospect does. In that way, you deflate the power of potential objections and his using that power to take control of the meeting. It also makes your prospect feel that you are not out to get him and are bringing up all the possibilities, even some that are not good for you. And even more important, along the way, you don't reveal any of the details about your product until you want to, essentially denying your prospect from accomplishing his number one goal, to get information without making a commitment.

Your prospect wins because he, too, relaxes into the meeting. He never feels challenged, pushed, prodded, tied down, manipulated or *closed*. In fact, he feels that you keep finding reasons for him not to buy your product. In a flash he finds his real dilemma: that he has to discard his plan of selling you *hope*, and now has to chase you just to get the information he wants. Along the way he reveals much more information to you than you reveal to him. And it is not only technical information or data, but also information about his emotional charges. In the prospect's mind, sharing emotions with you is a very personal experience. If you handle those emotions gently and honestly, the prospect will feel the beginning of a real relationship, igniting feelings of trust. Once he gains that trust, the chances of making a sale are substantially and meaningfully increased.

There's a glint in my eye. "Can I ask a question?"

"Sure."

"How do you keep from laughing?"

Chronicle #7
I Don't Walk in My Prospect's Shoes

He's an interesting kind of person. On the surface he seems pretty laid back. Perhaps I should say, at peace. Yet, when he says something, it carries a certain weight to it, a fire, a certain point of view that encourages me to look at things in a totally different way—something, by the way, that I don't always want to do. His voice tends to be soft, almost therapeutic. Yet his words have a cutting edge to them, and a certainty, that makes me want to listen. Normally, I would say that he is challenging, but it would be more correct to say that his ideas make me challenge myself, because, he, himself, is not challenging. It's not like he gets up there on a soap box and says, "I am going to challenge you with my ideas." That's not the feeling I get at all. It's more like he says, "Look, here's another way to look at it, here's why, here's the reality. Now, what do you think?" And when he asks that question, it's not with some kind of an uppity attitude. He's really asking, "What do you think?"

The other thing I notice about him is that he doesn't care what I ultimately do. It's not actually that he doesn't care; it's that he does care and doesn't care at the same time. Perhaps a better way of putting it is that he cares and is careful not to try and demean or downgrade what I am thinking, even if he thinks differently. Sure, he may present another viewpoint, but when he hears my viewpoint, he really takes it in. Put in his words, he doesn't seem to have a big negative emotional charge to things that he doesn't agree with. At least on the surface it looks that way. So nothing seems to faze him and he always appears to be in control—not in an uptight way, but in control because he maintains his balance, maintains an equilibrium and perspective that is well rooted in principles. The image I get is an iceberg, where you see what's on the surface, but most of it is below the water line, and it usually goes pretty deep. It has a strong foundation, so it is very stable. I wonder what he would say if I called him an iceberg?

Speaking of icebergs, it's not that he's cold like an iceberg. In fact, I find him to be very warm, very kind, embracing. It's like he wants to explore the way I look at things in relation to the way he looks at things. I always feel like he is willing to go where I want to go. And interestingly enough, just as I am thinking that thought, he starts our meeting.

I Want to Get to Yes, They Want to Get to Stall

"At every meeting, you and your prospect are going in opposite directions. As you continue to try and get to yes, your prospect is trying to get to stall.

Stall
The prospect's developed ability to delay a decision while getting as much information from you as possible. Also a place where salespeople go to hang their heads in shame when their sales end up in the toilet.

The more you try to get what you want, the more he tries to get what he wants. Compounding the difficulty is that every time you try to get to *yes*, your prospect will increasingly feel that the conversation is not going well. He will feel that you are not listening, you don't care, or you are ignoring him. Each negative feeling reinforces his desire to implement his game

Chronicle #7

plan to *stall*. You are walking one way, he is walking another. You keep your fingers crossed that you will both meet at the *close,* while he keeps hoping that your paths will never cross at all.

"Now, you're going to argue with me that you are a good listener and that you think your communication skills are well honed and that your prospects feel like you are on the same path, walking together, sort of friend with friend. You're going to tell me that all your caveman brethren have focused on listening skills; that good salespeople must be good listeners and that you are a good salesperson, which, by the way, you are. You believe this so much, these are the kinds of things you hear inside your head when you're with a prospect: 'Boy, I'm really listening to this person. This is a good meeting. He or she really likes me. We're getting along. We are moving in the right direction.' You say all this to yourself, don't you? But nothing could be further from the truth."

The words spill from my lips before I can say them more politely. "That's a lot of crap! I *do* spend a lot of time with my prospects. I *do* talk to them. We *do* develop good conversation. They *do* like me. That's why they refer people to me. So, that's a bunch of bull. If there is anything I do well, it's listening to my prospects."

He doesn't react. I think he is Mr. Spock. No emotions! But he is very empathetic as he says, "Steve, I believe you. And I believe that you do an excellent and conscientious job with the materials you have. There is no doubt in my mind that you are sincere and kind and that you wouldn't intentionally hurt anyone else."

He is not patronizing. But, I'm expecting that he's going to give me another angle, another point of view real quick. And of course, he does.

"Let's think this through together, and you tell me. Okay?"

I agree, then breathe deeply, trying to loosen the tension I feel.

"While it is true you are listening," he begins thoughtfully, "can you give me an idea of just what you are listening for?"

"Sure," I answer confidently. "I want to hear what their problems are. If I can find the problem that needs to be solved, then I know what their *hot button* is and I can offer a solution, which would then turn into a sale. It's all based on finding a problem and offering a solution."

"I see. So, you have a simple game plan: Listen for the problem, find the hot button, close the sale. Hmm. Not bad. Not bad. But let me ask you a question: Did you ever find a *hot button* and *not* make a sale?"

"Of course."

"And did you ever consider how that could happen? Logically, it shouldn't."

"Well, yeah. Sometimes the *hot button* is just not hot enough, or my product just won't solve the problem in a way that they want. So, no sale." Then I quickly add, "Why do I feel I'm about to get hit over the head with a sledgehammer?"

"Probably because you know the truth. Remember that little whisper that we were talking about a while ago?"

He stops for a moment and then goes on.

I'm a Good Listener, or So I Think

"You see, Steve, while it is true that you have been trained to listen to your prospects, you are listening for one reason and one reason only: to find your prospects' hot buttons. Once a hot button is identified you can then use tie-downs and pre-closes to move closer to making a sale. Caveman thinking is predicated on what I call *quantum leap thinking*; that once someone expresses an interest in something, that is the something they want to buy. Unfortunately, this is

> **Quantum Leap Thinking**
> Making a psychic jump in believing that once prospects express a desire for your product, or reveal a hot button, they are going to buy. Kind of like smelling the aroma of good food and then believing that you already ate the meal.

Chronicle #7

rarely true. Indications of interest can be minor *emotional charges* that have very little, if any meaning in the selling process. These minor *emotional charges* erupt in the moment, but they have little staying power. They catch a prospect's attention and get him all enthusiastic for a short time. Then, like someone took a pin and punched a hole in their balloon, the positive *emotional charge* deflates to no interest at all, leaving you wondering how your prospect could turn on you so quickly.

"Prospects lose excitement, interest, and enthusiasm over features and benefits because it is not what they really want or need on an emotional level. Remember when we talked about *emotional charges*, that some don't carry enough power to sustain themselves for a very long time? Well, when you listen for *hot buttons*, or selling opportunities, or *closing* opportunities, and then hear what you believe is one of them, you get an unrealistic feeling that you know what your prospect wants. Then, when you act on that feeling, it backfires. Your listening has not gone deep enough. You have not found out whether the *hot button* you recognize, or the buying signal that you see, is really real. You react to a piece of information that is actually quite superficial and may not reflect your prospect's real thoughts and feelings. Steve, once you begin listening with the idea of finding what you want, like a *hot button*, your mind will, sooner or later, interpret something your prospect says as that *hot button*, giving you exactly what you set out to find. But along with that *hot button* comes a false sense of hope that you are on the road to a sale. I call this *loaded listening;* where your listening is loaded with a layer of energy that is looking to hear what it wants to hear; or to look at it another way, it is listening that is not listening, but listening that has a specific objective, like a *hot button* or *closing* opportunity; listening on a mission.

> **Loaded Listening**
> Listening that seeks a specific objective, like a hot button or a closing opportunity. Better known as selective hearing.

"Once your listening becomes loaded, then you'll automatically graduate to the next step, which is *psychic listening*. This is listening that believes it can hear what is not said, better known as mind reading. *Psychic listening* convinces you that you understand exactly what your prospect says, when the truth is, you really don't. Here, let me give you an example."

I Hear My Worst Fear First

"Immediately, as you are walking into to your prospect's home after a number of successful meetings with him, you are hit right between the eyes with a major objection: 'Steve, the fees are too high!' Instantly you say to yourself, 'Uh oh, I'm in trouble already. I'd better get this objection off the table real quick or it's over.' At that very moment, your *psychic listening* causes you to believe that you know where your prospect is going and what he is thinking. The information it delivers to you, that this sale is going down the drain, is your worst fear, and it puts you under stress that moves you into action to handle the objection, to relieve your stress, to rid yourself of the feeling that the sale is going to be lost, if not lost already. At the same time, you add to your own stress by concocting a mental vision of yourself, returning to your home, being confronted by your spouse, who innocently asks you about your day. In your mind's eye you hear him or her say, 'So, Honey, how was your day?'

> **Psychic Listening**
> The superhuman quality of hearing things that were never said. Sometimes called assuming and other times called mind reading. Most often heard are positive messages, especially buying signals.

"Instantly, you can feel the little sweat beads appear on your forehead. You know that the real question is, 'Did you make a sale today?' Now, if you haven't sold anything in a while, your internal thermometer really starts to rise and you blow an innocent question out of proportion. You say to yourself, 'Damn it, my spouse is worse than a sales manager.'

Then, you feel the sweat soak through your shirt under your arms.

"Finally, you turn your attention back to your 'fees are too high' prospect. You look at him silently while steaming inside, as you say to yourself, 'I thought I could count on you. You're a liar like all other buyers. You don't know what you are doing. How stupid can you be? I know better than you do! You should listen to me. The fees are priced right. What on earth is your problem?' You then reach into your well-trained mental resource center to find the appropriate comeback to the 'fees are too high' objection. And, as all these thoughts and feelings simultaneously explode through your brain, words spill from your mouth, the same words you have used hundreds of times before: 'Well, have you considered the quality of what I do …. And then there is the personal service I give …. And how about how much you liked the product …. And did you forget that you didn't like the other guy …. And aren't you buying quality over price …. You know that price is relevant to what you're getting, isn't it?' And on and on you go, acting with false bravado, confident that your rehearsed delivery of the appropriate caveman talking points will overcome this disaster-laden objection.

"Your prospect, after what seems to you an extended period of time, looks at you with puzzled eyes. 'Steve,' he says, 'slow down. Slow down. I said the fees are too high. If you had given me a chance to finish, I was going to tell you that, despite the fees' being too high, I am going to buy from you anyway! You have the sale. Relax.'"

When I Stop to Think about It, I'm Not a Pretty Picture
"You get the sale, but deep down, you feel like a jerk. More than that, you are left bewildered by the fact that you were well on your way to ruining a sale that was already made; that you were your own worst enemy; and, while you thought you understood clearly what your prospect was telling you, in reality, you had no idea whatsoever. Be that as it may, you

go back to the office, or back home, and create a story of how well you did and how you *closed* this tough one. You create a scenario within yourself that you did a great job in handling the *objection*. Co-workers and spouses listen intently as you weave your tribal story of conquest. And, although you know it is just a story, you will let them believe that, if they were really smart, they would walk in your footsteps.

"Steve, under the power of *loaded listening* and *psychic listening,* you cannot really learn any *reality*-based information about your prospect. Instead of seeing him for what he is, instead of seeing the true nature of his or her problems, his emotional charges, you see, instead, what you want to see. And, if you can't find what you want, your mind will make it up for you. And, remember, your prospect has the same *loaded listening* and *psychic listening* when listening to you. So, in the greatest sense, although the two of you are speaking nicely to each other, really paying attention to each other, laughing at each other's jokes, **you are hearing little or nothing of what the other person is really saying.** It's a self-fulfilling fantasy, invented with each sentence, by each of your own minds, depending on what each of you wish to get for yourselves. Although you believe you are walking side by side with your prospect, you and he have not a clue as to where each of you stand. In a great way, it is a miracle that you are able to communicate with each other at all, no less consummate a business transaction."

'Well,' I say to myself, 'there it is; me and my prospect dancing like ghosts in the night; me reading his mind, he reading mine; me hearing what I want to hear, he hearing what he wants to hear; each of us hiding behind a superficial disguise; each of us out for ourselves.' I see us wandering in the dark, bumping heads in one moment, locking arms in another, tripping over each other's feet in yet another. I have another vision of my prospect walking away from me, and me from him, but both of us believing that we are talking directly to each other. The whole image is kind of bizarre.

I remember when I was younger and upset, a friend put his arm around my shoulders and said let's go get a cup of coffee together. I told him I was pretty upset and didn't want to; that I'd rather go for a walk in the park. With a little nudge of his arm, he tried to turn me towards that coffee shop. With a little push of my body I tried to edge forward towards the park. Then he told me how good the coffee would be and that we could sit quietly and talk. I told him how great the park would be and how we could talk and walk. He nudged me again; I nudged him back. After a few minutes he took his arm from around my shoulder and said I should do what I want, that he was going for coffee. Off he went. The last words I heard were that he had been looking forward to having his cup of coffee all day. The last thought I had was about my walk in the park. So, off we went, and the friendship ended there.

Where Does Steve Go from Here?

The Sale That Makes Itself
"Steve," he says, everybody has their own point of view and will see things exactly the way they want to see them. It's like the young plumber who saw Niagara Falls for the first time, thought for a few moments, and then said, 'I know how I can fix this!'

"Remember, what we're doing here is trying to awaken from the sleep cast upon us via caveman selling ideology. We want to wake up to selling reality. To do that, a lot has to change. You have to look at the world differently than you do now.

"To start, it would be good to understand the difference between making a sale and letting the sale happen, and know that the difference is poles apart, like night is to day. Your caveman training is all about making the sale; requiring you to lead your prospect to the result you want. Letting

> **Walking in Your Prospect's Footsteps**
> Joining your prospects on their personal journey; exploring their lives with them; taking them to places within themselves that they would not normally go; seeing life through their eyes, from their point of view.

the sale happen is all about going with the prospect, walking in his or her shoes, following and investigating all the prospect's thoughts and ideas with him, without any preconceived notion of what might happen or where it all might lead. By doing so, by *walking in your prospect's shoes*, you will allow and support his innate intelligence to lead him to a place within himself where **he will see the insanity of his own thinking and choose to correct it by using your product.** All you will need to do is sit back, let his intelligence do all the work, and watch the sale create itself, as if by some magic or process or alchemy."

"So," I interrupt, "you want me to make a sale, but don't want to make a sale at the same time? I think you've said that before."

"That's right, and that's the dilemma: to know what you want, but to let it come to you rather than going out to get it, or forcing it. It's a matter of having confidence in the process, and letting the result take care of itself. When all is said and done, you know you can't control the results."

"I do know that. But, if I step into the prospect's shoes and start walking with him, how do I know that he will eventually turn and go in the direction that will lead to a sale?

"Well, Steve, you don't. You have no idea what's going to happen. That's the hard part, letting it evolve without being able to see the results. He may take you to places that you never expected, to places where you can't see how they could possibly turn into a sale, but they miraculously do."

"I don't get it."

"Right. Not surprised. So, let's go back to listening, not for anything in particular, but just to see where your prospect wants to go. Then, when he heads in that direction, you just go there with him. It's like that good friend that puts his arm around you and says, 'Look buddy, where are we headed now?' And then, when you get there, you both look around to see what it's like. By working with your prospects that way, it bypasses all of your *loaded listening* and *psychic listening* habits. It is the only way to develop a real relationship."

"Sounds like you'd have to have the patience of a saint," I say.

"Well, you'll find that *walking in the shoes of your prospect,* letting him lead the process, will be one of the most challenging things you have ever tried to do in your selling career. It *will* test your patience, faith, and belief system; it *will* conflict with everything that you have been taught and practicing for years; it *will* oppose all the ideas and patterns of old-time caveman selling to which you have become accustomed and from which you have drawn all your selling strength. And, finally, it *will* require you to go against a stream of caveman-selling consciousness that has grown in strength and been reinforced to biblical selling proportions for over a hundred years. In a great sense, you will have to let go of your entire selling belief system, put an instant stop to your world of *me-first selling,* and take a giant step into the unknown."

> **Relationship**
> Something that cannot be gained by intellectual discourse. Requires a significant and emotionally close connection between two people. Starts with the sharing of emotion. It's the kind of connection you have with someone whom you are willing to let look into your closets.

Everything he has said is a challenge to my thinking. Now, he's asking me not to think, but to just go along for the ride; and if I do that, I will make a sale.

"I'm not sure I'm getting this."

The Good Friend Personality/The Lethal Business Personality

"No problem, because there are a couple things you need to do while you are taking that little walk with your prospect. The first is to develop the right personality mindset; and the second is to make sure that you take them further than they want to go. Let's take a look at each.

> **The Good Friend Personality**
> The part of you that creates an unfailing effort to be kind and look out for the betterment of your prospect. If one is not careful, it can lead to becoming a nice guy who makes no sales.

"Steve, you'll need to develop two distinct personalities. The first personality will always put your prospect's needs above yours; it will be the prospect's best friend. During a sales meeting, this personality will put its arm around the prospect, listen to him, be kind to him, be gentle with him, let him go where he wants to go, support what he wants to do, and be uncritical and honest. It will believe in your prospect's inherent wisdom and adult ability to make good decisions and to make them at the right time. This personality will be called the *good friend* personality.

"Your second personality will be a business personality. This personality will understand that a key component of a successful selling career isn't your ability to *close*, but your ability to control the agenda of the meeting; to be able to make certain that the expectation of the meeting is to ultimately do business, to exchange money for goods and services. I call this personality the *lethal business* personality. So, you'll have two personalities, the *good friend* and the *lethal business* personality, each working side by side with the other to move the meeting to an effective conclusion."

"It makes me feel kind of schizophrenic," I say. "Sometimes I think I have enough personalities already."

He ignores my comment and continues.

"Caveman salespeople often fake the *good friend* personality in order to get to the *close*. To *walk in the prospect's shoes*, you will have to give up the idea of faking anything, and actually become the *good friend* that your prospect would like you to be. The *good friend* personality will be just that, a good friend; and good friends walk with their buddies and support them in what they are trying to accomplish. At the same time, good friends will be candid with each other, respectfully trading opinions and beliefs. When you become the *good friend* of your prospect, there will be little or no *selling barrier* through which you must fight. Your prospect will never feel defensive, or that you are trying to put something over on him or that you're being disingenuous. If you can't see how easy you and your prospect's life will be in a meeting without a *selling barrier,* if you are always afraid that you might not get what you want by letting go of your tribal selling concepts, you will never be able to create a genuine *good friend* personality; you will continue to live as a fake.

"But, you need to be very careful in developing the *good friend* personality. If you do, and you don't develop your *lethal business* personality at the same time, you will become a very good friend, but a very poor businessperson. People will like you, but you won't make many sales. You will have many good and friendly meetings, get people to feel very relaxed, spend hours talking, and then get the traditional stalls and objections that you got as a caveman selling professional.

> **The Lethal Business Personality**
> The part of you that creates an unfailing effort to create a solid business meeting and sales transaction. If one is not careful, it can lead to becoming a cold-hearted salesperson whose only interest is in making the sale.

"Now, it's relatively simple to develop a *lethal business* personality. You just have to keep in mind one thought—that the ultimate purpose of your meeting is not social, but business. Being social and friendly is a part of business, but it is not the end goal of business. Remember, until there is a trade of money for goods or services, there is no business. The goal of any business meeting is to consummate a trade or to get out of the meeting as quickly as possible if no trade is possible.

"Unfortunately, many sales professionals like you, Steve, who are naturally 'good guys or gals,' or who develop a sincere interest in helping people, also have an undeveloped or misdirected *lethal business* personality. They are able to *walk in the shoes of their prospects*, but their meetings stay social and never turn to business. They think they are in business meetings when they really are not. You have to come to see that sitting and having good conversation, having everyone feel good, making everyone happy, sort of like a host at a party, often ends in just that: a good party, but no business. You can no longer believe that by using your *good friend* personality, that you will win people over and sooner or later they will buy, because they won't."

> **The Five Elements of a Lethal Business Meeting**
> Procedures that must be agreed upon to move a meeting from a social meeting into a business meeting.
> - *Purpose* for each meeting.
> - *Time* allotted for the meeting.
> - *Bail Outs:* How each party may end the meeting.
> - *Decisions:* When decisions will be made and what those decisions can be.
> - *People* who need to be present to accomplish the above.

"So," I say, "I need to be friendly and lethal at the same time. An interesting combination. I need to *walk in the shoes* of my prospect with my *good friend* personality, and, at the same time, make certain that every meeting turns into a business meeting rather than a social club visit. How can I do this—be lethal and friendly at the same time?"

"Great question! It's just a matter of understanding the elements that make for a good business meeting; making certain that those elements are clear to your prospect; making certain that your prospect is agreeable to all the elements; and, finally, to say it all with the friendliest personality you have. It becomes your job, while being friendly and *walking in your prospect's shoes,* to be constantly aware of just where you are in the business aspect of the meetings and to what extent your prospect agrees or disagrees with that aspect."

Chronicle #7

Five Elements of a Lethal Business Meeting

Lethal business meetings are meetings in which all parties *understand and agree, right at the very beginning of the meeting,* to follow the lethal business meeting elements: Purpose, Time, Bail Outs, Decisions, and People. Let's take a look at each element:

1. Purpose

What is the overall purpose of the meeting? What are the underlying purposes of the meeting that are required to reach the overall purpose? It might sound like this:

Steve: Mr. Prospect, thanks for coming in to visit with me (or for inviting me into visit with you). Before we begin, perhaps it would be a good idea to clarify the purpose of our meeting today. Is that okay with you?

Prospect: Sure, that sounds like a good idea.

Steve: Well, the way I see it, the purpose of our meeting today is just to talk, see if we are a good fit for each other, ask each other a lot of questions and then, at the end of the meeting, look at each other and decide whether we should have a second meeting or not. Does that make sense for you, too?

Prospect: That works for me.

2. Time

How much time is allocated for this meeting? How many meetings will it take to find out if business will be transacted or not? It may sound like this:

Steve: Mr. Prospect, I have us scheduled to meet for about an hour today. Does that still work for you?

Prospect: That's good for me, but you can't run much longer than that.

Steve: *(Sees a yellow flag regarding time. You lean on your "no man" training and try to bail from the meeting.)* Sounds like you might be under some time pressure. Are you sure that we're okay for the hour, or perhaps we should reschedule?

Prospect: No, you've got us locked in for the hour and we're okay, but thanks for asking.

3. Bail Outs

How, when and under what circumstances can either you or the prospect end the meeting? If you act like a *yes man* you will try and hold onto the prospect. For that reason, most prospects have never been given permission to end a sales meeting and always feel defensive during the meeting. You, however, as a *no man* salesperson, are not trying to make a sale or hold onto your prospect. If anything, you want to encourage your prospect to end the meeting or go buy somewhere else. So, you give your prospect a great deal of psychological relief and freedom by saying:

Steve: You know Mr. Prospect, while we are talking, you might be thinking that I am taking you down the wrong path and we are not a fit for each other. I hope you'll be candid enough to tell me if that should happen. At the same time, if I come to the conclusion that I don't think I can help you or that you are doing fine as you are, I'm going to be frank and let you know that. Do you mind if we are really candid with each other that way?

Prospect: Actually I would find that rather refreshing.

4. Decisions

What decisions will be made at the end of this meeting? What decisions will be made by the end of the meeting process? It may sound like this:

Steve: I can appreciate that. I find having candid prospects is refreshing for me too. Speaking of being candid, by the end of our meeting, one of two things will happen: If we look at each other and determine we are a good fit, we'll schedule another meeting. On the other hand, if we are not a good fit, we'll part ways as friends.

If this is a second meeting then it might sound something like this.

Steve: Mr. Prospect, at the end of this meeting today I am going to give you some solutions to the issues we've discussed. One of two things can happen then. You may not like what I've recommended and we can part ways. If that's the case, I want you to know that I'm okay with that and won't be offended; on the other hand, you may like the solutions as they are and decide that we should implement your program. I want you to know that I am, of course, okay with that too. Mr. Prospect, do you see any reason why we can't reach either a clear "no" or clear "yes" conclusion to this meeting?

Prospect: Yeah. We should be able to do that.

5. People

Who needs to be present to make it possible to transact business? Steve, I know you understand that if the decision makers are not present, the meeting, no matter what business is discussed, is still a social meeting and cannot turn into a business meeting. In that case, your *lethal business* personality will not want to stay long and bail out as soon as possible.

Steve: Mr. Prospect, is there anyone else that we need to involve who is part of your decision process?

Prospect: No, I make all the decisions on this end, too.

If it is a one legged appointment e.g. an appointment where one or more of the decision makers are not present, then you must add:

> Mr. Prospect, I understand your spouse is not here, and that is of concern to me. Are you saying that you can write a check without reviewing anything with him or her?

"Steve, do you see how you have now taken control of the meeting and created a balance to your *good friend* personality? By laying out and getting agreement on the five key elements of a business meeting, you can now *walk in the shoes of your prospect* without faking it and have confidence, assuming you keep reinforcing the business agreements of your meeting, that the prospect will deliver either a no-fit, implement, or next-appointment decision at the end of each meeting. If you don't follow this game plan, you will either fall into a *social meeting,* which will end in a *think about it,* or a pressurized business meeting, which will end in a *think about it,* too. If you make up your mind that you will only accept these three possible outcomes, absolutely nothing else, and keep making this clear to your prospect using your best *good friend* personality, you will have eliminated the biggest caveman stall in history, 'I want to think it over,' and, created a safe environment in which you can *walk in your prospect's shoes* to wherever he or she wants to go."

I feel like I've been blown away. I've had all these meetings in my selling career and I could have eliminated so many problems, so much *chasing,* and *close* so many more sales had I just turned those meetings into *business meetings*. I can't wait to get into my next sales meeting and see what it's like not to get a *think about it,* just clear decisions, nothing else, over and out. Refreshing. And exciting!

The Discomfort Zone

"I can see, really see, how this can work; but I still don't see how to take

Chronicle #7

people further than they want to go when I walk in their shoes. How do you do that?"

"Well, remember, you want to walk with your prospect, but both for his benefit and yours too. Then we need to rearrange what you listen for, and convert each meeting from a *social meeting* into a *business meeting*. And you're right, the question still remains: What do you do with the prospect, once he takes you to where he wants to go? I'll give you a direction now but won't be able to give you the how-to's until we cover some more ground and get you much more into reality than you are.

"The direction is this. Once your prospect takes you to the place he wants to go, your job is to then ask the appropriate questions to take him further, into a *discomfort zone*. Again, we'll talk about this in more detail in another meeting, but remember that your prospects will only go where they are comfortable going. Your sale, however, resides in the place that they are not comfortable, their *discomfort zone."*

He leaves me on that note. I am elated, bewildered, and frustrated. Elated, because I'm beginning to see myself as I really am, or, as he would say, *waking up*. Bewildered, because I am waking up into a territory I don't know anything about. And frustrated, because I can't see the whole picture, just bits and pieces; I can't see how you put the whole puzzle together to make it work in a nuts and bolts way, to make it very executable, very practical, resulting in more sales and a better and more balanced life. That's how I feel at the end of our meeting. And, I must say, I can't wait for the next one.

The Selling Chronicles

Chronicle #8
I Am Fearless, or So I Think

I'm a family man who's been around the block a few times. I was born in the Bronx, in New York City, and grew up in middle-income housing, playing games like stickball, ring-a-leevio, stoop ball, and sewer ball. Fun was running along the railroad tracks, or crashing down Dead Man Hill in St. Mary's Park. It was called Dead Man's Hill because it was a huge, long, straight hill with an equally huge, old, four-foot-wide tree at the bottom. If you started at the top and hit the tree on the bottom, well, the hill's name tells the rest of the story. We didn't have gangs at that time, but we did have fights—lots of them. It's not that it was a terribly bad area, because it wasn't. It was more that we lived in a tough part of town and you just had to prove that you were tough. So, we did. Or, at least we tried.

When we moved to Queens, another borough in New York, I met a new class of people. We stepped up in the world into a row house. To me, it was a castle compared to our apartment in the Bronx. Better schools, better teachers, better people, better everything. Of course, even though I didn't have to, I kept up my fighting spirit, because that's just what I had always done. Why not continue?

Mom was traditionally doting; and Dad was traditionally hard working and distant. She spoiled me, against his wishes. I kind of enjoyed that in some way. He tried to discipline me, but how could he? Mom wore the pants. They fought like crazy—or should I say, until they were crazier than they had been to start with. I guess fighting was in the Lewit blood.

Then came college, girlfriends, marriage, work, new friends, new neighborhoods, new restaurants, and new ideas. Fighting turned inwards, so I spent more time fighting with myself than other people. With a spirit like mine, I found it difficult to work for anyone so I ventured out on my own. I became a playing tennis pro, but not a very good one. When I finally ran out of tennis gas, I made an illogical career move: I became an opera singer. That's right, opera; a Wagnerian tenor. While I sang my heart out, my family cried their hearts out and suffered more hunger pangs than I would like to recall. So, when my singing gas tanks were financially empty, despite still having a lot of my heart left, I decided I needed a real, down-to-earth career. I was tired of starving, traveling, and getting paid nothing for it. All I needed was a fleeting idea of getting into sales to move me to answer an ad. In less than a week, I was officially one of the tribe.

Then came all the trainings, books, lessons, classes, seminars, rah-rah meetings, leads, and you know, everything that comes with trying to learn how to sell. I immersed myself and practiced what I learned. I became pretty good at what I did. What I mean to say, is that I was better than when I started, much better. But I was unhappy. I was unhappy with my production, my feelings, the negativity, and the amount of energy I was pouring out. The problem is, I didn't know how deeply disappointed and tired I was until I met *him*.

Now, this is our eighth meeting. He's certainly put a lot on the table for me to consider. I do see bits and pieces of a very hopeful picture of a new me and a new destiny. But is he just selling hope like everyone else, or is this the real deal? I know I won't know until I give it a committed shot, which I am prepared to do. Why? Well, why not?

Chronicle #8

The Standard to Which I Achieve Is Set by Others

He starts directly. "Steve, you have been brainwashed to measure yourself both as a human being and as a professional against measures set up by your tribal selling ancestors and fellow cavemen selling professionals. **These standards, these measurements, however, are like the fashions of the day, arbitrary and easily changed.** When you aspire to meet these standards, you find that they're a moving target. They provide nothing substantial or permanent by which a true measure of your success or accomplishment may be made. In that way, you always feel defeated, or not good enough, or unappreciated. In the end, they cause you to be desperate and afraid—desperate that you are not doing good enough and afraid that by not doing good enough you are going to lose the sale.

"As you well know, there is always someone out there who reaches the pinnacle of selling and is a superstar. When that happens the tribe holds that person out as an example, a poster child, of what you can be, if only you would work harder, abide by their selling rules better, buy more of their training materials, and attend more of their training seminars

"In fact, these standards of measure have nothing to do with you, your goals, your abilities, or the balance of your life outside of selling. Yet, these measures become more than a standard; they become a golden standard to which you aspire. They are engraved, like an Olympic medal, in your psyche and held in there in high esteem. Upon closer look, however, they are just empty fabrications which are causing chaos in your sale calls."

His words ring a bell that I don't want to hear. I am an achiever; I like to excel. And when measuring my excel rate, my achievement, I have never thought about the measures I used, where they came from, or why they were the measures everyone used. If the best closers were at 80%, I wanted to be at 85%; if the top production were at level A, I wanted to beat it at level A+. I looked at the world kind of like mountain climbers look at mountains: If it was there, my job was to beat it; just like if a mountain is there, the mountain climber's job is to climb it. But, why I should be holding myself up to someone else's merits and then feel like I wasn't somehow good enough was a good question, one I had never considered.

"In fact, Steve, if you think about it, you are a basketful of theories, opinions, and beliefs that you have adopted from others, both in your personal and professional life. Just think about all the ideas you currently hold about your profession, about selling, about approaching prospects, about closing. How many of these did you develop yourself and how many did you acquire from others that you have adopted in some way that now you have come to believe are *your* own ideas, *your* own goals, *your* own requirements for success? And how have these then led to your own feelings of inadequacy, low self-esteem, desperation, lack of confidence and feelings of failure?'

I Am a Double Loading Pain Dumper

"Steve, don't feel bad. It's hard for anyone to see the truth of what's going on inside him or herself. And, on top of that, there is always the *denial* which makes it even harder. We talked about this some time ago. But now I can tell you that your *denial* is much deeper than you think. So deep and so confusing, that it has the capacity to turn little fears into major phobias; the capacity to cause you to blindly react to fears that you cannot see and cannot understand in a way which eventually undermines your sale and, all too often, your sales career.

"Steve, let's say you discover that you are desperate to make a sale. You feel that desperation in many ways. You might feel personal pressure from home, competitive pressure from within yourself, professional pressure from your boss, financial pressure from your credit card companies, pressure to meet your mortgage payment, or disappointment in not being able to keep up with the top salespeople in your field. That's one level of desperation that is very real. Now, on top of that, is another layer of

Chronicle #8

> **Double Loading**
> The unique ability to make matters worse. Adding more pressure to an already pressurized situation. Letting your own personal issues confuse matters and create more pressure.

desperation caused by the phantom standards that we have been talking about that you have adopted to be your own. That's what *double loading* is. Adding more pressure to an already pressurized situation.

"Now, let's look at all this in an actual selling situation. You are in a sales call and, of course, feeling the pressure of the meeting itself. Then you prospect brings up an objection which, in itself, creates pressure in the meeting, because objections ignite the fear of losing the sale. You instantly recognize that if you don't do a good job in handling the objection, well, the sale might collapse completely.

"On top of that, since, in this example you are already desperate to make the sale, your fear of losing the sale is compounded by your desperation. Now that fear goes through the roof.

> **Pain Dumping**
> Relieving your own pain, especially the fear of losing the sale, by dumping it on someone else, which, in selling, will be your prospect. Often leads to feeling better about losing the sale.

"Then, it all gets worse. On top of that, you unconsciously feel the pressure from not meeting the artificial standards you have adopted. Now your fear of losing the sale literally jumps off the charts and makes you almost jump out of your skin. You are in deep pain. And, like any other human being, you don't like pain and begin to look for ways to quickly get rid of it. So, what do you do? You dump it on your prospect in the form of more pressure, in one way or another, to buy now. That's called pain dumping. So, you have become, in moments like this, a double loading pain dumper.

I Begin to See Myself, and I Don't Like What I See

"Well, what do *you* think of all this?" he asks.

"Man, it's a lot to think about; there's a lot going on. It's like there are layers upon layers. Pushes from the past, pulls from the future, denials, pain dumping, double loading, and fear. It's a wonder anything gets done at all, that sales get made at all, and it's a bigger wonder that this is going on all the time and I've never really seen it. So, to answer your question, I can relate. When I look back at lots of my sales meetings I can see where I overreacted, pushed when I didn't need to, prodded when I didn't have to, or thought that a sale was going down the tubes when it really wasn't. It never occurred to me that I was reacting to something that I couldn't see or understand I tell you, it's easier for me just to say that I had a lousy prospect, or that he was in a bad mood, or I caught him on a bad or good day, or that he woke up on the wrong side of the bed, or that I was really on my game and all kinds of things like that, than it is to look at myself and see that I'm a percolating, incubating, festering mess of a lot of stuff that makes my selling life difficult."

"And I can relate to all that."

He stops to think for a few minutes and sits quietly. I don't interrupt because I need the space too. The quietness is refreshing.

After a time he says, "You know, there is another layer to this that I'd like to share with you. Okay?"

"Sure."

"We now know that things like *double loading* and pain dumping make your meetings much more difficult than they need to be. Because of that pressure, prospects will see and experience you as difficult, argumentative, defending, not listening, and as a poor communicator. In a short time, they will develop a distaste and loss of respect for you, making it much more difficult, if not impossible, to buy from you. And when they don't, your negative feelings about yourself are reinforced. Unable to make the sale, seeing your fear of losing the sale come to pass, causes

Chronicle #8

you to see yourself as a big loser. Then, as a loser, you see the world as an increasingly greater threat to you. In your eyes, prospects get more difficult; competition is much too keen; your company is never supportive enough; you don't ever have enough leads; the market is always tougher in your community than anywhere else in the world; and you have a million other excuses just why you can't make enough sales. You say to yourself, 'If only I could get some prospects that are any good.' And you keep repeating these words of woe until you accept your level of success, give up trying, or leave the business. Steve, that's how insidious fear and its underlying irrationality can be. It can drive you right out of the business!"

While he is talking, I'm remembering how many times I almost quit, but somehow resurrected myself and got on with it, only to be led to quitting time again. What a nasty cycle that was. And these are memories I don't like to remember. While I always try to keep the good things in mind so that the other stuff doesn't pull me down, sometimes it feels like I'm holding back the dam with one finger and that I'm about to get overwhelmed by everything that is going on in my selling career. Other times I feel all this internal stuff is hiding behind a big door, but if I open that door, even a little bit, a whole mess of stuff—stuff about me, stuff I won't like—will come pouring out. Yet, from what he's saying, if I don't address it, don't let it out, it will taint and color everything I do or say in my selling. It's kind of like trying to carry this tremendous weight while attempting to get to the top of the mountain. It's not that the mountain wins, it's that the weight, the bad decisions, the poor planning, the inaccurate sense of reality—all that and more, defeats me. I defeat myself. Isn't that a terrible thought? I am, as he says, my own worst enemy. Me! Likeable, smart, intelligent, friendly, hard-working, fearless me. Isn't that a kick in the butt? Sure it is. And right now, I can feel the foot heading my way again!

The Selling Chronicles

Where Does Steve Go from Here?

"Steve, let me tell you a story. Just let me know if you've heard it already. This man is skiing and skis off the edge of a cliff. On the way down he latches on to a tree branch that is growing out of the side of the cliff. So, there he is, dangling, hanging by one hand, alone, cold and frightened. He yells out, 'Help! Is there anyone out there?' There is no response. So, he yells out again, this time louder, 'Help! is there anyone out there?' Again, no response. His hand is tiring. He looks down and there is nothing but the emptiness of a long fall into the darkness of the trees far below. With a last gasp, he yells out again, 'Please, help! Is there anyone out there?'

"Suddenly he hears a deep, low, thunderous voice. 'My son, I am here. I am with you. Just let go of the branch and all will be okay.'

"The man can't believe what he is hearing. He says, 'Are you kidding, let go of the branch?' The voice, stronger and more thunderous than before responds, 'My son. I am here. I am with you. Just let go of the branch and all will be okay.'

"The man's thinks for a moment. He has no time to lose. He yells out, 'Is there anyone else out there?"

I've heard that story before, but not for a long time. It's good to hear it again. Our laughter is kind of like a harmony between us, and it feels good. It raises my spirits.

He continues. "Steve, now how's that for denial? And, if you look closely enough, you will find that the **root of all denial and virtually every emotional pain you have is fear—fear of losing the sale**, as we have been talking about, plus a host of other fears—fear of losing control, fear of not being liked, fear of not being respected, fear of not knowing the answers, fear of saying the wrong things, fear of missing a closing opportunity, fear of failure, fear of peer opinion, fear of not making the grade, fear your prospect won't do what you want, and fear of fear itself. For selling pro-

Chronicle #8

fessionals, fear is the root emotion behind every selling issue you have.

"Admitting and recognizing fear is going to be very challenging for you. After all, cavemen are brutally brave. Fear is not part of your portfolio. As a caveman selling person, even if you could be aware of how much fear you really have, you are too embarrassed to admit your fear, not to any of your peers, not to your spouse, not to your friends, and of course, not to yourself. Yet, we now know that fear expresses itself as double loading and pain dumping, and that it is that fear that will bring you to the edge of failure and eventually to failure itself. Steve, you must learn to see your fear, taste it, own it, admit it, and deal with it. Only in that way will you be able to extricate yourself from the havoc that fear causes in your sales calls.. Does that make any sense?"

I've never thought of myself as a fearful person. Growing up, when I was with my friends, you could never admit that you were afraid. Fear just wasn't part of the portfolio. And, even if it was, you could never talk about it. We were macho men, indestructible, fearless. I'm not sure I don't have that same mentality today. If you really think about it, lots of the guys I meet or hang out with act like they drink testosterone for breakfast instead of coffee. They are very protective of their manhood. It's like if they lost their manhood they would somehow lose respect from the rest of us. Who knows, maybe they would. But, I think I'm in the same boat. At least I can recognize some things in me that I do fear, like not making a sale, just like he said.

No way am I going to admit that to anyone, especially my peers. No way! But it's there. I wonder if they can see it anyway. I can see it in them, plain as day, right out there, obvious, like the moon on a dark, cloudless night. You can't miss it. But they miss it. Or, at least, they never talk about it. Never! I can't remember anyone ever saying to me, "Man, when I go into that sales meeting I'm really afraid of losing the sale, it scares the hell out of me. And man, that fear affects everything I do and say." No, I never hear that. But, I do hear the *denial*. "Man, I was good. They should have bought. What on earth is wrong with them? Doesn't bother me, I'll go get the next one." What a load of crap. They're scared, just like everyone else, just like he says. I think we're all afraid of a whole bunch of things when we're selling.

Quietly I reply, "I can see what you're saying. In fact, I can see it more clearly than I would really like."

Selling Systems Are Supposed to Help Me with My Fear. Right?

"Okay, good. Now, what can you do about it? As a beginning step, you need to come to grips with the fact that your ancient tribal selling and *closing* techniques were developed to try and eliminate all the fears that you and your tribal buddies have living within them.

"**Closing**, for example, is supposed to eliminate your fear of not making sales. That's why the idea of being a 'good' *closer* is so important to caveman sellers. It's really not about *closing* sales and making money, although you think it is. It's really about eliminating your fear of not making money, of not being respected, of not making the grade. Thinking you're a good *closer*, a well-prepared closer, gives you tremendous confidence, and confidence eliminates fear.

"**Tie-downs** and **trial closes** are supposed to eliminate the fear of losing control of your sales meetings. In your head you figure that if you can get little bits of agreement, you are on your way to making your sale. So, that's what you try to do via *tie-downs* and *trial closes*, get people to agree on little things in order to get to the larger agreement.

"**Warm-up** is supposed to take care of your fear of being seen as a salesperson wanting a sale and losing respect in the eyes of the prospect. *Warm-up* is supposed to be the beginning of you building a relationship with your prospect. It is based on the idea that your prospect is somehow cold and that you need to warm him up. It's supposed to get you and him to like each other, demonstrating that you are just another human being and a nice person, so that he will be more willing to do business with you.

"When a **buying signal** is recognized, it is supposed to eliminate the fear of missing a selling opportunity, missing the *close*. It's like your prospect raises some fictitious flag, or gives you a secret signal to let you know that he is ready to buy. When you see that flag, you can then jump in to go for the *close*. So, you are confident that once you see the signal, like hearing drums from your tribal neighbors, you are ready to attack and go for the *close*. This gives you strength and confidence and supposedly, eliminates your fear.

"**Handling objections** is supposed to eliminate your fear that the prospect won't like your product. You believe that when you have learned all the moves to handle objections, you will overcome them, like a hurdler overcomes hurdles in a race. From your perspective, you see the end game—making the sale—and objections as things that you must get through or jump over or get around in order to reach the finish line that you want to reach. Knowing that you can leap the highest and most difficult of these hurdles takes away your fear that you won't get to where you want to go.

"**Staying 'up' or excited** about your product is supposed to eliminate the fear that the prospect will resist buying from you. After all, when people are excited about doing something, they do it. Moreover, when you're excited, they'll get excited. You believe that excitement is a disease, and that little excitement germs float through the air. If you get enough of those germs out there, your prospect will catch them, and succumb to them, in the form of getting excited and buying.

"**Giving a great *presentation*** is supposed to eliminate objections, get your prospect excited, and eliminate your fear of not having good answers or not knowing your stuff. You work hard at building your *presentation* and rehearsing it, giving it to friends over and over again to make it shine.

You are diligent in its delivery, believing that the greater it is, the greater your likelihood of *closing* your sale. Because it is something you can do and control, your *presentation* becomes your fear-eliminating focus for control. Once you get to the *presentation*, the meeting is all yours."

"So," I say, trying to get to the heart of what he's just told me, "you're saying I have this fear that I won't admit I have. Okay. There's lots of stuff I seem to have that I won't admit. I feel a little like a garbage can and I won't dump myself out. You know it's not like I can just turn myself over and empty myself of my history, the way I think, how I feel about things, what I'm afraid of, and what I can't see about myself."

"No," he agrees, "it's not an easy thing to do. These things become habits, second nature, and feel like they are part of us, like our arms and legs."

"Actually, I prefer my arms and legs to some of the stuff you're bringing to my attention. What makes it worse for me is that everyone I talk to is in the same boat I am. No one talks about these things. It's like it's taboo in the selling world."

"Taboo," he says emphatically. "Taboo, that's a great way to describe it. You see, you think if you push it away, ignore it, or deny it, it will go away. But it doesn't. It just festers there. Taboo puts a lid on the garbage can so that it can't be emptied.

"If you're still okay," he says, "let's go a little further."

I make no attempt to stop him.

Caveman Selling Delivers More Fear than It Eliminates

"Steve, when you really see caveman selling clearly, you will see that it is built to eliminate the subconscious fears that broil inside of you as a selling professional. **It is a fear-based system, to produce fear in a prospect, to eliminate fear from you.** Unfortunately, it doesn't get the job done. These caveman techniques do nothing to address your fears. They are built to do one thing: either bypass your fears or make you feel better. But

Chronicle #8

they do not eliminate or deal with them. Moreover, these old-fashioned techniques give you an artificial sense of security and confidence. Once you feel really confident, you are more inclined to deny that you have any fear at all, which turns you instantly into a *pain dumper* and a *double loader*. That's why, when we first began talking, one of my goals was—and it wasn't a pleasant thing for me to do—to bring things to your attention that would allow you to undermine your own confidence. Once your confidence was shaken, especially at the core, you would start to look at yourself in another way."

"Well, you've certainly accomplished that. I'm now looking at myself inside out, upside down, and right side left. I don't know if I should be happy about that. It's not easy. But that's the way it is."

He seems pleased at what I've just told him—not in an egotistic way, like he's just proven something or gotten me to do something; but in a way a friend, a true friend, would be pleased that his buddy has just done something very good for himself.

Then he adds, "Steve, your first step, which I think you have already taken, is to stop buying into a misguided system that, instead of dealing with your fear, actually avoids it and thereby reinforces it. Your second step is to understand that your prospects know exactly what you are going to do, and when and why you are doing it. After all, it's not the first time they've been in front of a caveman seller. In fact, some prospects have seen more caveman sellers than the sellers have seen prospects. You need to respect your prospects' intelligence and experience in dealing with salespeople. They can see your old-time selling moves coming far before you even start using them. So, here's what happens:

"The prospect sees and feels your *close*. It's not something new to him, and he knows that somewhere during the sale you are going to go for a *close*, so, he's waiting for it. When you go for the *close* he feels pushed or pulled by you. He knows what you want and, at that point, that you are going for it. The more you try to *close*, the more stubborn or distrusting your prospect becomes, all leading to a bigger and deeper *sales barrier*. The more stubborn or distrusting your prospect becomes, the more fear you feel that you will not make the sale. The result of *closing* may be a sale, but most often, since you don't sell everyone, *closing* actually reinforces the fear it is meant to eliminate.

"The prospect sees the *tie-down and trial close* as quickly as the words leave your lips and instantly feels manipulated by your trying to get what you want, closer to the *close* and a sale. Once your prospect feels the *tie-down*, he or she feels boxed in, cornered in, or a sense of being led into a corner. At that moment all of his defenses go up, since he feels that he is losing options and losing control of the meeting. In actuality, *tie-downs* often create a dogfight for control, rather than a lead to the sale. Once there is a dogfight for control, you have, in fact, lost control of the meeting. You spend more time defending, trying to regain control, than you do in solving your prospect's problems. The fear and feeling of losing control, along with the sale, is reinforced with every unsuccessful *tie-down* attempt.

> **Tie-Down**
> Something usually done when capturing a criminal. In selling, it's a way of cornering the prospect. Similar to a trial close. Relies on the idea that prospects somehow need to be tied up in order to get a sale.

> **Trial Close**
> The act of testing your prospect's willingness to make a positive decision. Similar to polling a jury to see if they are going to convict or acquit a prisoner. In both cases, rarely will you get the truth.

"The prospect knows that when he first meets with you, you are going to spend time doing *warm-up*. You know, and your prospect knows, that this is an old selling technique that's been used for centuries. All caveman sellers do *warm-up*. So, while you are doing *warm-up*, your prospect is getting increasingly uncomfortable and wants to get down to business. You feel his discomfort and will always make a decision to try and unravel that discomfort by spending more time, or working harder, at *warm-up*. But, what really happens? Your working harder at *warm-up* makes the situation worse. Your prospect wants to get on with it, while you want to get more 'buddied up.' You feel, and are seen, more and more like the salesperson you don't want to be seen as. Warm-up ends up reinforcing your fear of having a salesperson's image, exactly what you don't want, with every warm-up word you say.

"Now, let's look at *buying signals*. First, I want you to realize that your prospect, and only your prospect, knows what a *buying signal* is. While you try to read your prospect's mind and interpret what he is saying and whether it is a buying signal or not, your prospect is trying to read your mind to determine what you are saying and whether your are going for the close or not. The prospect asks about a delivery date. You say to yourself, 'I got it. I didn't miss the buying signal.' You are very proud of yourself, elated with yourself.

> **Buying Signal**
> A mythical flag or beacon raised by your prospect to let you know that he or she is ready to buy. The flag is said to contain the words, "I am ready to buy and I want you to know that."

You go for the close. 'Well, Mr. Prospect, if I could get it here by blah, blah, blah, does that mean I could earn your business today?' The prospect answers, 'Hell no. I wanted to know the delivery date so I could spreadsheet it with your competition. It's just one component.' You, with your tail between your legs, retreat, and your fear of losing a selling opportunity goes up instead of going down.

"The prospect knows that it's your job to **get excited** about your product. And sometimes the prospect actually gets excited because he catches a little bit of your enthusiasm. So what? At some point your prospect is going to come down to earth. He has to. He's just watching you and your excitement. But, it's your excitement. Not his. So at some point he's going

> **Get Excited**
> The process of lighting up your prospect's enthusiasm for your product or service so that he will continually say "yes" to almost anything you propose. Sometimes used as a sexual term that is applied to selling.

to say to himself, 'Wait a minute. What am I getting so excited about? He's just doing what every other salesperson has done, trying to get me excited. I'd better calm down or he's going to get me to buy this thing, and I don't know if I really want to.' So, at the sales meeting, or after the contract is signed (calling to cancel), he comes down to earth. Boom. No more excitement and you have shot your excitement wad. So, instead of having an excited, buying prospect, you now find yourself in a corner with no more ammunition to get yourself out. As your prospect deflates, your fear inflates, as you believe more and more that he won't like your product and won't buy.

"Your prospect expects a **presentation**, a **dog and pony show**. They count on it. Often, they plan their time around it. They know that during the presentation, you will spill your guts, give up all your information, answer all their questions, give them all the data, and do all that work without any agreement to do business. So, the prospect sits there, nods

> **Dog and Pony Show**
> A circus with dogs and ponies. Also, a presentation given before you know you have the sale. Something you should never do unless you are in the circus or own a dog and a pony.

his head in agreement, smiles when you smile, gets excited when you get excited, sees all the features and benefits just as you want him to, and, asks everything he wants to know. Yet, with every well-crafted answer you give, you seem to get another question or another objection. Soon, you are plum out of answers, plum out of energy, and plum out of control. And then, at your prospect's whim, he will bail from the meeting by leaning back, folding his arms, and grunting out one of his standard 'think about it' stalls. 'Uh, oh, um, you know, that's great stuff, Steve. Let me run the figures and crystallize my thinking. How about you give you a call in a couple of weeks?' Once again, your fear, like a thermometer on a hot day, rises to the rooftops."

As is beginning to be usual, I feel he's hit the nail on the head. Or, better yet, he's hit me directly on *my* head. I remember one sales meeting where I skipped *warm-up* because I was pressed for time. But, during the meeting, I would interject personal questions about my prospect, but do it as they came up naturally in the conversation. Boy, this customer had no problem getting right to business and actually was more open with me about his personal stuff. Now that I think about it, it was probably because he saw me as being more genuine and not doing the same "selling thing" that everyone else had done to him, not doing blah, blah, blah just to hear myself talk and feel good about myself.

> **Blah, Blah, Blah**
> Much of what salespeople say. Can be replaced with Yap, Yap, Yap.

Admission Is the Better Part of Valor

If I'm being really candid with myself, it is true that the last thing on earth I want to do is lose a sale. It is my biggest fear. I think about all the hours of prospecting, telephone calls, and then finally getting them to see me. Tons of hours. So, when I finally do get together with a prospect, I really want the sale. Getting the appointment was all the work. Now it's time to make money. The idea of losing the sale after all that work gave me all kinds of agitation. It just couldn't happen. So, what did I do? That's right, work harder at *closing, tie-downs, warm-up, getting excited,* and all that stuff. And what did that get me? A more stubborn and distant prospect and a lower *closing ratio*.

"Okay," I begin, "so I'm afraid to lose a sale and I'm willing to admit it. Really willing to admit it. A part of me is saying to myself, big deal, everyone is afraid to lose a sale, or just doesn't want to lose a sale. But, I think the difference for me now is that I have a much better understanding of what that dislike or fear does to me and how it impacts my prospect. You know, I work so hard to get a meeting with a prospect, I just don't want to lose the sale. And, if I'm short on prospects, that dislike turns to fear because there aren't enough prospects behind him to make up the loss. And when the fish are really running, lots of prospects, well, with my competitive nature, if I see myself losing the sale I really get down on myself. I ask myself, 'Why didn't I win that one?' 'I'm really not good at what I do.' 'I should have had that one.' And so on. So, that's that. What now?"

"Steve, if you mean all that, that's a very big step. Because, to eliminate *pain dumping* and *double loading*, **you must first have the courage to admit your dislikes and fears.** And, second, when you make those reality-based admissions, it helps you give up on the selling system you've been brainwashed into believing. You have to realize that you're like a man watching a movie; you're so captured by it, you believe that it's real and that you're one of the players. You need to get out of your chair, get out of the movie, turn it off, look yourself in the mirror, see yourself as you really are, look at your old-time selling system, and see it as it really is. You have to stop living in denial, burying your real feelings, and hiding in a caveman selling system's cave."

Chronicle #9
I Can't See I'm Getting Exactly What I Want

So here we are at another lesson. I choose to keep quiet and not let him in on any of my thoughts, which, by the way, he always seems to know anyway. Well, let's see where today takes us. He'll probably look me in the eyes and pick up what I'm thinking anyway. He has the ability to do that.

"Steve, it's good to see you. You have a kind of bewildered look in your eyes. What on earth have you been thinking?"

My resolution to keep quiet quickly fades. I want to tell him what I'm thinking, and I do.

"When I look back at the meetings we've had, I am surprised at the amount of territory we've covered. There are so many different facets to what you've been saying that I wonder how you're going to put it all together for me so it weaves into a meaningful system that I can use day in and day out. I mean, I don't mind being hammered, molded, prodded, and investigated, but, at the end of the day it's got to turn into more than good conversation. It's got to turn into something productive, financially and personally. After all, some of this stuff is pretty subtle, or, at least, *I* think it's pretty subtle. So I don't want to get lost in the minutia and lose sight of what this is all about—making more sales in less time and having more fun along the way."

"We've ranged pretty far and wide, haven't we? It reminds me of the six-year-old little girl who went to the library and asked the librarian if she had any books on airplanes. The librarian disappeared for a few minutes and came back with a big stack of books. The little girl looked at the stack of books and walked away. The librarian, quite surprised, asked her where she was going. She said, 'I'm leaving. I didn't want to know that much about it!' So, Steve, I hope that you are not like that little girl, not wanting to know this much about selling, because we still have a good way to go."

"No, it's okay. You know, when someone is chiseling you into a different mold, it's a lot to take in. But, let's keep on trucking, or should I say chiseling?"

It's Not the Sale Stupid!
"It is a lot. How about we truck and chisel this way today? Let's talk about what you really believe when you go out to make a sale, because what you believe is that you really, really, want to make a sale. That it is your top priority, right?"

"Of course!"

"But do you really? Is it possible that you really want something else, more than you want to make a sale? Is it possible you are like the king with no clothes? You believe one thing, but the reality is another. Is it possible that you actually sublimate your desire to make a sale for something that is really more important to you? Is it possible that boiling within you are deeper desires that, without your knowing it, take greater priority than making a sale? Is it possible that you think you want to make a sale, **but are blind to the fact that making a sale is often a lower priority on**

Chronicle #9

your scale of important goals than you think?

"Perhaps you're like the man who goes fishing, thinking that he really wants to catch a fish, but finds that his greater priority is drinking beer and laughing with his buddies. So he drinks and laughs a lot, while fishing very little. Perhaps you cannot fathom that you, not your prospects, are the cause of your selling failure because you don't really get what you really want, something more important to you than the sale."

"I find that a pretty interesting concept. But, what could it be that I really want more than a sale? After all, that's how I earn my living. I live to make sales."

> **Priority Killers**
> Land mines in your personality and emotions that blow up your true goals. Unconsciously switching your primary goal for a lesser goal. Leads to winning the battle but losing the war.

"That, Steve, is the question of the day. What is it that effectively and silently takes over your 'make the sale' priority and puts itself first? Okay, let me give you some ideas. I call them *priority killers*. They live in you like bacteria, gathering together until it's time to pop themselves up, usually during moments of higher pressure. Of course, they take on a different order for different people, but they look much like this:

- You want to be liked.
- You want to show how smart you are.
- You want to please others.
- You want to feel important.
- You want to control other people and conditions.
- You want to feel better about yourself.
- You want to avoid confrontation.
- You want to help people.
- You want to look professional.
- You want to feel needed.

"Think of it this way. In every moment of every conversation you have a sea of these *priority killers*—thoughts, feelings, and emotions that, if you permit, will supersede your desire to make the sale. In the instant that one of these *priority killers* surfaces to a priority position, you are a goner, along with the sale that you think you want."

Look, It's Me, the Real Me

"Let's take the *priority killer*—you want to show how smart you are—and see how that works. Suppose you let this thought drive itself into your number one priority position. Now, as the conversation between you and your prospect evolves, you begin to take every opportunity to prove to your client the vastness of your wisdom and intelligence. If the prospect brings up a small technical question, you give an encyclopedic answer. 'I am really smart,' you say to yourself. 'That was one great answer I just gave—didn't miss a detail!' While it is true that you really did show how smart you are and didn't miss one detail, it is also true that you took one big step closer to killing the sale. How so? Easy! Your comprehensive and technical tirade actually causes your prospect to ask more technical questions than he otherwise would. You, thinking that the prospect is really interested in this technical stuff, jump in and give him another technical display of fireworks, which, in addition to creating even more questions in your prospect's head, reinforces in your own mind just how smart you really are. You say to yourself, 'I am really smarter than I thought I was.' Now your prospect, immersed in an ocean of technical details, is stupefied into a hypnotic confusion and forgets the real purpose of the meeting. You then get a response that sounds something like this: 'Boy, you really know your stuff. Let me mull this thing over, check out a few things, and get back to you.' You've won the battle but lost the war. Smart, but no sale.

"Now let's take a look at your *priority-killer* list and fill in what happens to you and the interactions with your prospect that you just don't see.

Chronicle #9

You want to be liked.
"With this *priority killer* working, your conversations will avoid candidness and honesty because you think being candid and honest is difficult for people to handle and they therefore won't like you if you are that way with them. At the heart of your thinking is the idea that if people like you they will buy. So you spend your meetings with your prospect, trying to get him to like you. While it is true that people would prefer to buy from people they like, what you don't understand is that people really buy from people they respect. Your prospect ends up saying you are the greatest guy in the world. They don't buy, but you get what you really want, to be liked."

You want to show how smart you are.
"We already talked about this a little earlier. But, in this priority killer, when you give so much information and answer every question in so much detail, you either bore your prospect to tears or raise more questions than they would otherwise think about or ask. Your show of intelligence results in all the stalls and objections you are trying to avoid, especially if you're in front of a prospect who is more interested in showing you how smart he is than in buying something. It's a never ending cycle, because when your prospect shows his intelligence, you use that as a launching point to show how smart you are again. Your meeting becomes a proving ground for your smartness. While you always end the meeting feeling better about yourself, you lose the sale and, in so doing, classify your prospect as just being 'dumb or stupid' for not buying."

You want to please others.
"This *priority killer* is about being such a nice person that you want your prospect to be happy. So what do you do? You please him by giving him what he wants. If he asks, you deliver. If he wants a brochure, you have one handy. If he asks a question, the answer is out of your lips in an instant.

If he wants you to call him in two weeks, you are quick to say, 'Okay.' If your prospect has a time pressure but wants to meet anyway, you try to satisfy him by squeezing everything in. You give and keep giving and then, if you have to, give more; all to please him, and indeed you do. Everyone has a good experience when they meet with you. The only problem is that they don't buy. You go home at night proud of your ability to make life pleasant for others, and upset that you go home with nothing for yourself, except the feeling you have about yourself that you are a pushover!"

You want to feel important.
"Steve, this *priority killer* is the result of the caveman mindset believing that importance is gained by monopolizing the sales meetings. Here, you want to be the center of attention in every meeting. You tell stories about yourself, you talk freely about your knowledge, you interrupt your prospect's thought processes, and you put on a phony attitude, all in an effort to raise yourself up in the eyes of your prospect. You raise yourself, but only by pushing your prospect down, by making him somehow lower than you. You don't understand that the sales meeting is never about you, but is always about the prospect. It is your *prospect* who wants to feel important, be the center of attention, feel intelligent, be respected—all the same things you want. And what happens is that you lose sight of the fact that it is your job to help him feel that way. Now, as the meeting continues, your feeling of self-importance grows. You say to yourself, 'This is great. I am really important.' As your prospect leaves without buying, you can't understand why you lost the sale. You can't see that you let your desire to feel important take priority over your desire to make the sale. Mission accomplished: You feel important, and you feel poorer, because you are."

You want to control other people and conditions.
"Here's a *priority killer* where you try to gain control of situations and peo-

ple through manipulation and pressure tactics. You make pronouncements about the benefits of working with you and your product, and at the same time you devalue everything and everyone else. You want to take your prospect down the path that you want to go, thereby disrespecting and devaluing his goals. By pressuring your prospect, you bring upon yourself the buying resistance that you are trying to break down. By trying to control things, you actually lose control, and then you try even harder to gain control back. In the end, your tactics work against you, giving your prospect the control that you want for yourself. You push for control, but you know deep inside yourself that you are hanging on by a thread, or actually losing control quickly. Making the sale is soon forgotten as you spend more and more of your time trying to get what you really want, control."

You want to feel better about yourself.
"In this *priority killer,* your low self-esteem causes you to categorize your prospect as either being less than or greater than you are. You are always comparing yourself, in some way, to your prospect. As long as you are in a comparison mode, evaluating your prospect in terms of yourself, you can't develop a clear line of communication and a solid relationship with him. Because of this, you fall back on your technical savvy, your enthusiasm, and your manipulating tactics in order to make the sale. All these tactics are designed to make you feel better about yourself, but it is only a temporary satisfaction. Soon you see your relationship with your prospect floundering. You don't see that while you are feeling better about yourself, your prospect is feeling worse about himself. Since you are more concerned about taking care of yourself, you, of course, forget to take care of your prospect. Soon you and your prospect have a floundering, non-caring, all-about-me meeting. You get a good feeling about yourself, and along the way develop bad feelings about your prospect. In your mind, you are okay, but in your prospect's mind, he is not okay. As your

prospect is walking out the door, you say to yourself, 'Man, if I could only get some good prospects.'"

You want to avoid confrontation.
"Steve, this *priority killer* stems from the idea that the key to building relationships is to make certain that you don't upset people by confronting them. Here, you don't understand that confrontation is actually an important component of healthy relationships and can be positioned and communicated in a friendly and nurturing way. You've had such bad experiences with other poor communicators that you think confrontation will ruin any possibility of making a sale. You can't fathom that healthy confrontation actually builds rapport and solidifies relationships, giving you a better chance of making the sale. You interpret confrontation as being abrupt, too direct, too risky, too much to deal with. You would rather skirt around issues; you shy away from being direct. Your conversations with your prospect always seems to wallow in a gray area that sooner or later increasingly bogs down you and your prospect until the whole meeting becomes confused and unfocused. In the end, the meeting feels purposeless and your prospect doesn't buy. More important, the prospect doesn't respect you because, in many ways, he just feels you are not being straight with him. In his mind, you are really very nice and very friendly but offer nothing that moves him. You don't confront, you don't get the sale, but you do get what you really want: no confrontations."

You want to help people.
"Now, with this *priority killer*, let's say you have a wonderful helping quality within yourself. You want to do good in the world and help people out. Unfortunately, you would rather help people than make a sale. So you go overboard in the help arena. If your prospect wants something, you give it to him; if he wants to proceed a certain way, you say, 'Okay'; if he needs help in his personal life, you become a great listener; if he

wants more information, you are ready to provide it; if he wants something mailed, the stamp is on the envelope. You love to feel helpful, so much so that you allow this feeling to take priority over the sale. You don't realize that helping is a wonderful quality, but in sales, if helping is the singular goal, it will lead to selling disaster. You become known as a great helper, a kind person. You also get known as a lousy salesperson, and will soon leave the business."

You want to look professional.
"In this *priority killer* you think you are the consummate professional and that you know everything you need to do to make certain your prospect sees you that way. You are the boy scout of selling, always prepared. From head to toe, you are dressed like a professional salesperson should dress. When you enter a meeting, your calling card is instantly on the table. You come through the door with your bag full of all the materials, everything you are going to need. They could ask for anything; no problem, it's in your bag. You also have all the answers, know all the data, have the right bag of jokes, and, of course, know your selling system like the back of your hand. In fact, you are so busy being professional you forget that selling is all about communication, understanding, and relationship. In fact, you can't see that your professionalism actually turns your prospect off. Why? Because they have seen that same professionalism from every salesperson they have ever met in their lives. In fact, when you walk through the door, the first words that pop into your prospect's mind is, 'Uh oh, here comes another salesperson!' And why not, you are the spitting image of the stereotypical salesperson. The result? The more you look like a salesperson, the more your prospect feels like a prospect. The more your prospect feels like a prospect, the bigger the sales barrier and the harder the sale. You are in trouble the minute you walk through the door—very professional, but with less chance of making the sale."

You want to feel needed.
"This *priority killer* comes from the simple fact that you are human, and it is human nature to want to feel needed. Everyone has that feeling. But your need to be needed is out of bounds. Your happiness and self-esteem are dependent on establishing, with everyone you meet, that you are needed by them. At the end of the day, your need to be needed, like most excesses, turns on you and produces the exact opposite result. By wanting to be needed, instead of working diligently with people to solve their problems in a respectful and nurturing way, you quickly establish, in your mind, that each prospect has no idea what he is doing, and that he needs you to solve his problems. So without knowing it, you really upset people by minimizing their intelligence, by not expressing appreciation of their thoughts, their processes, their feelings, and their solutions. You think that your prospect's inability to think for himself requires that he turn to you. In actuality, all you do is make your prospect feel bad and subtly, or not so subtly, insult him. Sometimes your prospect doesn't even know he is being insulted or disrespected, but deep down he feels uncomfortable with you. He doesn't buy into your niceness. It is almost like you are telling him how great he is on the one hand, and stabbing them in the back with the other. Sooner or later in the meeting, you don't feel needed enough and work harder at making your prospect need you more. In the end you never succeed at making them need you by forcing your help upon them. The meeting ends in failure, with you mystified at why they didn't buy from the person they needed most, you. You've made yourself feel needed, but they thought otherwise. You got what you wanted, but the sale went somewhere else.

"Steve, here's the problem in a nutshell. **You are constantly blindsided by priorities that overlay and preempt your priority to make a sale.** And although the signs are all around you, you are either blind to them or you choose to ignore them. When you lose a sale you have no real idea why. Because you think you were focused on making the sale, and that was your priority, you study your caveman selling techniques with greater fervor and commitment. But, that same study blinds you further from the truth. You are in the dark but think the sun is shining."

I am thinking about all the things percolating in me that I have never talked about. It's like there's a part of me that relates to almost everything he's saying. I can remember meetings where I wanted to be nice, or wanted to be liked, or wanted to be seen as a professional instead of just a salesperson, or didn't want to confront people because I thought they wouldn't do business with me. What a load of baloney. All that stuff really has to go. And when you really think about it, my prospect is doing the same thing. So, if I don't somehow hide or control all these *priority killers,* and my prospect doesn't either, then we really have nothing going on. Pretty hard that way to end up in a trusting relationship and a willingness to transact business.

I get this image of myself and say, "You know, if all this stuff is boiling below the surface, I can see myself like the little Dutch boy with my finger in the dike, plugging a hole here, only to have the water punch another hole in the dike there. So, if, in every other minute one or the other of these *priority killers* bubbles up to the surface, how do you deal with all that?"

"Well, Steve, let's see where to go from here."

Where Does Steve Go from Here?

He Calls a Spade a Spade, and I'm It!
"Steve, do you remember the old saying, 'Even a fish wouldn't get caught if he kept his mouth shut?'"

"Sure I do. After what we've talked about, I'm getting to think I really need to sew mine closed permanently."

"Well, not quite as bad as that. But, you need to come to the realization that you are really a person out of control. I will say this as kindly as I can, but you are a *pain dumping, double loading, priority killing, unconscious, caveman salesperson* living in *total denial.*"

I look him square in the eyes. He did say it with kindness, but it still upsets me. I guess what upsets me the most is that the little whisper inside of me telling me that there is a lot of truth in what he's saying is now a loud voice saying, "Yes, he's right. You are just like that." Sarcastically I say to him, "Okay. Is there anything you would like to add to that?"

"Actually, yes. And this will probably upset you more than you already are. I am truly sorry for that, but, in truth, you have very little clue, if any, what you are going to say next, how it will impact your prospect, why you are saying it and how your prospect will react. That's the reality."

Again, our eyes square off. The kindness is still in his voice. The loud voice in me, telling me he is right, has now upped its volume to a gentle scream, or at least as gentle as a scream can be. This time, however, I'm not sarcastic; I am just pissed off. I don't hide it either, when I say, "You know, keeping one's mouth shut is not something new, something that you invented. I've heard that many times and in many places," I add, "*especially* in my caveman training."

"Steve, Steve, you are quite right. And you also need to know that all the stuff going on inside you is quite natural, and that your emotional feelings about the things you didn't recognize in yourself are very natural, too. Denial is like a curtain. When it rises, when the real show goes on, you are moved from one reality, the reality of illusion, into the reality of reality. You put yourself in the real play, right into the drama. That's a big step, with big emotions and sometimes a lot of inner defense and turmoil. I just want you to know that you're not the only one who is experiencing what you're experiencing."

His words are comforting. It's nice to know I'm normal. But the emotions are still there, and I want to blame him for what I'm seeing in myself. I continue to give him that look.

Chronicle #9

The Reality of Win-Win

He continues, "Caveman selling *has* evolved to a level of recognizing that talking can get you into trouble. Unfortunately, *not* getting into trouble is *not* what selling is all about. **Selling is about consummating a business transaction in which both parties** *win*. To get to that level, a *win-win,* you need to do more than just stay out of trouble. You need to *co-create* a meeting, its content and its atmosphere, which allows a human level of communication in which both parties feel a sense of freedom, mutual respect, and care. If you keep your mouth shut just to get

> **Co-Create**
> A mutually respectful effort to achieve an agreed upon goal or goals. A shared responsibility. Often thought of by caveman salespeople as a sure road to a lost sale, because they have to keep their mouths shut in the process.

what you want, just to make sure you stay out of trouble, you are missing the point of what keeping your mouth shut really means.

"Look, the idea of *co-creating* a *win-win* sales meeting is foreign to most caveman sellers like you. Although they all would defend their position by saying that *win-win* is all that they want, it's just not true. They either want to make a sale or they want get something else from their prospect that supersedes their desire to make a sale. When you keep your mouth shut, it gives you a chance to see your prospect more clearly. More important, it gives you a chance to see yourself more clearly, to become more aware of yourself, to begin to

> **Win-Win**
> Something you think you strive for as a salesperson but really don't. Face it: You're out for yourself.

wake up. The less you talk, the more you see. The more you see, the greater your awareness. The greater your awareness, the greater the possibility you will do the right thing. The more you do the right thing, the more your prospect will be responsive to you and you to your prospect. The more responsive you and your prospect are with each other, the greater the possibility of co-creating a *win-win* meeting. That's what reality looks like.

"Steve, true *win-win* meetings are difficult for the caveman selling professional's intellect to grasp. You see, you want to win, period! If the meeting ends in a *win-win*, it is a nice by-product but not your real goal, no matter what you may say otherwise. Your real goal is to make the sale, nothing else. But *win-win* meetings can either result in a sale or not. It doesn't matter. It can't matter. It can't matter because as soon as a certain end result is the goal, the meeting will end far from a *win-win*."

I remember all the conversations with my selling buddies about *win-win* and that we were pretty serious in trying to find ways to make our meetings work out that way. What is interesting is that, in those same conversations, we would tell all our tales about how we got each sale, what kind of close we used, how we manipulated the prospect to get what we wanted, not what they wanted. Now *is* that a *win-win*, if someone buys something they think they need, or, even actually do need, and we convince them, or push them to do it? I think it is, even though we might have manipulated the meeting somewhat. I got what I wanted and they got what they wanted. So, I'm not certain I see the difference here. If my real goal is to make a sale and I do, and my prospect is happy, that's a *win-win*.

So, I ask him, "If they buy and I sell and everyone's happy, isn't that a win-win?"

He answers, "Not really. What is their experience? What is your experience? How much life energy did you both put into it? How much needless aggravation did it cause? It's just not about end of the journey; it's about the journey itself. What was that like? Was it really worth it for both of you, just because it had a good ending? Does the end justify the means? And these are just the questions for a positive outcome.

"But let's say they don't buy and you can't make the sale. Is that a win-win? Or, are there the same questions and more? I think so. What about you?"

"No. If they don't buy, I certainly didn't get what I wanted, and I don't know if they got what they wanted."

Every Meeting Must End in a Win-Win ... a Real Win-Win

"That's right. You see Steve, in the caveman system, *win-win* only happens when there is a transaction, a sale. And, even then, there could be times when a sale is made but the people who bought only bought because they were trying to satisfy one of their *priority killers* like, for instance, buying from you because they did not want to hurt your feelings. How is that a *win-win*? *Win-win* means that every meeting, every single meeting, ends in a way that both parties win."

"Every meeting?"

"Yes, Steve, every meeting."

"No matter how it ends."

"No matter how it ends," he says emphatically. "Just imagine if I was looking out for you and you were looking out for me and we were both committed to that. You see, no matter what happened, no matter the result, the meeting would be a win for both of us. The result becomes incidental to the meeting, instead of the meeting revolving around the result. Now, let's be clear here. The only meeting that is not a *win-win* is a meeting that ends in a *think about it*. In this case there is no clear end to the meeting, and without a clear ending the meeting cannot be a win for both parties."

"If that's true, then making the sale is incidental to the meeting and the meeting is not to make a sale."

"There, you've summed up all our work in one sentence. Everything else we're talking about is just how to accomplish that. Should we go further?"

"Onwards and upwards," I answer, actually with some enthusiasm. This is starting to sound like it could be a lot of fun.

The Selling Chronicles

My Mouth Moves, My Sales Go Down

"Okay now. When you talk too much, you're emotionally loaded, unconscious priorities take over your thought processes. Every word you speak is loaded with an emotion that is neither beneficial to you or to your prospect. **By zipping your lips, you give your emotional and thinking energy a chance to ground itself in** *reality*. *Reality* is an unbiased, accurate, independent picture of what is happening at any point in time. *Reality in a sales meeting is really the ultimate goal of the meeting. Reality-based sales meetings* should be your first and last goal. You need to see the *reality* of yourself, the *reality* of your prospect, and the *reality* of the words and actions flowing between both of you. Your first priority is to see the *reality* in yourself, to become aware of yourself, your feelings, your loads, your pressures, your thoughts, your opinions, your needs, your neediness, your dreams, your biases, your tendencies, your strengths, your weaknesses, and your motivations. That's what being aware is about.

"So when you're in a sales meeting, obsessed with your caveman tactics, you don't—actually, you can't—experience *reality*. You are too involved with trying to get what you want. You are so involved with yourself—what you want, how you're doing, what you will or won't get, your success, your failure, and all the other *stuff* floating around inside you—you cannot really see what is happening with your prospect. You hear what you want to hear and look for signals that you want to look for. Your emotions, like a roller coaster, capture your attention with highs, lows, curves, and bumps. And with each turn, you think you are doing better, worse, going nowhere, scared, happy, okay, not okay, all hinged onto one critical and selfish thought: Will you get what you want out of this meeting, a sale?

"Steve, to experience *reality*, you have to disengage with all the *stuff* that

> **Stuff**
> Your talk during a sales meeting, which doesn't improve on the silence it interrupts. (See *Blah, Blah, Blah*.)

is boiling within you. You need to come to the realization, as a first step in developing a sense of awareness and *reality*, that what you think, feel, and experience is nothing more than *stuff*. And, when you see all your *stuff* as *stuff*, that all that *stuff* is very transient and really means nothing to you, you can begin to disengage yourself from your *stuff* and start to see yourself, your prospects, and the world around you as it really is."

Trying to be very realistic, I say, "Looks like we are back to *reality*. In fact, I can see all of our conversations as your helping me; or should I say, you're providing me with information so I can help myself, see through a lot of the fog surrounding my selling, especially the fog around me. I must say, it's pretty thick fog; more like soup. Remember you talked about that whisper. Well, I think that it's hard to hear what is being whispered because of all the noise, the fog that is going on during the meeting. Lift the fog, hear the whisper, and you're there. Maybe it's as easy as that?"

"Steve, I remember someone saying to me once that things are either easy to learn and easy to do; or easy to learn and hard to do; or hard to learn and hard to do. And, do you know which one most salespeople choose? That's right, hard to learn, hard to do. This stuff is not hard to learn, there is just a lot of it. And, it's not hard to do. It's just a matter of practicing and coaching, which we'll get to soon."

It's the Sound of Silence

"So, you're asking yourself, how do I do this? Well, that's what silence is all about. Silence is the single best way for you to begin to see your *stuff*. By not talking, you can sit back, let your prospect do all the work, and, instead of being a caveman salesperson, become an *active observer* to everything that is happening within you, within your prospect, and what is happening as you interact with each other. **As an *active observer* during a sales meeting, you will not react to your *stuff*, and you will not react to your prospect's *stuff*.** (Everyone has *stuff*.) Non-reaction during a sales meeting gives a tremendous opportunity for creative conversation and planning. You don't know what it is like not to have *knee-jerk* reactions to your prospect. Although you crave that kind of freedom, you can't get to it because you are so identified with your *stuff*. You believe your *stuff* is real, while it is not.

"Steve, you can convince yourself that your *stuff* is not *reality* based by just watching it as it pops up now, disappears later, then pops up again and disappears again, *ad infinitum*. One minute you see your prospect interested, and you feel good; the next moment your prospect raises an objection, and you feel danger; the next moment you say something you think you should not have said, and you feel stupid; the next moment your prospect says something you don't like, and you feel attacked. Everything is changing. *Reality* is seeing the *reality* of change, of how undependable your *stuff* is. Yet your *stuff* drives you throughout your sales meeting, throughout your life. By becoming aware, by seeing the reality of things, you can take hold of yourself, release yourself from the misery that you create for yourself, become proactive instead of reactive, make better decisions, learn new methods, and extricate yourself from the habits and brainwashing of the tribal consciousness fostered by your caveman predecessors."

> **Silence**
> What you get to hear when your lips are not moving. That from which reality springs.

I remember the times I would kid myself about making a mistake and say that I can't walk and chew gum at the same time. In this case, I can see that if I talk, talk, talk, I won't be able to see, while I'm yakking away, the reality of what is happening. And, there are millions of ways to keep me so occupied, out of *reality*, other than talking. On a simple level, how about a good movie? That's a great escape. Or, how about computer games? I don't play them, but I know enough kids who know more about them than they know about what they ate for breakfast. Or, how about

Chronicle #9

a mystery novel? I can read a good one for hours and have no idea about what is going on with the entire universe while I am doing it, totally absorbed, totally escaped. Take all that and apply it to my sales meetings and, for sure, there is no *reality* there. Not with me, not with the circumstances, not with my prospect, and probably not in my prospect either. Maybe he should have called it fantasy selling, or dream selling, or non-reality selling instead of caveman selling. You know, if he practices what he preaches, he lives in a totally different world than I do. If he lives in *reality*, and I live in non-reality, we are living in two different worlds. He can see what I see, but I can't see what he sees. I guess, in the end, I have to pick which world I want to live in. No problem though, I've already made that choice.

The Selling Chronicles

Chronicle #10
I Don't Know That the World Works in Reverse

"Steve, let me start with a pretty challenging statement, okay?"

"Well, it's not like you've held back in the past. Every road we go down is pretty challenging to me."

"I'm not surprised. But there's challenging and there's *challenging*."

He says the last "challenging" with a very challenging tone of voice and look on his face.

"Okay, let me have it."

"Good. Here goes. I submit to you that everything you experience in the world you live is not as it appears. Things that look solid, are not; the stars that you see, are not there; what you see now is not what you saw a moment ago; the sun doesn't rise in the morning and the moon doesn't rise at night; you see the world as flat, but it isn't; you think you live in the present, but you don't; you think you're independent, but you're not; and to top it off, you think the world works in a straight line, and it doesn't.

"Now, you're probably saying to yourself that this sounds like a lesson in quantum physics. Well, to a certain extent it is. But for selling, it is a lesson in reformulating your vision of what works and what doesn't, when meeting with a prospect.

"For our purposes as sales professionals, let's focus on the last example I gave you; that you think that the world works in a straight line, and it doesn't.

"Think about it. In your world, you believe if you want to get from A to B, you just put it in forward, make a few adjustments along the way, and there you are. Then, if you want to get from B to C, again you make sure you're facing in the right direction, turn you're marching feet on, and soon you'll be at your destination. Now, I know you're wise enough to know that nothing works the way we plan it to work. You might have to move left a little bit, go around a little bit, hurdle a small or large barrier or two. But in the end, as long as you keep those feet moving forward and don't give up, you'll arrive. It's a 'pound the rock' mentality. You've heard sales gurus say, 'You just need to pound the rock, work the system; pound the rock, work the system.' Right?"

"Oh, yeah. I was just reading an email blast sent to me from a guy who considers himself a super coach. That is exactly what the message was. If you want to succeed you just need to pound the rock and work the system. That's all you need to do. There was a lot of focus in that message, but there was no wisdom. Which rock are you pounding? With what kind of tools? With what mechanics? With what level of effort? Which system? Does it need adjustments, fine tuning? To which market? There was nothing like that in the message, just work your butt off and you'll be okay. Well, maybe, but at what expense? Now, I know, and every other salesperson knows, even though they keep looking for it, there's no silver bullet in marketing and selling. But just to pound the rock, like you said; that doesn't make much sense to me either."

I Believe the World Works in a Straight Line

Quickly, he adds, "Now, if you really think about it, you'll see that in your mind you believe that the world works in an essentially straight line and

Chronicle #10

> **Linear Thinking**
> Believing that to get from A to B you can walk in a straight line. Thinking that the world will adjust to your wishes so you can accomplish your goals. In sales, focusing on the close and going directly for it, no matter what.

you can always get to where you want to go by moving forward. Actually that is a kind of pound-the-rock mentality. But, why would you or anyone else think that way? Because that is the way, in your eyes, the world appears. You look down the highway and put your foot on the gas pedal; and except for a few curves and hills, boom—sooner or later you're there. It's the thinking that extends from the caveman hunter's mentality. You say to yourself, 'I'm just gonna go out there and kill that sabertooth tiger (or wooly mammoth) knock the cover off the ball ... no matter what! Just give me my club, point me in the right direction, give me my marching orders, and I'll do the rest.' In your world this is called *forward* or *linear thinking*. **It's the Neanderthal mentality football macho mentality: Put your head down, dive into the dark of the cave, and head for the beast.** You and everyone else are taught, from the moment you can think at all, to look forward, set your goals, get there as fast as you can, and leave everyone else in the dust.

"Okay? Now, let's apply that to your selling. You set a goal to *close* the sale. You plow ahead like the selling shaker and breaker you are, and put all the moves you can on your prospect. These are supposed to lead to the end game, the goal, *closing* the sale. But they don't. Too often, although you set a good target, take good aim, and shoot your arrow as straight and as true as possible, you miss the target. In selling, more often than not, starting at *A*, with your eye on *B*, and marching like a true soldier towards your goal, just doesn't get you there. In fact, all too often it gets you to places you are absolutely trying to avoid. Did you ever notice that?"

"Notice that?" I say. "I'm a living example of that! You know as well as I do that in selling you're failing more than you're succeeding. Otherwise

I would *close* every qualified prospect. So it's true, I don't end up where I want to go. I end up chasing people, trying to get them to buy—exactly, as you say, where I *don't* want to go."

"I'm glad you see that, Steve. The problem for you and most everyone using so-called modern selling techniques is that those techniques are based on *linear thinking*. It never occurs to you that your belief in how the world works, that to get from *A* to *B* requires you go forward, is exactly opposite to the way the world really works. You never see that most of the world doesn't work that way at all, and, in fact, that the way to get from *A* to *B* in selling is not by going forward, but by going backwards. You see Steve, the world really works in reverse.

"Look at it this way. In the old days, your caveman buddies looked at the sun and thought it revolved around the earth. They wove such a good myth about the earth and the sun that it lasted for thousands of years. It was hypocrisy to think otherwise. Now you're in the same boat. You're wearing blue sunglasses and think the world is blue. If you could take your sunglasses off and disengage from the myth of how the world works and look at the reality of what is happening to you in selling, you would find that the world, especially your selling world, is *not* linear. Understanding this concept of *reverse world thinking* sits at the heart of your being able to revamp your selling methodology to better fit with the mindset of modern-day people and, of course, make more sales. Some of the ideas of *reverse world thinking* may strike you as being absurd or making no sense. You'll feel like you have to put your car in reverse to go forward. For now, don't worry about how you feel; just open your

> **Reverse World Thinking**
> The understanding that you often should do the opposite of what you think you should do to get where you want to go. To get the prospect to "yes," for example, you push him to "no." To get the prospect to buy your product, try to get him to buy a competitive product first.

Chronicle #10

mind and listen, okay?"

Before, he kind of turned my selling world upside down. Now, he's turned it from forwards to backwards. Pretty soon he'll have me walking on the ceiling or standing on my head to walk at all. And, after that, he'll probably just turn the whole thing inside out. What the hell; I've already jumped off the cliff with this guy.

"Okay," I say, shrugging my shoulders to indicate that there's nothing else I could do anyway except just walk away, and I'm not about to do that.

"Good. So here's what *reverse world thinking* looks like in comparison to *forward* or *linear thinking*:

Your Linear Thinking	Your Experience	Reverse World Thinking
To make more sales, you need to work harder at closing.	Instead of more closes, you get more stalls and objections.	Instead of working harder at closing, you must work harder at opening.
You have to get the prospects to move in the direction you want them to move, or you will lose the sale.	The harder you try to get the prospect to go in the direction you want them to go, the more they dig their feet in and want to go in the direction they want to go.	To get the prospect to go in the direction you want them to go, you have to first go in the direction they want to go until they do not want to go any further. Then, on their own, they will go in the direction you want them to go.
If you get the prospect to say "yes" during the presentation, they will say "yes" when you go to the close.	The prospect says "yes" during the presentation, but then says "no" at the close.	To get an ultimate "yes" at the end of the meeting you have to push them to "no" during the meeting.
To control sales meetings you have to control and somehow manipulate the prospect along the way.	The more you try to control the prospect, the less control you have over him or her.	To control meetings and prospects, you have to give them the freedom and respect they deserve; then they will give you control.
To get prospects to trust and believe in you, you have to prove yourself in every moment and in every possible way.	The harder you try to earn trust and prove yourself, the more wary of you your prospect becomes.	To get people to trust and believe in you, you must trust and believe in them.
To make more sales, you must at all times encourage prospects about the features and benefits of your product.	Encouraging prospects in this way actually puts them on the defensive, making them less apt to buy.	To make more sales, you have to discourage people from buying so that they eventually encourage themselves to buy.

155

"Steve, *linear thinking* dominates every aspect of your selling. You believe that if you say what you're supposed to say, you'll get what you're supposed to get in the end. When you get something different from what you're supposed to get, you write it off as the fault of either bad luck, needing more practice, your own shortcomings, the economy, your spouse, the weather, the stock market, or the size of the orange crops in Florida. You never say to yourself, 'The kind of thinking I'm prone to think, and the view of the world I'm prone to view, just doesn't have any basis in *reality*. I need to change my thinking and the way I view the world.'"

I Only Know One Direction—Forward!

When he stops speaking, it gives me a chance to think about how I was brought up from childhood and, more importantly, how I'm bringing up my children today. I can see where I learned, even as a young boy, to never give up, never turn around and go backwards, never retreat. I remember getting a singular message, as did all my friends, of how to diligently march forward in my conquest of the world. Indeed, it was not just a benign world that I was being trained to conquer, but it was a terrible world, with terrible people that you couldn't trust. Conquest! That's it. It was about conquest. And it's still about conquest. And that's the message I subtly, and not so subtly, send to my children. Just the other day I gave my son a talk on how he can't give up; how he had to march forward in his business; how failure was unacceptable; how he had to set his sights and train his mind to get what he wants. But it's not only my message; it's the message of the day. It's everyone's message for success. Why? Because that's how the world seems to work. And both of us are passing this wisdom of life down to all these kids about how to get along, how to move forward in life.

I take a moment and try to recall a time, any time, that I ever heard someone tell me that it was okay to retreat; that by reversing direction, I might really get further forward; that although a path might look like it was going backwards, it was really going forwards; that it was possible that life was an optical illusion and that the paths we were treading were not necessarily the paths that would take us where we want to go. While my mind churns to find just one memory indicating the benefit of going backwards, I realize that none are there. Finally, I give up thinking about it at all. Retreating is absolutely foreign territory to me.

Now, as a well coached and well trained selling soldier, I have learned that selling requires me to go forward, to move on, and to always follow the rules of engagement. I will conquer; I will close; I will make the sale; I will win. And what's he telling me? Hogwash! It's a lot of caveman baloney. Take off the glasses Steve, open your eyes, see what's real. The world doesn't work that way. He's saying, "Relax partner, selling is easier than that; control is easier than that; people are easier than that; you're easier than that; your life is easier than that; all that, if you would just turn around and go in the other direction. Because that's where the action is: behind you, not in front of your nose. To get into the action, you need to go exactly in the opposite direction of where you think you need to go. How about that?" Well, how about that?

"Looks like I need eyes behind my head so I can see in reverse."

"Not really, my friend. But to let people inspire themselves to buy from you, to guide them to their own motivation to change, you have to look in different places than you've been looking. In fact, you don't have to look at all. You just need to let your prospect take you there, and that begins by seeing that your *selling world works in reverse.*"

I think the little light bulb in my head is turning on, and I decide that I shouldn't tell him what I want, because that would be the way I would normally say things. Instead of asking him directly, "So, what do I do; how do I fix this?" I choose to go in the reverse direction, to tell him what

I don't want to happen to see if it gets me what I do want.

With a combination of apprehension and excitement in trying something new, I say, "So, you probably don't want to tell me right now what I can do about it. It's probably premature or the wrong time."

His laugh starts as a heave in his stomach, and by the time it reaches his mouth it's like a little volcano erupting. It is catching, and mine starts in about the same place. In a moment we are both howling.

"Steve, I'm really proud of you. Now it sounds like you're working me over. To answer your question, it's absolutely the right time and it is not premature at all. I'd love to tell you what you can do.

My thoughts are clear about what I just did. If I had asked for what I wanted, I could have been rejected, let down, disappointed. By telling him it probably wouldn't happen, I couldn't lose, no matter his answer. I got what I wanted. But, more importantly, he gave it to me without my asking. Now, how about them apples?

Where Does Steve Go from Here?

Giving Up Desire

"Steve, as you *wake up* to the reality of your selling, you'll find that you are locked in and driven by *four overriding, dominant, unceasing desires*:

- Your desire to win.
- Your desire to be right.
- Your desire to control.
- Your desire for your dreams to come true.

Do those sound familiar?"

"For sure, I like to win. I like to be right, I certainly am a control freak, and I've been known to have a dream or two that I would like to come true."

"Okay. Now, as you learn to see the reality of your prospects, in fact, people in general, you will see that they too are locked in and driven by

Chronicle #10

The Four Overriding, Dominant, Unceasing Desires

Desires that are part of the inner nature of you and your prospects: winning, rightness, control, and dreams coming true. They are like children who want something in the toy store—they never give up.

the same four *overriding, dominant and unceasing desires*. It is human nature. Now, here's the problem. *Reverse world thinking* asks you—or better yet, demands—that you swim upstream against human nature. To take advantage of your new understanding of how your selling world really works, you must eliminate—completely give up—your desire to win, to be right, to control, and to have your dreams come true. If you could do that, put your world in reverse in this way—let others win, let them be right, let them control the meetings, and let them get their dreams fulfilled, even at the expense of your own, you would make more sales than you ever imagined. And, ultimately, you would turn out being a winner, being right, controlling the meetings, and having your dreams fulfilled too.

"Now, what most people are saying to themselves at this point is something like this: 'How on earth could that be possible? It makes no sense. How can you get what you want by not trying to get what you want? This sounds like a lot of mumbo-jumbo nonsense!' Some other types of people will be thinking, 'Man, this is a lot of psycho-spiritual hogwash that I've heard before, but it really doesn't work in the business world.' Yet others might say, 'Sure, I've seen a lot of people let other people win, or reach their dreams and stuff like that. You know what they got for themselves other than a good feeling and really being liked? Nothing! Absolutely nothing. A big fat zero! So why on earth would I want to do that?'"

Once again, he seems to be reading my mind. "Well, I can't say that I'm not having those same thoughts. After all, all that's very nice and very kind, and very good natured, but I don't see how that makes sales."

I Start to Put the Pieces Together

"Actually, by itself, *reverse world thinking* could get you into a lot of selling trouble. Remember that *reverse world thinking* is only one part of a system. It's an approach, a method, a path to follow that will work for you and your prospect's mutual benefit only if it is tied and used in conjunction with the rest of the things we've been talking about. For example, using *reverse world thinking* and not turning your meeting into a *business meeting* will lead to almost certain selling failure."

"I'm glad you reminded me of that. It's easy to get so involved in some of the ideas and concepts you're talking about, that I forget that each one at some point has to be tied together with the others and woven into a working plan. Is that right?"

Business Meeting
A meeting in which all parties agree on the process that leads to the goal of exchanging money for goods or services, better known as a sale. The opposite of a social meeting, which unfortunately many salespeople prefer.

"That's exactly right," he says. "And, there will be a point when I put the whole thing together, like a game plan, and a lot of this will become even more clear and understandable. Right now it's more like an intellectual exercise to try and get you to open up to new views of yourself, your selling world, or the world in general. If you can do that—and you are—then we can piece a new selling system together for you. But let's keep going.

"Steve, soon you will come to realize, by putting on the brakes and reversing your thinking, that the *four overriding, dominant unceasing desires* are really a lot of needless gibberish and the cause for much of your selling and personal pain. Let's look at the examples I gave you in a little more detail and give you some more ideas and examples of why and how this stuff works."

Linear Thinking:
To make more sales you have to work harder at closing.

"Steve, most people don't make it in sales. The turnover is horrific. Worse yet, you see many bright, articulate, professional and well educated people fail at our craft. I'll bet that each time a new crop of salespeople arrive at your company, you and your buddies take bets on how long each one will last. And, you always guess wrong. There is no telling who will win and who will lose. But one thing is for sure, and you get told this over and over, when someone fails in selling it is because they are weak closers. That is the single, biggest and most common explanation for selling failure. Since *closing* is the key, if you can't *close*, you can't sell."

Reverse World Thinking:
To make more sales you have to work harder at opening, not closing.

"Steve, caveman sellers like you think problems occur at the end of the sale when you go for the *close*. You can't see that all the objections, stalls, and put-offs that you get at the end of the sale are a result of how you handled your prospect right at the beginning of the sale. In fact, to take this a little further, if you could really understand what stalls and objections are all about, you could get rid of most of them at the very beginning of your very first meeting with a prospect. This is the job of your *lethal business personality*. The

> **Social Meeting**
> Yap, yap yap; blah, blah, blah. All without any business meeting agreements such as those found in the *Five Elements of a Lethal Business Meeting*.

very first set of objections are removed right at the beginning of the meeting by making certain that you turn your meeting from a *social meeting* into a *business meeting*. We saw the elements of a *business meeting in* Chapter 6: Purpose, Time, Bail Outs, Decisions, and People. *Reverse world thinking* demands that you get agreement on these elements at the beginning of the meeting, rather than at the end. In the process, typical objections that you would get when you go for the *close* are eliminated."

I See How and Where Objections Fit in

"Now, let's extend this thinking to objections in general. If you take a look at the kinds of objections you get, you'll find that they fall into four broad categories:

> **Objection**
> Something the prospect doesn't like and that you usually get defensive about.

- Objection to one of the elements of the *lethal business meeting.*
- Objections to the product.
- Objections to the cost or the plan.
- Objections to you.

"*Linear thinking* dictates that each of these should be handled as they come up during the meeting, in whatever order they come up, and provides specific language to handle each type of objection. Steve, you can buy books with hundreds of pages on different 'great' things to say to handle objections. You may own some already. So, with linear thinking, there you are, sitting and talking with your prospect, waiting for him or her to bring up some kind of objection, many of which you have heard before, some of which will be new to you, prepared with your list of memorized responses—the same list, by the way, that every other salesperson has memorized too.

"To make matters worse, the prospect's game plan is designed to wait until you have done most of your *dog and pony* show, answered most of his questions, revealed your most important information, and do all that before bringing up his standard objections and stalls. So, you'll find that a great deal of time passes before you discover what your prospect is really thinking. And you, like a conscientious parent shoveling food on the table for your child, dicing, microwaving, broiling, defrosting, baking, messing up the whole kitchen, creating a lot of dishes, pots, and pans to wash, keep all your information coming without even knowing if your kid, or prospect, is hungry or not and wants to eat what you are serving.

"Now, in the linear selling world in which you live, when your child says, 'But Dad, I'm not hungry,' what do you do?"

"Knowing me, I'd probably say that he needs to eat to be big and strong; or that it's lunchtime and if he doesn't eat now he'll have to wait until dinner; or man, this is the greatest peanut butter and jelly sandwich ever; or, if you don't eat this there'll be no desert; or something like that."

"Right, you try to overcome the objection. It's a natural instinct for a parent. You might even try laying a guilt trip on your kid, 'Gee, I've worked so hard, and now I've done all that work for nothing? Or, look how beautiful this peanut butter and jelly sandwich is, how can you resist?' And you will keep the pressure on until he eats a little bit of something. Right? And then what does he say? 'Dad, I'm really full; or I really don't like the way it tastes; or some other stall or objection that little kids develop to combat the selling tactics of their parents. So, you cook the food too early, just like you give up your information or presentation too early. Then, when the objections come, you've already done the work, and for what reason? They may not even be really interested."

I Bring Up the Objection First

"Steve, *reverse world thinking* requires you to handle as many of these objections as you can at the beginning of the sales meeting, before you go to work. In fact, it becomes your job to raise objections that are typical for your product, or your personality, or your price, or whatever, **before your prospect does**. I'm going to say that again. You need to raise objections that you hear all the time about you or your product before your prospect does. You need, early in the meeting, to put all those objections on the table to see what your prospect will do with them. Do you see that?"

Quickly, I answer, "You want me to think of all the objections that I usually get and bring them up early in the meeting, right?"

"Exactly right."

"And the reason I do that," I ask as I tip my head slightly, "is to prevent myself from doing a lot of work and then, after I've done that work, find out that this guy might not be a buyer at all. Is that right too?"

"Exactly right too. Then, what happens, is that *reverse world thinking* reverses the selling world in the eyes of your prospect, and thereby confuses him, which diffuses his game plan—the same game plan he has used on every salesperson he has ever met. If you were willing to commit to *reverse world thinking,* despite how much sense it makes to you or not, you would eliminate most objections before you volunteered important information that your prospect wants.

"Now, let me show you how you can get many of your objections out of the way at the beginning of the sales meeting, before you've given critical information to your prospect, rather than at the end of the meeting, after you have given critical information to your prospect.

Agreement on the elements of a business meeting:
Eliminates objections and stalls that usually happen at the end of the meeting that sound like this:
- I want to think it over.
- I need to consult with my current financial advisor or competition.
- We're just shopping around.
- We need to do some research.
- I'll get back to you.
- We always wait 24 hours before we make a decision.
- We need to look at other options.
- I don't buy on the first appointment.
- I don't have any money.
- We've been with them for years and won't leave.
- My uncle is in the business, let's see what he says.
- Oh, we're not really ready yet.

Chronicle #10

When you bring up typical objections first at the beginning of the meeting you will:
- Dissolve the negative influence of the objections the client is thinking about.
- Make certain that your prospect does not take control of the meeting by raising objections and putting you on the defensive.
- Let the prospect know at the beginning of the meeting that there is nothing to hide.
- Lower the prospect's guard.
- Immediately increase trust.
- Take the worry away and pressure off you, since you know you would have gotten the objection or stall sooner or later and would have had to handle it then.

Bringing up objections to fees, costs, or pricing, early in the meeting, before the prospect does, eliminates these problems:
- Cost issues that inhibit the prospect from really listening to you as he or she inwardly spends time thinking about them, or waiting expectantly for the issue to come up.
- Many prospects' reluctance to discuss fees. When you bring them up first, it gets them out of the way, causing your prospects to relax and hold a more realistic conversation.
- False ideas and pressures you may have within you about how this prospect feels about your price. It may be okay and not an issue to your prospect at all.
- Many of the standard objections and stalls that we discussed earlier.

Bringing up issues of relationship early in the meeting, before the prospect does, allows you to:
- Diffuse any difficulties that may undermine your ability to establish

rapport between you and your prospect, such as quirks in your personality. For example, you might say, 'Mrs. Prospect, I tend to be a very candid person. I hope you won't mind that. And, of course, you can be candid with me too!' Or, 'Sometimes I kid a lot. I hope you won't be offended by that. And you can kid me, too!'
- Lay the ground rules for communication so the prospect will feel more at ease. 'I tend to ask a lot of questions. Some of them might be quite specific about your product and business. Will you be okay with that? And, of course, you probably have a lot of questions for me, too.'
- Communicate to the prospect that you are transparent, not hiding or faking it, very much unlike other salespeople that the prospect has met with.

"Steve, when you put *reverse world thinking* to work for you, you eliminate major stumbling blocks to a successful business meeting. Moreover, you eliminate them when and how *you* want to eliminate them, creating, along the way, chaos in your prospect's game plan; clarity of purpose in the meeting, in your communication, and in the goals of each meeting; and a prospect who really likes and is comfortable with you—all this, perhaps, in the first fifteen or twenty minutes of the meeting, before you have given your prospect one iota of any important information, which is, of course, all the prospect wants from you."

He's just turned my selling process 180 degrees in reverse. It's like he wants me to start at the end; to make the end the beginning and the beginning the end. I have never, ever seen anyone sell anything like that. Every training I've been to is based on the same system, just with different quirks. No one sells backwards; or at least, no one but him. I wonder what it would be like to get as many objections as I can up front and then have clear sailing. It actually sounds pretty relaxing. I'm usually waiting, like a little kid anticipating a visit to the dentist, for my pain to begin, for the prospect to break out with an objection, and then another and another. I'm

Chronicle #10

> **Motivation to Buy or Do Business**
> The prospect's inner emotional drive to do business with you. Leads to a sale where the customer decides to buy based on his or her own emotional drive to change rather than your ability to 'close'. In other words, they close themselves as you sit back and relax.

on the defensive before I even begin, because I know, sooner or later, the objection will come. So, why not when *I* want it to come, especially before I've spent a lot of time giving the prospect an education. But then, if I'm selling backwards, that means that I would be really *closing* the sale at the beginning, instead of at the end. Hmm, *closing* up front. I wonder ….

"So, are you telling me that, when I've learned all of this stuff and how to use it, that I'll be *closing* up front, at the beginning of the meeting, instead of at the end?"

"Well, it's sort of like that. First, though, there is no *close*. The whole idea of *closing* is foreign to this system. Second, you are right in that the first part of the meeting clears the way for your prospect to buy at a later time or date. It sets the groundwork for their *motivation to buy*. Once you show them how your product justifies that motivation, they just buy. No close, just the buy. Cavemen systems wait until the end to clear up the mess of objections and stalls and then go for the close. You know Steve, if you're traveling by car and want to get somewhere fast, if at all, you better make sure the road is clear, that there are gas stations along the way, motels to sleep in, no construction, and so on, *before* you take the trip. If you just try and work it out along the way, well, that might be very adventurous, but in selling, it's very dangerous. Here, you will always find the sale at the beginning of the meeting."

"You mean I've got my head screwed on backwards."

"Actually, I'm trying to screw your head on backwards so that it can be forwards."

"I see," I say, and wonder how I missed all this in the first place.

The Selling Chronicles

Chronicle #11
I Guarantee Myself Failure

"Steve, let's step back for a moment and summarize where caveman selling is bound to lead you. Bottom line, no matter how hard you work or study, no matter what you do, you are working off a blueprint that creates and reinforces a *chain of events* that automatically skyrockets your failure rate far beyond acceptable levels of performance. Notice I said *automatically*. It has very little to do with you. Failure just happens, like the building that collapses because it was built on a bad foundation. Your selling processes itself something like this:

1. **You meet your prospect.**
   You do your greeting and your 'getting to know' you dance known as warm-up.

2. **Your prospect sees you no differently than any other salesperson.**
   You say and do exactly the same things that all other salespeople do.

3. **You think you are in control of the sales meeting.**
   Since you are well practiced in your caveman techniques of handling

objections, stalls and put-offs that your prospect may throw at you, you are, on the surface, genuinely confident.

4. **The prospect begins to jerk you around.**
   Your prospect is all over the place. Now he is laughing; now he is objecting; now she is demanding; now he is offended; now he is excited; now he is depressed; now she is putting you off; and so on. Soon you don't know if you are coming or going. Little by little you feel you have less and less control of the meeting. It's a feeling you don't like.

5. **Your feelings of frustration are loaded by other hidden feelings.**
   You can't live with your frustration. Your frustration lights up your fear, the greatest of which is that you're going to lose the sale.

6. **Fears from other parts of your life compound your fear of losing the sale and feelings of loss of control.**
   You don't have control of many things in other aspects of your life. You are subconsciously very upset about this. When you see you are losing control of your sales meeting, something you are absolutely supposed to control, you get even more upset. This kicks your fear of losing the sale up another notch, a cycle which keeps repeating itself until you or your prospect can't take it anymore.

7. **Your desperation causes you to try harder.**
   You, being desperate not to lose control of the meeting and to make a sale, clutch harder at your antiquated selling techniques. The prospect feels, as you use more and more of your techniques, that you are just another salesperson, like all the rest. He now feels pressure from you, so he tries to protect himself by jerking you around even more.

Chronicle #11

8. **Your fear and loss of control of the meeting and the sale deepens.**
    You are on the slippery slope and can't get off. You say, while keeping your fingers crossed under the table, 'Maybe it will work out anyway.' For you, hope springs eternal!

9. **Now your self-esteem hits rock bottom.**
    You feel now like you are begging for the sale. In a very big way, you are. You have lost control, you're living in fear, and the only thing you have going for you is your hope that your prospect will buy anyway. You feel like a beggar on the street corner, hoping someone will drop a quarter in your cup.

10. **Under pressure, you switch the meeting's priorities.**
    You, not knowing what to do, embarrassed and lost, and feeling bad about yourself and how your meeting is going, change the priority of the meeting from making a sale to saving face. Your goal now is just to take away your pain and feel better about yourself.

11. **You lose the sale, but rationalize why you can feel okay about yourself.**
    You compound your denial to save you from yourself.

12. **You make adjustments at your next meeting, which makes you feel temporarily better until the same chain of events takes over and you lose another sale.**
    You have a big heart. You pull yourself up from your bootstraps. (You, of course, have been trained by your predecessors to be sure to always have the strength to do this.) You reload your enthusiasm, review your strategies, and start all over again. Except for the moment when you make a sale (which of course you will do), you never really feel

great about yourself or your craft.

13. **In your caveman thinking, you feel you must become more aggressive, close harder, or work harder.**
    You will do one or all of these. Many of you end up quitting, justifying your failure as you mumble, 'It's not worth it. Who wants to be a salesperson anyway? Selling is for idiots.'

14. **You fail.**
    Even if you make a sale, you live on a continual battlefield with your prospects. Except for those moments when you finally close one, when you feel the thrill of making a fresh kill, you live in incessant frustration, pressure, confusion, and fear. You live the roller-coaster life: up when you make a sale, down when you don't, and chasing in between. Even in your selling success, a big part of you still feels like a failure. At some point, you just run out of steam. You become paralyzed from the effort of sustained battle, incessant frustration, and continuous waves of roller-coaster emotions. When you can't take it anymore, like a dog with your tail between your legs, you run for hiding via a promotion to sales manager or, more often, to another profession.

"Steve, this is your story and the story of millions of sales professionals just like you. And unfortunately, there's still much more to come."

It *is* my story. I must admit it. And it's a story I don't like. I feel like a barbecued chicken—poked, prodded, cooked, basted, but still on the fire; his fire. Then he says there's more to come. As if these ten meetings haven't been enough. More to come? What more could there be? Actually it's kind of depressing and exhilarating at the same time. It's kind of like throwing out an old car that you're still attached to, and, at the same time, really looking forward to the new one you've ordered. You know the old one has to go, but it's hard to give up, like an old habit. Is that what my selling is: just an old, bad habit? I think so. I really do. But I also know that breaking old habits is not an easy thing to do. And how quickly can I do it? And, to what end? I feel like a giant question mark. Now, I am really looking forward to his answers.

Where Does Steve Go from Here?

By Doing Nothing, I Get Everything

I look at him, probably with a little bit of dismay in my eyes. I'm not certain how to proceed. Habits are hard to break. I say to him, rather directly, "Here's my problem: I can't even throw out an old pair of my favorite jeans, no less my entire selling system. So, how do you suggest a person like me goes about demolishing his selling self, and then reconstructing his selling self, all at the same time?"

"Steve, first, you need to understand that there is nothing you have to do, absolutely nothing. In your mind you have a system which you now want to dismantle, and then you have a lot of ideas from which to construct a new system, and then you have to get used to using it. Now please hear this clearly: **All that is just your mind creating a lot of garbage in an effort to keep you from doing what is best for you.** You see, your mind kind of has a mind of its own, and it's basically lazy, so it likes habit. Now, it sees all this stuff coming and says to itself, 'Whoa, what is this? If I let this stuff in, I'll have to do a little work. I can't stay on cruise control. I'd better create a diversion to keep this stuff away.' And that's exactly what it does.

"Now, here's the trick, and it's the same trick that will happen in your selling. There's nothing you have to do, nothing you have to force. Just by being *aware* of what you are doing; by connecting to the *reality* of what you say and how you act with a prospect; by understanding your prospect and connecting with the *reality* of him or her; by having the internal motivation to do better, to have a more peaceful life, to have higher self-esteem, to produce more sales, to have more fun—all that will create an internal drive that will naturally, by itself, change the direction of your mind. The best thing you can do, just as you will do with your prospects, is not to force anything on yourself. Just let yourself take care of yourself, and it will. Just like you can let your prospect take care of himself, and he will. You will buy this system and put it in place of your old system if you believe it will do better for you. You don't have to sell yourself on it, just like you don't have to sell your prospects on anything, either. It's your belief system, your knowing that what I am teaching you will take away a lot of your selling pain, that will provide you with the motivation and energy to change. It just happens by itself. You just stand back and enjoy the process."

"I've never thought I would enjoy getting the *you know what* kicked out of me."

"I understand. And, I think you understand that what is getting kicked out of you is like bad food, drugs, smoking, rubbish, and junk, and that you yourself are doing the kicking. I'm just the catalyst. Do you see it differently?"

"Actually, I would like to blame you, but I'm beginning to think that it's more about me than it is about you. Like you said when we first started to meet, *reality* is not easy. At the same time, what I'm seeing is that staying in this mess is far worse. I'll take *reality*."

Systems Always Deliver Something, But Not Always What You Want

"Okay, let's go a little further. We've been talking about a system and referring to your type of caveman selling as a selling system. Steve, you need to understand that even though you call your system a *selling system*

> **Caveman Chain of Events**
> A series of steps, developed to be performed in specific, pre-determined situations, in a linear world, all leading to unreliable and unpredictable results. In short, a system that does not work well.

it really is not a system at all. A system, by definition, is *a method or set of procedures for achieving something specific and predictable.* Caveman selling *systems* define a method, specific procedures, and what it is to be achieved—making a sale. But the system delivers inconsistent results. Inconsistent results are the result of an inconsistent system. An inconsistent system in selling delivers more frustration than it does sales. In fact, an inconsistent system is not a system at all. It is just a façade, an empty set of steps squashed together to look like the system it isn't.

"Inconsistent selling systems focus on global results like making the sale, rather than a *chain of events,* the successful steps and mini-results that lead to the sale. If all of the mini-results were in place and assured by the system, you would not have to worry about the global result. Making the sale would take care of itself. It would be similar to your starting the engine of your car. If

> **Selling System**
> A chain of events that delivers predictable results. In selling, those results are either a buy decision, a no-buy decision, or a continuing appointment.

you have gas in the tank, put your key in the ignition, put your foot on the brake, and turn the key in the right direction, a *chain of events* is put into motion that assures the engine will start. If the engine doesn't start, it's a simple matter to trace back through the *chain of events* to identify what is wrong, fix it, and then start the engine. Likewise, in a true selling system, when the global result is not delivered, you can trace back through the *chain of events* to see what went wrong. You can then fix it for your next sales call. Then, the global result of making the sale will take care of itself.

"Developing a *chain of events* that delivers accurate results is what scientists count on for everything, from flying rockets to the moon to making your faucet work in your bathroom. Without accurate results delivered from specific *chains of events*, life would be totally unpredictable and absolute chaos. Likewise, selling systems that deliver inaccurate results make selling life unpredictable and chaotic. Sure, it's possible to make sales, but your selling life is chaos during the process.

> **Reality Based Chain of Events**
> A series of steps, linked to reality, that may occur in any order, but which lead to reliable and predictable results. Akin to great systems like FedEx, McDonald's, and Starbucks.

"In order to design a *chain of events* that delivers accurate results in a selling situation, you need to understand and learn how the two most important components of the meeting—you and your prospect—work. That's why we have spent so much time, so far, revamping your view of yourself and of your prospect."

The Five Core Principles

"Steve, being aware is **the secret**. Seeing things as they really are, reality, is **the key**. Letting go of old theories, opinions, and beliefs is **the method**. Stepping fearlessly into the unknown is the mystery, **the excitement**. Satisfaction and happiness are **the motivation**. When you put all of these on the table before yourself—*the secret, the key, the method, the excitement, and the motivation*—and compare them to how you sell now, you may decide, without making any effort whatsoever, to buy into all the stuff we have been talking about up to this

> **The Five Core Principles**
> The central aspects of yourself from which your selling journey is formulated:
> • The Secret: Awareness
> • The Key: Reality
> • The Method: Letting Go
> • The Excitement: The Unknown
> • The Motivation: Satisfaction

point, and all the stuff to follow. *The secret, the key, the method, the excitement, and the motivation* are what I call the ***five core principles*** for building peak

Chronicle #11

sales performance and enjoyment.

"As you recreate yourself, your goal is to keep reminding yourself of the *five core principles* whenever you are in a selling situation—whether it be on the phone, at a formal meeting, or in an elevator. You may think that selling is your first goal, but it is not. Making a sale is beyond your control. As hard as you try, you cannot force someone to buy. When your prospect writes a check, or says 'yes,' or fills out the application, it is, when it's all said and done, his or her decision. Instead of focusing on the end result, here we are addressing the quality of the journey and the reliability of the results. The *five core principles* begin the process of assuring the best journey ever; the *chain of events* gives results that take care of themselves. Once you are on this journey, it's a matter of sitting back and enjoying the scenery. The more you do to get to a goal you want—a goal that does not naturally evolve out of the process—the less you will get what you want and the more difficult the journey will be. It is *reverse world thinking* at its best."

To say I am relieved would be an understatement. I had this vision of a demolition ball slamming into my head to get me to change. You know, I *can* be pretty hard headed, and sometimes it does take a demolition ball to get me to see things differently from what I want to. But, hard headed or not, the demolition ball is nothing but me, seeing a better me and then letting myself evolve into the better me that I see. If I told him this, he'd probably say that I sound like Yogi Berra again. I'll bet I do. Maybe that's not so bad. At least it's more fun.

The Selling Chronicles

Chronicle #12
I Don't Understand My Role as a Sales Professional

He starts quickly. "Steve, you think that your role as a sale professional is to *qualify* prospects and ultimately to *close* sales, no matter what system you are using. Is that right?"

"For sure," I answer, without giving the answer much thought.

"Now, let's look at *qualification* from the perspective of *reverse world thinking*. What do you think that would look like?"

Qualifying the Prospect
An undependable, old-school, doctor-like examination performed on a prospect to determine if he is worthy of your selling efforts. Actually the opposite of what you should be doing: disqualifying the prospect and then letting him qualify himself. (See *Disqualifying the Prospect*.)

"That's not exactly rocket science. If regular thinking says that I should *qualify* my prospects, *reverse world thinking* would have to say that I should *disqualify* my prospects. But what does that really mean? Should I get rid of prospects as quickly as possible?"

"Steve!" he says. "Did you hear what you just said?"

"Sure, I heard what I just said. I said, 'Does that really mean that I should get rid of my prospects as quickly as possible?' And then you said,

'Did I hear what I said?"

"OK wisenheimer, maybe I should ask that differently. Steve, do you realize the importance of what you just said?"

"Well, I'd like to say 'yes,' but right now I'm not sure."

"Think of it this way. *Qualifying* means that you are looking at your prospect and looking to see if he or she qualifies for you to make a sale. You are trying to find all the reasons that they qualify to buy; hooks that you can hook yourself and your product into that lead to a *close* of some kind. You are kind of looking at the prospect and saying to yourself, 'Is this person capable of buying my product?' Right?"

"Right! So?"

"So this! By trying to qualify your prospects, by trying to find why and when they will buy, your natural caveman inclination will be to try and get them to buy, to try, somehow to corner them, to ambush them, to prepare them for the kill, to attract them, to get them to like you, or to do business with you. By qualifying with the intention of making a sale, you will, without knowing it, pull at your prospects and tip your hand that you are really out to make a sale; and they will, in the end, actually feel cornered, or ambushed, and know that you are leading them down the selling path.

"But, while you are trying to qualify them, they are trying to qualify you. They are asking themselves, 'Is this a good guy or a bad guy?' 'Is he on my side or on his side?' 'Does he care or doesn't he care?' Once they feel pulled, pushed, cornered, coerced, cajoled, or anything like that, up goes the sales barrier, and the salesperson-versus-prospect game is on.

"Steve, here's a typical qualifying scenario after you do your *warm-up*, getting-to-know-you routine:

You: Well Mr. Prospect, how can I earn your business today?
You, after doing your traditional warm-up, try to turn the meeting into

Chronicle #12

a business meeting. Good idea. Unfortunately, you are too early into the meeting for this move and the prospect knows what you are doing and your selfish, albeit true, intention.

Prospect: Well, let's see what you've got!

The prospect, having heard this from all the other traditional salespeople he has met, begins to hide behind the selling barrier. He's done this hundreds of times before. He's a master of hiding.

You: Okay, but let me do some data gathering first, so I know what to show to you. Okay?

You know that you shouldn't just go ahead and present your stuff. You, in fact, are proud of yourself for not showing your hand, even though you would really like your prospect to see how smart you are and how good your product is.

Prospect: Sure, just ask away.

He doesn't mean it whole heartedly.

You: Tell me about this…? How about your income…? What about those CDs…? Who's managing your money…? How much did you make…? What did you lose…?

You do your traditional data gathering, looking for a hot button to qualify your prospect as someone who might buy from you. As time goes on, you become more and more impatient to find the hot button or to get some kind of an indication you can make a sale. At some point you start to feel like you're looking for Waldo in a Where's Waldo *book.*

Prospect: Blah, blah, blah blah …. Yes, I've got a little problem, now that the market's down.

He admits something, anything, throws you a bone, just to keep you interested in him. He shows the tip of the iceberg, hiding the real problem deep behind the selling barrier. He knows you are after him and he has to give you a bone to satisfy your hunger. By satisfying your

	hunger and giving you hope, he knows he can get the information he wants from you.
You:	Oh, we're real good at handling that kind of an issue. In fact, we have products specifically built to protect you in a down market. Let me tell you how.
	Your selling fire is ignited on hearing a hot button. You bite on the hook set by your prospect, you chomp on the bone. You think there's a problem and that you have the solution. Now it is time to show how good your product is and how it can solve your prospect's problem. And you do! Yap, yap, yap and more yap. The dog-and-pony show starts. He is qualified to buy.
You:	Well, the way we design portfolios, we prefer to have a diversified blah, blah, blah. Now when you combine that with the fact we use our nationally known software for planning, it is a sure win for you. Now, let's take a look at blah, blah, blah.
	Your mouth keeps moving and your tongue can't stop wagging. You are on top of your presentation game. You are good. You also are giving all your information away.
Prospect:	Wow, that's great. … Hmm, that's real good too. … Oh, I didn't know that. … Geez, can it really do that? … This all sounds real good to me.
	While his agreement energy is bubbling over, your selling energy is bubbling about how good a prospect this is. You've got him eating out of your hand. You start to calculate your commission or bonus from making this sale. You begin to see yourself as a hero in the office; a winner, by all means. Your ego tips the top of the ego thermometer. This is your day. Or is it?

"Steve, this sale is destined for disaster. Think about where you're at. You've given away all your information in the interview, believing that you have a qualified prospect. But, you don't really know if that's true or not. You want so much to believe that your prospect is qualified, the moment you get any indication of interest, a gong goes off in your head that says, 'Gotcha. I can fix that. This is a hot button. Time to go for the sale.'"

When he stops to think for a moment, I jump in. "Well, you're not going to spend time with someone who isn't qualified. So, if I can find the problem they have, and I have a solution, and they have the money, to me that's a qualified prospect. Why not go for the sale?"

"That's just the point. You are still doing all the work. You're putting a lot of pressure on yourself. And, you're doing all that work, under all that pressure, with one overriding goal, the goal of making a sale. When your prospect sees you heading down this path and feels your ever-so-slight push or pull towards the close, he begins to erect his *selling barrier* and starts to hide behind it. Then you have to work even harder, which causes him to hide more, and so it goes. Now, qualifying the way you qualify is certainly better than doing nothing, but it simply is not enough, and leads to all kinds of problems."

My Qualifying Is an Uneducated Guess

"Steve, you don't realize that qualifying, caveman style, is just a feel-good methodology that denies *reverse world thinking*. Qualifying is your way of determining if there is a sale on the table or not. *Reverse world thinking* says that *you* cannot make that determination. *You* can't see if there is a sale on the table or not. **You are the blind man feeling around the elephant.** *You* don't know anything about what you're prospect is really thinking and feeling. You are making nothing more than a fairly uneducated guess.

"You don't see that the world works in reverse. Only your prospect can see if there is a sale present or not. Only he knows if he is ready to buy or not. Only he knows what his real problem is. Why? Because it is the *prospect's* ultimate responsibility to find his *motivation* to buy and to ultimately agree to pull the trigger; no one else, not even you, can make that decision for him.

"Look, you've had plenty experience with this. You know that if you continue down this path what your prospect will do. You know he will come up with all kinds of *stalls and objections* that you will eventually have to handle and overcome. And, as we have seen, with every *stall and objection* it's likely that you'll feel less and less in control of the meeting and feel more and more pressure as you watch your sale slowly fall apart. In the end, when you finally get a *think about it* or some form of *think about it,* such as a *'maybe,'* it then puts you in a position where you now have to *chase* your prospect to get the sale, or, more likely, to just get in touch. *Qualifying, caveman style,* starts a *chain of events* that cannot deliver what you want it to deliver with any consistency at all. It's like a crapshoot where the odds are stacked against you and for the house."

> **Maybe**
> A *think about it* in disguise. A placating remark prospects use, designed to give you hope for the future so you will give your prospects what they want now—information. Often used with children to placate them in the same way.

He's right on. I've got vivid memories of too many prospects who seemed perfectly qualified but didn't buy. It's as if, somewhere during our meeting, they just turned off. Now I'm thinking they turned off because they got the information they wanted. Once they got what they wanted, they didn't need to play anymore. So, out came the stalls and objections, putting me through my paces to try and get to the *close*.

"Okay, if I don't qualify my prospect, how can I know if I'm going to make the sale; or, better yet, if there's even a possibility of making a sale?"

It's Not Me That's the Problem, It's the System

"That gets back to what I was saying before. It's not your job. It's your prospect's job, and you have to give it to him or her. If you take away his

Chronicle #12

job, then you think you need to do all the work and, in a great way, really disrespect your prospect's ability to make decisions and solve his problems. You need to get out of the way.

"Actually, to compound the matter, and make it a little more difficult for you, **when you feel like you did a good job** *qualifying* **and recognizing** *hot buttons* **and then don't get the sale, you feel like you lost.** You end up flabbergasted that you didn't get the sale and can't figure out what you did wrong. Then you take the leap off the cliff by assuming that because you did right by your system and it still didn't get the sale, then there must be something wrong with you. The more you believe there is something wrong with you, the more your self-esteem plummets. Again, you find yourself in a vicious negative cycle with no way out. You are only as good as your last sale, and the cycle will continue until you get one.

"Steve, if you understood *reverse world thinking*, you would see that the problem is just the opposite of what you think it is—it's the system, not you. Of course, if you're some kind of a jerk, the system won't make any difference and nothing short of therapy could help you. But, since you don't fall into the jerk category, it is the misunderstanding of *reverse world thinking* that makes you decide that you're the problem. A logical guess, but absolutely the wrong one."

For years I've practiced and learned how to qualify my prospects. I've always felt it was one of the best things that I've done in my selling career. From my point of view, prospecting was like panning for gold, and once you found the gold, the next step was to determine the quality of the gold. So, I would qualify hard. After all, I was the one looking for the gold, so I had better look and evaluate what I found. I assumed that no one would just walk up and give it to me. Now, from the perspective that he's putting on the table of *reverse world thinking*, he is saying that I am wrong; that someone will just come over and hand me the gold, tell me all about it, have me understand its quality and its value. So, I'm saying to myself, that

that's a pretty neat trick if you can do it; just sit back and collect the gold.

"Okay. I think I've got it, but it sounds too simple. What's the trick?"

"Not a trick," he says, "just a different kind of thinking, a paradigm shift. Let's take a closer look."

Where Does Steve Go from Here?

The Path Less Traveled: Getting Rid of Prospects

"Now,' he says, looking squarely into my eyes, " *Reverse world thinking* demands that your role be just the opposite of what you believe it to be. It says that your job as a sale professional is actually to try as hard as you can to *disqualify* prospects. What that means is that you are going to look at prospects and try not to make sales. In fact, you are going to try to get rid of them as quickly as possible."

"You want me to get rid of my prospects as quickly as possible?"

"In a sense. I want you to have a different mindset. Instead of spending all your time looking for all the reasons that your prospect *will* qualify, I want you to focus on finding all the reasons why they *won't* qualify. You're looking for a needle in a haystack. One way to do that is to push the straw this way and that, looking for the small glimmer from the needle, and then pluck it out. The other way is to remove each piece of straw and set it aside in another pile, and sooner or later the needle will show itself. You don't have to look for it at all. It just pops up. Kapow! It's there, right before your eyes, and all you did was focus on getting rid of straw instead of looking for the needle. In the same way, if you try and disqualify your prospects, at some point, kapow! There they are, sitting there with their qualification shining through, your sales opportunity staring you right in your face, without your ever looking for it. They do it themselves. And, if they can't do it, if they can't find all the reasons why you should spend your time with them, bang, they are out and you are on to the next prospect. No fuss, no muss, no waste of time, no searching, no extra effort."

"Right," I say quickly, "but I need prospects. They're so hard to get, that I don't want to miss a sale because they didn't like me, or warm up to me, or I didn't show them some ideas that might pique their interest to buy."

"*Absolutely*, you need prospects," he says. Then he adds, "And you are absolutely right that people like to do business with people they like. But ask yourself this: When you're sitting with a prospect and being nice, does he see through your niceness, does he see it simply as a ploy to get something from him? Now, before you answer that, ask yourself this: When you think that your prospect has warmed up to you, why is he still hesitant to share all his problems and information with you?"

"Obviously," I say, "he still doesn't trust me enough."

"That's right. But it's worse. Ask yourself this: What doesn't he trust?"

I think about that for a moment. "That's a much harder question to answer. I would guess he doesn't trust that I'm on his side."

"That's right too. But it's worse than that. He's thinking that every time he gives you some information about his problem, you're going to use it against him as you try to make your sale. Does that ring a bell?"

"More than a few!"

"So why should he give you any information? In his eyes, if he does, he's creating his own problem with you. So he holds back. You see, he gives you a little crumb, you take it, try to turn his attention to buying, reaffirming his initial doubt about trusting you, and then he's off to more secrecy, while you then go off on your caveman seek-and-destroy thing."

Dr. Jekyll, Meet Mr. Hyde

"You see, Steve, the idea of attracting prospects as potential buyers is one thing. Trying to attract them *into* buying is quite another. In the former, you lay a healthy and respectful groundwork for making a sale. You set an atmosphere of absolute integrity, whereby, if the prospect wanted to buy from you, he or she would be comfortable enough with you to do so. He would say to himself, 'Man, I like this guy; not only is he a nice person, but he's talking to me about things that no one else has ever talked to me about. He must really care and he must really know his stuff.'

"The trap you caveman guys fall into sounds something like this in your head: 'Boy, I can tell he's really comfortable with me. Now, let's see if I can find out what he wants to buy.' And, with that thought, off you go, trying to show the best features and benefits of your product. You talk about quality, dependability, manufacturing standards, delivery dates, growth rates, and all your other good stuff. You work hard at getting tie-downs in place and finding buying signals. Convinced that your prospect likes you, you step over the line and spend hours trying to convince your prospect to like your product.

"And what happens virtually all the time? You can tell me, I know you know the answer."

"I do know the answer. Somewhere during the meeting they seem to turn on me. Sure, they like me, but their liking me seems to go out the window when we start talking business."

"Exactly, your prospect is like Jekyll and Hyde. First you get this part of him, and then, the moment you try to turn the conversation into liking your product, to turn the meeting into a *business meeting,* you get that other part of him. Your prospect immediately changes his view of you from someone they like to someone they inherently don't like, a salesperson. The prospect will say something like this to himself: 'There he goes. Now he's out to get me. I'd better watch out or I'll wind up buying something here. I knew he was just salesperson disguised as a nice guy.' You see, once you turn your salesperson switch on, your prospect turns on his own switch, his prospect's switch. He no longer thinks of himself as human being talking to you. He begins to feel like a commodity, and behaves accordingly.

"Now you, sensing the onrush of defensiveness from your prospect, immediately interpret that as losing control of the meeting and probably losing the sale. In time, the sales meeting that began with optimism, good humor and friendliness, turns into a battle between caveman, the hunter, and prospect, the hunted. And, sitting between the two of you is the *selling barrier*, all the *stalls* and *objections* behind which your prospect can effectively hide. And hide he does as you, bewildered and mystified, try to pull every trick out of your bag. Soon the sale is over. What started well ends poorly. No one wins, everybody loses. The caveman *chain of events* delivers its unpredictable result. "

Qualifying Reversed = Disqualifying

I'm a little agitated because I want the solution. "So," I say, "I'll ask you again: What's the trick?"

"Steve, here's the trick. Once you buy into the idea of *reverse world thinking*, you'll see that your role as a salesperson is not to *qualify* prospects, but to *disqualify* prospects. Trying to *disqualify* prospects before making any kind of a *presentation* sets a new kind of *chain of events* into action.

> **Disqualifying the Prospect**
> The process of trying to end your sales meetings as fast as you can. It is your first job as a modern sales professional and the most fun you could ever have in a sales meeting.
> Allows the prospect to qualify himself and sell you and close himself.

Disqualifying prospects reverses your natural inclination to pull prospects towards you so that you can make a sale. The process of trying to *disqualify* prospects actually pushes prospects away from you, away from making the sale, exactly opposite to what you would like to do and to what your prospect expects you to do.

"In *linear thinking*, you think that you must pull prospects towards you, only to see them run the other way. The goal of *reverse world thinking*, and *disqualifying* prospects, is that by pushing prospects away from the sale, they will, at some point, want to go in reverse themselves, and walk themselves towards you and the sale, without any manipulation from you. The process of *disqualifying* tests the prospect's *determination to do business* with you by presenting all the alternatives to your product, all the reasons they might not want to buy. Now, if your prospect bites on any of these alternatives, you know he has no *motivation* to do business with you. You send him away to do business where he should be doing business. But, if he doesn't bite on the alternatives, or he finds himself hung up on objections that you bring up, then you know that he has some *motivation* to do business with you. The amount of motivation will be a direct reflection of the depth of his problem. And that's what will drive the sale. Nothing else.

"Now, when you walk into a sale meeting, your mindset is quite different from that of your caveman predecessors. You say to yourself, 'I've got to test this prospect's *motivation* to do business with me. If he is not *motivated* to do business with me, I want to get rid of him as quickly as I can. I only want to work with people who really want to work with me. I want to feel like I am working with the best. I want to feel like I'm *cherry picking* at every meeting I have.' Based on that, you set out to see if you can get your prospect to buy your competitor's product, give him reasons why he might not like your product, or suggest that he keep doing what he is currently doing and not make any changes at all. You will do almost anything to get your prospect not to buy and to let *reverse world thinking* bring your prospect closer to you and the sale."

"Sure," I say. "With an attitude like that, I'm almost assured that he'll buy somewhere else. Sounds to me that an attitude like you're suggesting will just make people mad."

"It could, if you're not careful. Remember, we always talk to our prospects with the deepest of respect, the friendliest part of our nature that we can find, in the kindest and gentlest way. Otherwise, the prospect

Chronicle #12

will balk. He will walk away, not because he wants to, but because he just doesn't like your attitude. By putting your arm around him, *walking in his shoes*, being a true friend, as you push him away he won't understand what is happening, but he won't resent or be unhappy with the process. Let me give you an example of what it would sound like:

You: Mr. Prospect, I want to thank you for inviting me over today to talk about our retirement services. That's been the focus of our business for quite some time. But you know, on the way over here, I was saying to myself that we have some pretty big competition with some major-name, nationally known companies that have a bigger share of the market and a bigger sales force than my company does. And, they are really good at what they do, too. So, on the way over here I almost convinced myself that you would, at the end of the day, even if I could help you, and I don't even know that yet, that you would certainly elect to go with one of the big companies and not with me. Am I making myself crazy for a reason?
You surprise your prospect by touting the competition. This is the last thing he expects you to do. He is unprepared for this approach, as no one has ever talked to him like that before.

Prospect: Well, we did look at some other companies and you're right; they did have some terrific stuff. But, at the same time, we felt that we might get lost in the crowd and not get the personalized service that we really want. We thought you might do better. *Caught off guard, the prospect tells you more about your competitor's misfit than he had planned to. His original plan was to tell you nothing to keep his negotiating upper hand. He gets a little upset with himself because he understands that he just gave you a selling opportunity and suddenly feels he is now going to get selling pressure from you, pressure that he wanted to avoid.*

You: Oh, I appreciate that Mr. Smith. But you know, while many of these companies are big, they can give personal service. I'm sure you've had some good experience with them.

You push harder to see if the prospect has any determination to do business with his competition. If he does, you will disqualify him immediately and bail out from the meeting. You only want to do business with people who are determined to do business with you.

Prospect: Well, that's true. But when things go wrong they seem to disappear. At least that's been our experience. Why, now with the down market, haven't we heard from our person in 6 months?

If the prospect was dumbfounded before, he is even more dumbfounded now. He thinks, 'This guy is not a very good salesperson. He's actually telling me that his competition can get the job done.' The prospect, feeling no selling barrier, begins to feel that you and he are now on the same side, looking at the competitor's product together. He tells you more about their shortcomings.

You: Well, to tell you the truth, and this is hard for me to admit, but that can happen with any company. Perfection is really hard to come by. But it does sounds like the service was okay up until that point.

You have to be careful here. You cannot sound like a wise guy. In actuality, you are dead serious that no one is perfect. At the same time, you're giving your prospect a little push back to the competition. You know that prospects are not dumb, and that if the other company was more suitable, they would go to that company, no matter what you do. But, you also know that if he's going to consider the other company as an option, it is better if he does it with you, at your meeting, than without you.

Prospect: I guess we'd be okay. But, you know, we just want to have a little more confidence. Now, tell me about what you do.

Chronicle #12

	He is totally confused with you and decides to turn the conversation back to your product so he can get the information he wants. This is the prospect's attempt at regaining control of the meeting.
You:	Hmm. I'd be happy to do that. We actually take pride in the level of personal service we provide, even though, as I said, we are not perfect. But, as we were talking here I had another thought that ran through my head. The fees associated with our products and services tend to be higher than average. And, you know, some people are just looking for the lowest fees… which isn't us. Again, I don't know if I can help you yet, but where do you stand when it comes to fees?
	Now you agree with your prospect, but then present him with another problem that might come up about your fees. You push your prospect away from you by raising an objection about your product and continue to upset his thinking about you and expectations from you. When the prospect told you that he was unhappy with his current company, he was expecting you to launch into a dog-and-pony show about how great your product is. Instead, you bring up another objection. The prospect is mystified as his traditional game plan dissipates like the morning fog.
Prospect:	Well, uh, we don't want to pay through the nose, but we'll pay what's fair. I don't mind paying as long as I'm getting what I expect.
	Now the prospect reveals more information, to your delight, about his decision process about fees. He is losing his negotiating position by revealing more and more information. He thinks that you and he are just talking, one person to the other, one human being to another; he has no sense of the selling barrier that he normally experiences with other sales people.
You:	You know Mr. Prospect, I really appreciate that. Would it be okay just to share with you one other thought that's been running through my head? Have you considered, instead of using a

nationally known big company, or a small company like mine, that you self-manage your portfolio through one of the trading houses? They actually are known to do a very good job, too. And they have pretty good quality and usually a pretty good price.

Even though you know that your prospect is ready to turn his determination directly to you and nobody else, you must still be careful. It could be a smokescreen. So you gently push him just a little further away, waiting for reverse world thinking to perform its magic.

Prospect: No, no, no … we looked into that and it won't work at all. Look, I think we can probably handle your fees, especially if the quality of your company is what you say it is. It would be easier for me to work with someone I can talk to right away. Quite frankly, it would take a lot of pressure and worry off of me. Tell me what you need to know and let's see if we can do business together.

The prospect does not see that the roles have now been reversed between him and you. Here's how:

- *The prospect is doing most of the talking.*
- *The prospect is revealing most of the information.*
- *The prospect is selling you on why you should tell him about your product.*

You: Well, if you insist. Would it be okay if I asked you just one more question before you begin? When you say we can do business together, are you suggesting today or sometime in the future? *You sit back and relax. The thought goes through your head, 'How much better can this get?' You feel like you are cherry picking. And you are! And, it can get much better than this.*

"Steve, you need to follow one simple rule—no *motivation*, no meeting. By trying to disqualify your prospect, you force him to show his *determi-*

Chronicle #12

nation for doing business with you. **In reality, it is the prospect qualifying himself.** You just sit back and let him do most of the work. In this way, you never feel that you are a losing a battle; or that you are losing your self-esteem; or that you are putting extra pressure yourself. When you see that your job is to try to *disqualify* prospects instead of selling them, you will find that you will make more sales, and make them much easier than you ever imagined possible. You get the results you want by doing the opposite of what is expected. *Reverse world thinking* lets you see whether your prospect's *motivation* to do business is with you, someone else, off sometime in the future, or never. As soon as you learn that your prospect is unwilling or unable to turn the meeting into a *business meeting,* you get what you want—quickly, without wasting time in a meeting in which business could not be transacted. You are better off on the golf course or in the gym or spending time with your family than sitting with a prospect in a *social meeting.*"

He continues, "I'm reminded of the story of the husband who finds a magic lantern and rubs it. Out pops a genie who says to him, 'Thank you for letting me out. I will give you one wish; one wish for anything that you want.' The man thinks for a while, looks at his wife, and says, 'Honey, you're not going to like this one bit, but I'm 65 years old and I would really like a wife who's 30 years younger than I am.' His wife gets very upset and implores the genie not to give her husband his wish. After all, what will she do? She is also 65 and has been married to him, it seems like, forever. The genie turns to the man. 'Are you sure that's the wish you want? Look what it's doing to your wife!' The man looks at his wife, then looks back at the genie and says, 'Yes, that's what I want. You said I can have one wish, and now I want it.' 'Okay,' says the genie; and Puff!—the husband instantly becomes a 95-year-old. Steve, things aren't always what they appear or come out like we plan them!"

I wonder about the world working in reverse, about things coming out backwards, exactly opposite to what I've planned or expected. And I keep wondering about that, right up until our next meeting.

Chronicle #13
I Am Linked to a System That Guarantees Loss of Control

While I'm waiting for him to show up, I have a lot of time to think about everything we've talked about. Actually, I feel that he's really done most of the talking and I've done most of the listening, questioning, and defending. He said it would be that way; that I would defend myself. He was right. It's not easy to get yourself out of a rut you've constructed for yourself by doing things over and over again a certain way. Boy, that rut is pretty comfortable, even though it might not be a great rut to be in. At least I know what to expect. My rut is, after all, *my* rut, not anybody else's. And, I'd rather have the rut I know than the rut I don't know.

I remember, as a kid, wanting to play football for my high school. So, I went home with the permission slip, eased it before my parents, and asked them to sign so I could play. "No," they said. "But Mom, Dad," I argued, "that's what I want to do. Please sign it." "No," they said, even more emphatically. "But Mom, Dad, why not?" "Because people in our family just don't do that." And that was that: No football, because we just don't do that. And it wasn't only football; it was the food we ate, our vacations and other travel, the things we said, the people we hung out with, and on and on. What a rut they were in; and I was pulled into it, too. That's how they controlled me, keeping me straight and narrow in their straight and narrow rut.

When he arrives, I am still in the rut of my past and present and wondering how my rut for the future will look. As has come to be usual, he starts talking about the things I'm thinking about.

I Have Control Issues

"Steve," he says, "*control* is a deep issue for you; in fact, for everyone. You want things to go your way You want your world to be predictable. In your sales meeting, you want to get in the heads of your prospects and have them see what you see; have them agree with what you suggest; have them get excited about what you get excited about; have them hear your advice, take it, and implement it. You want to lead the way, keep control of the meeting. And, when you sense you are beginning to lose *control* or have lost control of your sales meetings, you can sense it immediately, often through nervousness in your gut, or a bunch of negative thoughts circling through your head. Something in you instantly identifies when things get out of hand and you can't make happen what you want to happen."

> **Control**
> The ability to maintain your balance in a sales meeting. Has nothing to do with controlling anything or anybody but yourself. A sense you would like your prospects to feel but not actually experience.

"Yeah, I know. Actually, I'm starting to feel that way right now. Every time you start these meetings, you always come up with something that rocks my world, takes my sense of control away. Then, you kind of give me control back at the end of the meeting. So, I feel a little like a yoyo with you at the other end of the string. Okay, where are you taking me now, up or down?"

"Let's agree, Steve, that I'm not taking you anywhere that you don't

Chronicle #13

want to go. But I am taking you to places you never visited; strange places that initially make you very uncomfortable. Can we agree on that?"

"Sure, we've been doing it for quite some time now. Sometimes I'm not sure where I am at all, but I always seem to get my feet back down on the ground."

"Great. Let's go to a new place."

"I'm on the train."

"Steve, loss of control for you means that your prospect is getting what he or she wants, but you feel like you're not getting anything you want ... no *hot buttons*, no *buying signals,* no *tie-downs that work,* and too many *objections*. Moreover, you find that you can't quite get a handle on your prospect's ever-*changing* attitude, level of enthusiasm, thinking, mood, thoughts, or feelings. Then, in your *disrespect* for your prospect, you take on the job of managing all these different aspects of your prospect's thinking and feeling, instead of letting your prospect manage them himself.

> **Change**
> Here now, gone in a flash.
> "Look, I see my prospect. Look again, uh-oh, he's different. And now he's changed again. Is this ever going to end?" No!

Now, each job you take on makes you feel less and less in control. It's inevitable. You know it's impossible for you to manage what other people say, do, or feel. Yet you take on that responsibility in order to keep control of the meeting. As usual, however, you get exactly the opposite of what you intended. And, you will continue to get results that are backwards until you recognize that the world works in reverse.

"Now, to add to your discomfort, **you experience an additional loss of control every time you give away a little bit of information** about your product or service before your prospect has laid all his cards on the table. It's subtle when it happens; and before you know it, the prospect knows infinitely more about your product than you know about his needs, circumstances, or *motivation* to do business with you. Here, let me give you some typical scenarios that you might experience. In each scenario, remember: Looming in the back of your head, like a great storm cloud, is your biggest fear, the possibility of losing the sale. Also remember, that your prospect knows this, and plays on your fear like a bow on a fiddle to get his way."

Prospect: Gee, I'm a little short on time. Could you get right to the point of what you've got?

You feel the pressure of time. You say to yourself, 'I've spent a fortune in marketing to get this appointment. I'd better come up with something great real quick or I'm a goner.' You start talking about your product via a show–and-tell presentation. The prospect gets what he wants. Once you take on the responsibility of fixing the time problem for the prospect by speeding up whatever you want to do, you have lost control. At any time the prospect could look at you and end the meeting by saying, 'Ah, that's too bad, I'm really interested, but I'm out of time. Give me a call next week.'

Prospect: That's ridiculous. I read just the other day that mutual funds will outperform individual stock portfolios by a wide margin.

You see the objection as a hurdle. You take on the responsibility of fixing the objection in the prospect's mind. You say to yourself, 'I must convince the prospect to see my product in a better way or I'm going to lose this sale.' You go into defense mode, telling the prospect more than he should know, and probably raising more objections in the prospect's mind than he had before you started yapping away. As you talk you feel control slipping away, along with the sale. The more information your prospect gets, the less he needs you.

Prospect: Rachel has been handling my account for 12 years. I don't think I'm about to change.

You gulp and think, 'How am I ever going to make this an effective

Chronicle #13

> *meeting and end up making a sale!' You launch into a treatise of how much better a job you can do than Rachel. You don't say it outright, but you imply it in everything you say. The more your prospect hears, the more upset he gets, because he is happy and likes Rachel. The more upset he gets at you for criticizing someone that he appreciates, the more control you lose. By taking on the responsibility of evaluating Rachel, you lose control and, in the process, make Rachel the winner and make yourself the loser.*

Prospect: We could do that, or we could do this. I'm not sure which way we want to go, but we are leaning to you.

> *You, sensing that there is a closing moment, leap at the opportunity to tell your prospect how much you agree with him and why your solution would be better for him. By taking on the responsibility of encouraging your prospect to go with you, you feel like you are seizing control of the meeting. When the prospect says, 'That's real good stuff, but I, I don't know; right now I was actually thinking that the other way would be best,' your feelings of control evaporate. You are blind-sided by the prospect's indecision. Now you exhort the superiority of your solution and begin to press the issue. In the meantime, your prospect is getting more and more distant. You watch as control slips from your grasp and your sale mystically goes to the competition.*

"Steve, those are just some examples of how *reverse world thinking* plays havoc with your desire to control things, especially your prospect's thinking. We've seen this before: The more you dig into your arsenal of caveman tricks, the more desperate you find yourself. The more desperate you are, the more you crave and cling to control. The more you crave and cling to control, the more you dig for a new trick. You are stuck in a circular pattern, a rut, a mode of keeping control that actually backfires on you and ignites every negative selling feeling you can imagine."

There's a glimmer in my eye. "I get this!" I say. "It's like the story of the monkey who was given a banana through the bars of his cage, but he could never eat it, because while making a fist and clutching the banana he couldn't get his hand back through the bars. So, when I think I know where I'm leading a prospect, or that I'm in control, or anything like that, it's like reaching though the bars and having food I want in my hand. Then, because I'm afraid to let go, afraid that I might lose or not make the sale, I won't let go. By not letting go, I can't eat the fruit of my sale and I go hungry for a close. Well, now I'm hungry for more of this, so let's keep moving ahead. What do we do now?"

Where Does Steve Go from Here?

I Need the Wisdom of Strength, and the Strength of Wisdom

"First, let's make sure you understand that control is a huge issue in a sales meeting. If you can't maintain control of the meeting, you are bound to lose the sale. Put another way, whoever takes control of the meeting will guide the outcome."

"But," I interject, "we talked about every meeting being a win-win. So, if it's a good meeting, then no one should be in control; it should just evolve. Right?"

> **Begging for the Sale**
> What you end up doing when you lose control over the sales process. Prospects have internal antennas that immediately pick up any form of begging, a signal that you have now given control of the meeting to them.

"It would seem that way logically, but doesn't work that way in practice. Someone in every meeting is always stronger or weaker; stronger, in this sense, means that they have more control in the meeting than the weaker person. You might have a meeting that is agreeable, mutually creative, and respectful, but one of you will always be stronger than the

Chronicle #13

other. You both might feel like you are in control, but control is never equal. It is always shifting.

"Now, here you have to use your wisdom. Wisdom tells you that the stronger person controls the outcome. So you have to be one who is stronger, in greater control; not to be manipulative, but to get what you want to make it a successful meeting, which is a clear and predictable result. If your prospect is stronger—that is, if you lose control of the meeting and delegate it to your prospect—wisdom tells you that he is not interested in a clear and predictable result. He is just interested in getting information from you without making any decision at all. He is interested in a fog-shrouded result. So you have to maintain control."

"But we just talked about how, when you try to *get* control, you always *lose* control."

"Right. But once you buy into the concept of *reverse world thinking*, you know you must reverse the way you think. To get control, you have to do the opposite, give up control. When you hear or experience your prospect's thoughts, feelings, desires, and opinions, you have to give up trying to control what they are or the direction in which they go. **You need to realize that the only thing you are responsible to control, or can control, is you.** When you take the responsibility of fixing your prospect, directing his thoughts and feelings, trying to *correct* the way he should or shouldn't be, you are, what I call, *upstaging* your prospect. *Upstaging* causes all kinds of control issues and puts power squarely into in the palm of your prospect.

"Steve, *upstaging* is a word that comes from the theatre. When actors move to the back of the stage in order to get other actors to turn their backs on the audience, it is called *upstaging*. When you take responsibility for fixing your prospect's thinking or feeling, you are trying to get him to turn his back on his own ability to solve his own problems. You want your prospect to be dependent on you, rather than himself. Deep down,

> **Upstaging**
> Putting yourself in the spotlight. The process of making people dependent on you. Making yourself more important than you are. Basically, what you do most of the time, unless you're making an effort not to.

you feel that if he is dependent on you, it will give you a better chance of controlling what the prospect does and *closing* the sale. Once again, you make a fatal error by ignoring *reverse world thinking*. In *reality*, to get a prospect to be dependent on you, you must get the prospect to be dependent upon himself. Only in that way will the prospect discover his own weaknesses and then, once he makes that discovery in himself, will look to you for strength in the form of a solution and using your product.

"Let's look at it another way. You know you want to *walk in your prospect's shoes,* like a friend. But, you can't *walk in his shoes* because you are always trying to *upstage* him. At the root of *upstaging* is your *disrespect* for human intelligence, a concept we looked at earlier. When you look at your prospect as being somehow incapable of solving his own problems, or handling his own emotions, you feel you must take over the ship. And you do, only to find that you have a mutiny on your hands. The mutiny comes in the form of the *selling barrier,* a host of *stalls* and *objections* that just don't want to behave the way you want them to behave.

"So, what's your job? It's to use your *good friend personality* and your *lethal business personality* to make certain that your prospect takes responsibility for himself. This is what *walking in the shoes* of your prospect is all about. By *walking in your prospect's shoes,* you will bring him face to face with his own dilemma. That's good for him, and it's good for you. But, to lead him to that face-to-face place, you must walk with your prospect much further than your prospect wants to go. You must, in a great sense, put your arms around your prospect and let your prospect lead you in the direction he wants to go. But, when he decides he wants to stop walking in that direction, you must gently nudge him to continue farther."

Chronicle #13

Going Beyond Comfort Zones

"So you're telling me that if my prospects want to talk about how good things are, then that's what I talk about. Or, if they want to look at the competition's product, I do it with them. That I understand. But what do you mean when you say I have to continue farther? Farther than what?"

"Once again, good question. Steve, you must remember that prospects will rarely, of their own volition, go beyond their *comfort zone*. They will go right up to the edge, but they won't cross over. At the same time, you must also remember that you don't want to go beyond your *comfort zone* either. Your inclination is to go right to your *comfort zone* edge and stay put, too. So, at a sales meeting, you have two parties, each of whom has a natural desire to stay in his own comfort zone. It's kind of a 'comfort stand-off.' You won't move, and neither will they. Everyone is happy.

> **The Comfort Zone**
> Thoughts, feelings, and actions that are pleasant and feel good.

"Now, you ask, 'What do you do?' Simple: You move your prospect right into his *discomfort zone*.

"Now you're going to say, 'But how do I do this?' No problem; if you encourage your prospect and dig deeper into what he wants to talk about, the direction he has chosen, he will take you right to the edge of where he is comfortable. Your job, at that point, is to nudge him to go farther; to consider things that he doesn't want to consider, or never thought of, or denies the existence of. If you can do that, he will become uncomfortable.

"Now, you're going to ask, 'Why do this?' And I really want you to hear this reason, okay?"

"Okay," I reply, but with a sense of discomfort I can't identify.

"Good. Steve, it is in that *discomfort zone* that the prospect will come face to face with his thinking, feeling, or actions that cause problems for him, that cause him to be uncomfortable. When he gets into the *discomfort zone*,

The Discomfort Zone
The place within the prospect where he discovers the emotional motivation why he should buy from you. A place where thoughts, feelings and actions reside that don't feel good to the prospect. A place where he doesn't want to go because it is not an enjoyable place. It is also a place where *you* don't want to go because it is equally uncomfortable for you.

he will begin to identify things that he needs to change in order to get back to where he is comfortable. If your product or service can effect that change, then the prospect will change from a prospect into a buyer. If your product can't effect that change, or if your prospect's discomfort is sufficiently tolerable, then he will remain just that, a prospect, and you have no selling opportunity. In short, all sales are the result of a prospect wanting to change something to move himself from his *discomfort zone* to his *comfort zone*."

"Okay, I can buy that. People are more apt to change, the unhappier they are. But what do you do or say to get them into that unhappy zone?"

"Well, we've talked a little bit about that already. The first step is to be sure that you are *walking in your prospect's shoes*. Put your arm around your prospect; say, 'That's interesting, let's talk about that a little more, give me some more details'; explore with him; go where he wants to go. He will tell you everything you need to know about what is comfortable or uncomfortable for him. When the discomfort arises, he will want to give you a superficial explanation. For example, he might say, 'Man, I am so worried about my income for retirement.' And that's about what he will be comfortable telling you, that he's concerned about his income for retirement. The next step is to take him further into just what being worried or concerned really means to him, to look at that issue on a much deeper level than the intellect. Maybe it causes stress between him and his wife. Maybe he is concerned that he may have to lean on his children, or perhaps he and his wife won't take a much-needed vacation, or do some of the activities that they enjoy. The question is, what does worrying about future income do to his emotional life?"

Ignite an Old and Unfriendly Memory

"Your job is to take him back to that time, to refresh his memory, to ignite the emotions that he doesn't want to experience again. That's what it means to take him to his *discomfort zone*. Now, once he's there, once he is living that experience and feeling his real emotions, he will see for himself, without your telling him, his motivation to buy, his desire to get back to comfort—hopefully, a result of purchasing your product or using your services. But remember Steve, he must see it for himself, say it to himself, without your stepping in, disrespecting his personal wisdom, telling him about his own story, and robbing him of his own personal discovery."

"I'm getting uncomfortable just thinking about that," I say. "It's like he's going to get all agitated, right? And then, you think he's going to buy from me, the person that got him all agitated? I don't think so!"

"Actually, yes I do," he says, "for one major reason: You are not the person getting him agitated. He is getting himself agitated in front of you. You are just opening the door. He, of his own volition, is walking through and discovering realities about his life that he didn't want to discover.

"As to your discomfort Steve, that's another problem you will face. By *walking with your prospect* into his *discomfort zone*, you will probably walk yourself into your *discomfort zone*. **Most salespeople are really very kind and don't want to make their prospects uncomfortable.** They would rather take over the show and just tell the prospect what his or her problems are, instead of letting the prospect simmer or stew in his own, self-made recognition of his own problems and faults. This is a formula for selling disaster or, at least, selling chaos. Since your prospects live in *denial*, they really don't want you or anyone else telling them their problems. They would prefer to stay in *denial*. So, what do they do when you tell them what their problems are? They argue, fight back, and disagree with you as vehemently as they can. They may have a huge problem, but if you tell them they have it, they can't see it. It's a huge blind spot."

They Discover, I Win (and so Do They)

"On the other hand, if they discover their own problems, there is a much better chance that they will admit them into reality and ask you if you can fix them. So, Steve, to get what you want to get, a self-motivated buyer, you must be willing to get uncomfortable, willing to let your prospect suffer his own shortcomings, as uncomfortable as that might be for either of you. If you try to stay in your *comfort zone* by letting your prospect stay in his or her *comfort zone*, it's back to handling objections, trial closes, closing and the mess of caveman selling."

"And here I thought we wanted to have these neat and tidy, very friendly, easy-going sales meetings," I say, thinking back to all the work I've done with prospects to try to make them comfortable.

"Well, actually you do. The more uncomfortable your prospect gets, the nicer, more understanding, more pleasant and compassionate you need to be. That's how you can maintain your balance in the meeting while your prospect may be having fits of anger or disappointment. At the same time, you need to realize that the person who maintains his *balance* at a sales meeting is the person who keeps *control* of the meeting. Just like in a boxing match, gymnastics, swordsmanship, wrestling, hitting a baseball, stroking a tennis ball, or driving a golf ball, *balance* is the key. The nature of the sales meeting is that each party is trying to get the other off balance. From the prospect's point of view, that is what stalls and objections do. They put you on the defensive and throw you *off balance*. From your point of view, in *caveman selling,* you try to maintain your balance by having an arsenal

> **Balance**
> The secret of controlling a sales meeting. Out of balance equals out of control. Balance keeps you from being blindsided by your prospect.

Chronicle #13

of great responses to your prospect's offensive attacks. The problem, though, is that once you are off balance, and your prospect is off balance, both at the same time, your meeting is a mess and the battle for control becomes a tug of war.

"By *walking in your prospect's shoes* and helping your prospect go into his *discomfort zone*, he will lead himself to his own imbalance. The *discomfort zone* is unbalancing to the prospect because he is not prepared to go there and face his difficulties. It sets the prospect's mind in turmoil, taking him out of his game plan to keep you *off balance.* In this disruption of his normal thinking and feeling process, the prospect will reveal more of his problems than he would like, which in fact will add to his sense of being *off balance*. It is a vicious cycle in which the prospect finds himself. In the meantime, you sit back, in total *control,* watching as your prospect struggles to stop revealing all the problems that your product may solve.

> **Off Balance**
> The state in which prospects reveal more than they want, including all problems your product or service may solve. It also could be the state in which you reveal more about your product or service than your prospect wants or should know, in which case, he will thank you for the information and then give you a *think about it* stall.

"Let's take a closer look at this process; it isn't as complicated as it may appear."

Prospect: Well, I'm pretty happy with the portfolio that we now have.
The prospect may or may not be telling you the truth.

You: That's interesting, sounds like that has been working well for you.
You do not jump in with a promo on your product and why it is better than the product he now has. Instead, you begin to walk in your prospect's shoes, unafraid where it might take you, but knowing that it will keep you in control of the meeting.

Prospect: Well, it has. We've gotten a pretty good return, about 10% per year, over the years and are pretty satisfied.

The prospect takes your lead and begins walking on the positive path of his current product. He feels no defense or desire from you to move him in another direction. The prospect's defenses begin to go down.

You: 10%. Hmm. That's pretty darn good. You should be quite happy with that. There's probably a good story behind that. Could you tell me more?

You continue in your prospect's footsteps by urging him to tell you more of the details about how his current product works.

Prospect: Oh, it is an interesting story … blah, blah, blah. But, the bottom line is, we've gotten ourselves to a level we have never been before.

The prospect is now fully involved in telling his story about the history of his portfolio. He has completely let down his defenses and feels neither a push nor pull from you. The prospect is also building inertia, tending to talk more and move faster down the path he is taking you. He is proud of his portfolio and he senses that you are really interested and not playing a selling game. The prospect is still in his comfort zone, content and satisfied with what he has.

You: That's a great story. When the folks who are managing your portfolio gave you their proposal about keeping that rate of growth but lowering the risk in your portfolio, what did that look like?

You attempt to move the prospect further than he wants to go along this path. As of yet, the prospect hasn't said anything about improving on his current situation, most likely because this will take him into his discomfort zone. So at this point, both you and your prospect have maintained balance. Neither finds any discomfort in the communication taking place. You, however, understand that if your prospect stays

Chronicle #13

in his comfort zone throughout the meeting he will not buy anything, so you begin the process of moving him into his discomfort zone. You do this by using a method called 'assuming the competition did a great job,' in this case, a proposal for lowering risk.

Prospect: Well, actually, we never discussed moving the risk down. So, I certainly don't have a proposal from them and don't know what that might look like. Quite honestly, we've never discussed the downside, and we've had some pretty good ups and downs.

Suddenly the prospect has moved into a discomfort zone and feels out of balance for the first time. He is surprised by your question and confused that his current advisor has not made a proposal that you (knowing quite well that they probably didn't make such a proposal) had assumed he had done. Moving into a discomfort zone sends so many thoughts through the prospect's mind that it tends to confuse his thinking, causing the imbalance that you are looking for. If there is enough imbalance, the prospect will reveal deeper levels of problems and issues and then look to you to solve them so he can get back to the balanced feeling he prefers.

You: So, correct me if I don't get this right, but it sounds like living with those ups and downs is okay with you, and that lowering your risk is not much of a priority.

You take greater control of the meeting by walking farther yet in your prospect's shoes, to see how he will react. Notice that you take a 'no man—reverse world' approach rather than a 'yes man—linear thinking' approach that would sound something like this: "Well, I could lower the risk in your portfolio; wouldn't that be great for you?" But if you were to take the linear approach, your prospect would immediately feel the 'sell' from you and begin to erect a selling barrier.

Prospect: Actually you didn't get that right! The downs have always come back, and it's been pretty aggravating for us when the market is down. In fact we did look at some other information that showed that our portfolio went down more than the averages. That was a little frustrating! I would prefer to have a more even ride. I believe my wife would like that, too. Do you think it's possible to do that and still get a good rate of growth?

The prospect is now in a place that is further than he originally planned on going. His original game plan was to let you know that he was happy with what he had, see what you came back with, or have a quick courteous meeting and get you out the door. In that way he could continue to hide what he really wants and the difficulties he is facing. Now he is revealing his frustration and finds himself totally off balance in the conversation. His mind is spinning. He must now relive the frustration of previous market declines. You, on the other hand, just sit back and listen.

You: I'm not quite certain that we can. Could you give me some more details on what your portfolio has done in the past down markets? That's probably a good story too!

You want your prospect to get into an even greater position of imbalance before you reveal anything about what you can or can't do. You know that the more out of balance your prospect is, the more he will want to hear from you, and the greater the chance that he will turn from a prospect into a buyer. And, the prospect will do it all by himself, without your using any of your old caveman selling tricks or manipulations. It's reverse world thinking at its best.

Prospect: Blah, blah, blah, blah. So, that's our story. At one point, it was quite a mess and very discouraging. There was even one point when we asked ourselves what we would do if the market didn't come back this time. Can you help me out here?

Chronicle #13

The prospect is so out of balance, he feels himself ready to fall over. Without hesitation, he reaches out to you, hoping that you will lend him a hand to pull himself back up into a balanced position. Now all you have to do is make certain all the elements of a business meeting are present before you give any information. You have now discovered that this prospect has plenty of motivation to do business with you. You are in total control.

"Steve, your loss of control at sales meetings is the direct result of your playing by the wrong rules, your prospect's rules, non–business-meeting rules. The fear that comes with the loss of control and potential loss of the sale, reinforced by many other areas of your life where you don't have control and don't know how to get it, will feed your insecurity and your need to push or pull your prospect in order to make the sale. You can't control your kids, you can't control your spouse, you can't control your boss, you can't control your credit cards, you can't control your weight, you can't control your drinking, you can't control the parking attendant, you can't control the waitress, and you can't control myriad other events and things in your life; and now you can't control your sale. Emotionally, you're a loaded gun, and unfortunately it's aimed at your prospect. By changing the rules, moving with the prospect, moving far into the recesses of the prospect's thoughts and feelings, you can take control—easily, effectively, and without effort. In this part of your life, you can find deep satisfaction, and you can lead your prospects to that same sense of satisfaction—but only if you change your approach."

The Selling Chronicles

Chronicle #14
I Don't Know How to Use My Intuition

Sometimes, in moments of stillness, when the activity of business suddenly fades into the background and the thoughts about my successes, failures, and struggles to accomplish recede into the nothingness from which they seem to have come, I can look clearly at what he has been teaching me. In those moments I see that this is not really about selling, not really about me. It's really about understanding human nature and tapping into the more subtle aspects of how and why people do what they do, and how to use the power of that knowing to help people better reach their goals.

Now I don't know that much about him, but it seems to me that he has a knowing about him that can see things in a broader, more accurate, and genuine perspective. It's like I am looking at myself, my prospects, my customers, and my business from the top of a three-story building. But he has the ability to see from a much, much higher vantage point, so he can see more, and he can see farther than I can see. That's why I believe that he pretty much knows what I am going to say, how I'm going to react about what he is teaching, when I'll put up a fuss, and what I need in order to make an effective change.

As he arrives for our next meeting, these thoughts literally spill out of my mouth. I want to share them with him. I want to know why he seems so different, so capable, and so ... well, seemingly psychic.

"Psychic," he says without hesitation. "Psychic sounds like a lot of mumbo jumbo to me. But, if you had said intuitive, we would have a lot to talk about."

"Okay. I'm easy. Intuitive it is. Is that what makes you so darned—how shall I say it—competent?

"Not quite Steve, but it is a big deal. In fact, I'm always surprised that your caveman training didn't include the development of your *intuition*. After all, your caveman predecessors, when out hunting, often moved through the terrain based on their inner instincts rather than some predetermined path to their prey. And that's what *intuition* is all about: being able to negotiate through different situations based on inner instincts, gut responses, or feelings, rather than reacting to experience or data, or using some set of memorized steps or moves.

> **Intuition**
> Knowledge that is based on neither data nor experience. Comes in four flavors:
> - Directive
> - Analytical
> - Predictive
> - Impulsive
>
> Also a quality used by psychics who are generally fakes. Be careful with intuition. A necessary quality to be handled with wisdom.

"Regrettably, caveman selling has become nothing more than a pre-set drill of 'do this,' 'do that,' 'look for this,' 'look for that,' and along the way, 'go for the *close*.' The result is that your *intuitive* instincts have been deadened to the point where you don't even know that your *intuition* exists. You have become a *mechanical salesperson*. Just wind you up and off you go into your selling routine. It's the same 'yap, yap, yap' to every prospect, totaling ignoring the fact that every person, every situation, every conversation, every thought, every emotion, and every feeling is different and changing at every moment of the meeting.

Chronicle #14

"Now, you would argue vehemently that you aren't mechanical at all, that you are just following steps to make a sale, and that you creatively weave these steps to make your sale. Right?"

"That's right. Good salespeople are always thinking on their feet."

"Yes, that's true. But thinking about what? Look at it this way. You live, as we've seen, in denial. That keeps you from recognizing that the selling steps you follow are rigid and artificial. By performing them over and over, burning them into your memory, they have become second nature, habits that appear to be spontaneous and creative, but are the 'same old, same old,' in different disguises. You can't see that these types of habits have a powerful negative effect on your ability to be intuitive. You are unaware that your caveman selling habits, instead of reinforcing creativity and intuition, actually undermine and snuff them out. Please, don't be offended by this, but you are wrong about your creativity and spontaneity. Dead wrong!"

"Offended? Me? Are you kidding? Anytime I say I'm one thing, you show me I'm another. Now that's getting to be something I can predict. But," I add quickly, "when I go into a sales meeting I am prepared, as best I can be."

"Steve, I certainly understand, and I respect that fact that you've stuck it out as long as you have. Now, let's go even further. You see, you follow the creed of all *caveman selling professionals*—to be prepared. As far as you're concerned, as you said, you *are* prepared. So why on earth do you need to develop some mystical power like *intuition*? The problem is that you are only prepared for what you *know* to be prepared for, only for what you have experienced. You are well trained at giving pat answers to pat questions, responding with pat actions to your prospect's pat moves, and handling pat problems with pat solutions. Intuition brings in a whole other dimension. It gives you the skills to handle the unknown, things you cannot be prepared for because you don't know they're going to happen. That's where I'd like to take you now, into successfully negotiating the unknown. The question is, are you willing to go there?"

"If you're up for the taking, I'm up for the going. Just don't leave me behind, okay?"

"Perfectly okay."

I Need to Get Into the Mystery of the Unknown

"Steve, while you are prepared to handle what you anticipate will happen, you are totally unprepared for what you don't expect—*the unknown*. How could you be; it is *the unknown*! So, when confronted with something that you don't expect—a change in your prospect's attitude, an objection you've never heard before, a point of view you haven't considered, a personality you've never had to deal with, emotions that make you uncomfortable, interruptions you never thought would happen, competition you didn't know you had, and a host of other *unknowns* that you will encounter—you, with an undeveloped or immature *intuition,* will not have a clue what to say or do.

> **The Unknown Zone**
> Territory with which you are unfamiliar and which is seen as a mysterious place to you. Not to be confused with a similar sounding sexual connotation.

"The unknown often throws you off balance because you can't link it up with previous experiences and therefore don't know what to do. That type of unknowing is very uncomfortable to you and to most people in general. So, you want to make your world as predictable as possible—a place where you know what's going to happen, with whom it will happen, how it will happen, when it will happen, where it will happen. And you want all of that planned out ahead of time so you can relax, enjoy yourself, feel good about yourself and above all, stay away from your fear of the unknown. You are a creature of habit, and it is your habit to try and *stop the world. Stopping the world* is one of your greatest desires. If you can prevent change, secure and hold a picture of life and its prospects, you will always know where you stand and what you should always do. You will be unafraid. You will, in your mind, be prepared.

"So you use the same words and phrases in every situation. You are like a man driving his car at sixty miles an hour, despite how much traffic or how many yellow lights, red lights, or green lights you see in front of you. You have brainwashed yourself into believing that your caveman system is *the* system of choice, and that there is no other choice. You have no other tools. You have cornered yourself to use what you've got, and you 'don't got' any *intuition*."

I Share Fear of the Unknown with My Prospects

"Then, Steve, your problems deepen because you don't see that the very thing you are trying to avoid, *the unknown,* is also the very thing that your prospect is trying to avoid as well. Like you, your prospect is trying to fix his world so he can stay in balance and feel good about himself. Yet, it is in the prospect's *unknown* that the prospect will find the reasons to buy from you. Right now, you don't have the insight to see that your sale is not living in your ability to manipulate your prospect, but your sale, if there is one, is living in the *unknown* from which you and your prospect are running. That is why *walking in the shoes* of the prospect is such a powerful tool, but only if taken all the way into the mystery and *the unknown*, further that the prospect and you want to go. Think about it: If your prospect knew his own *unknown,* and knew that he had a positive *emotional charge* to fix his problem, he would just come to you and buy what he needs. Prospects, however, don't know their *unknown* (nobody can) and can't identify the *emotional charges* associated with a visible problem because they are buried

> **Stopping the World**
> The attempt to take the continuum of change and the unknown out of your life and selling situations. In other words, attempting the impossible.

deep in a prospect's subconscious. Often these are emotions that the prospect does not want to feel or experience. He doesn't want to go there. Your job is to guide him there to see if there is sufficient *motivation to do business with you*. If he does not want to go there because it is *unknown* territory for him, all is lost—or at best made extremely difficult.

"Let's look at an example of how poor intuition compounds your caveman difficulties:"

Prospect: This all sounds great, … but … uh, … I don't know … there's something really bothering me here about this plan, and I can't get my arms around it.

You don't know if the prospect is hiding behind a lie or is telling you the truth. Either way, you begin to feel a little uncomfortable because you realize that the real objection may be lurking around the corner.

You: Bothering you? Hmm … perhaps I didn't do a good enough job of explaining everything to you. It seems to me that it is a perfect fit for you. After all, when we talked about what you were trying to accomplish, we agreed that our product was absolutely the best choice.

Since you don't trust your intuition, or, it isn't working, you fall back to a practiced, mechanical, safe response, which unfortunately comes off somewhat defensive.

You're also torn between different thoughts and feelings that are now churning within you. On the one hand, some inner thought is telling you to let this statement alone, not to respond, to just wait a little; other inner thoughts are telling you that you are going to lose the sale; and yet others are searching your mental archive for something that has worked before in this situation. You are pulled in three directions at the same time, compounding your feelings of nervousness and causing you to react more defensively than you normally would.

Chronicle #14

Prospect: Oh, no, you did a great job! You really explained everything. It seems like it should work. But … I guess I just need a little time. *The prospect uses one of his standard stalls. Since you haven't got a firm direction in your mind, you can't lead the conversation into his unknown zone. At the same time, your prospect won't go there of his own accord because he has no compelling reason or motivation to make himself uncomfortable. You are now in a corner.*

You: Let's look at it this way—my product gives you the blah, blah you need; it gives you the yap, yap you want; and it gives you all the rah, rah that you could ever get. What more could you ask for? So, all I need is your social security number and we can get this moving forward.

Now the thought that you could lose the sale rings like a siren in your head. 'Damn,' you say to yourself, 'another think about it.' Your temperature begins to rise. You can feel the sweat starting to bead up. 'Think about it' are the last words you want to hear. You do, however, maintain a positive outer image. With your mind churning to figure out something clever to say, the phrase that pops into his head is, 'When in doubt, go for the close.' So, you do. You use your old friend that has worked before, the 'choice close.' You stay away, at all costs, from the unknown, the place where your prospect is hiding the real issues and, once again, go mechanical.

Prospect: I … uh … I really like you, and I'm pretty sure I like what you've put together. Everything you say makes a lot of sense. But … well … I just want to be sure I'm making the right decision. You know, you've been great. Let's talk next week after I've had time to mull it over.

The prospect feels pressure from you to get the sale. He butters you up to make you feel better about the stall. The unknown stays unknown.

You: You know …. How about we get going with half of your

portfolio instead of all of it? That will give you a chance to get to know and work with me better. All I need is some personal information and we can start to get your portfolio in better shape.

You are stumped. You ignore your intuitive little voice, which is telling you to back off. Instead, your mechanistic caveman training sets you off for the kill—you try to close again.

Prospect: Half the amount? That might be a good idea. You are really good. So let's definitely talk next week and I'll let you know what we are going to do. By the way, I really appreciate all your work, it means a lot to me. So, I just need to cross my t's and dot my i's. Next week I'll have that all in place.

The prospect will not budge and has you on the run. He won't talk about what is really bugging him (it would make him uncomfortable). And, if you don't really know what's bugging him, you can't guide him into his unknown zone to explore it. Now he has a better price and still did not make a decision. Life is good ... for him!

You: Gee, Joe, the best way of understanding this plan is to really experience it. Let's do something today, even if it's just a small piece. Okay? (You hold out your pen and contract.)

Now you feel brave, albeit, cornered and stupid.

Prospect: Boy, you don't give up. I guess I'm just going to have to disappoint you today. I'll give you a call next week.

He's acting nice, but he is a bit upset with you about the pressure you're putting on him. To protect himself, he digs in with both feet and ends the meeting.

You: Thanks for your time, Joe. If you have any questions, just give me a call. Oh, by the way, here is another brochure that will give you an even better explanation of why my product is for you.

Chronicle #14

Without effective intuitive skills and modern selling skills, you lose all control of the meeting. Neither you nor your prospect recognizes that success for both of you resides in that arena.

To make matters worse, something in you actually feels good about the meeting, despite the fact that you probably won't get the sale, because the prospect noticed your tenacity. And you also feel good because you remembered to give the prospect a great brochure to review. At the end of the meeting you somehow find a way to pat yourself on the back for a valiant effort. Along the way you fail to believe or listen to your intuitive voice telling you that something is radically wrong.

"Throughout the meeting, both you and your prospect cling to the safety of things with which you are both familiar and comfortable; for you, it's your selling method; for him, it's stalls and objections. Without the presence of intuitive guidance, neither of you has any inkling of what is really happening. In the end, it's the same old routine. Vaudeville in modern dress. Neither of you is willing to step into the *unknown* and explore more substantial and emotional issues at hand. Your *fear* of losing the sale, of not knowing what to say, and of looking stupid, combined with your prospect's fear of being sold, looking weak, or appearing in a bind, makes for a meeting where a sale feels like more of an accident than satisfying event."

"Yeah, except that I know guys who have lots of accidents," I say.

"We all do. That's what makes caveman selling so intoxicating. Salespeople are, for the most part, like little monkeys, all climbing the same tree because a few monkeys already on top are screaming about all the bananas up there. There might be a huge bunch of bananas right under their noses, but they won't see it. That's the power of group consciousness. No intuition there, no deep thinking, no creativity; nothing but mass madness."

When I was in the sixth grade we all took a test to see if we qualified for

The Selling Chronicles

SP—Special Placement in Junior High School 168, our next educational step. If you qualified, you went into a special program that graduated you into high school in two years instead of three. I was devastated when most of the kids who lived on my block passed the test, while I didn't. The group was marching on, and I couldn't go. Even while I cried, though, something kept telling me that even if I had passed the test, it would not be a good decision to accept SP. Just trying to make myself feeling better? I don't know. But, I do know this: A few years later the program was cancelled. Studies showed that the test was flawed and that kids in SP did not fare well in high school. Had I had the choice, I probably would have ignored my intuition, followed the crowd, and missed out on the rich and rewarding high school years I did have at a very special school, Brooklyn Technical High School, for which, by the way, I *did* have to take a special test to get in.

"So I see what you mean. How does this intuition stuff work anyway?" I then joke, "Palm reading, Tarot cards, a little crystal ball, maybe?"

Where Does Steve Go from Here?

At Some Point, It's a Gut Call

"Steve, first you need to know that *intuition* is a necessary and indispensable ally that can successfully guide you through the puzzle created by an ever changing world. Your whole world experience is magnified, put right in your face, in every sales meeting. Why? Because every sales meeting is filled with moment after moment when the unknown rears its head. It might be a question the prospect asks, an emotional reaction, a phone call interruption, an objection, something you didn't know about the competition, something you didn't mean to say, an article in the newspaper, a knee jerk reaction, a negative comment, a shift in attitude, or any of a host of other possibilities that bring the unknown, the unplanned for, right into the meeting. In those moments you will have to make a gut call about

Chronicle #14

what you are to say or do. **That gut call will be the result of your being able to identify and abide by the guidance your intuition gives.**

Most of us think that *intuition* is some kind of a mysterious power that only a few people have. That is simply not true. Everyone has *intuition*. It is built into the human system, just like bones, skin, brains, and blood. You don't know about it because no one has taught you about it. Because *intuition* is not an exact science and cannot be quantified or measured, schools don't teach it, corporations don't value it, and people don't use it. And, like everything else, if you don't use it, you lose it! For you, *intuition* is not only a lost power, but it's a power to which your selling ancestors have turned up their noses—so much so, that it isn't even a worthy or valued topic of conversation.

If you would look closely Steve, you would find that there are different kinds of *intuition* pursing through you during every sales meeting, begging to give you information and insight into what, how, and why you should say, act, or do at every moment, especially when you venture into *unknown* territory. By knowing the types of *intuition* possible, you will be better equipped to identify them and decide if you want to follow their lead. Here are four fundamental types of intuition that will be easy for you to recognize:

1. *Directive intuition:*

> **Directive Intuition**
> Knowledge that arises in the moment that tells you what you should do next. Not based on any pre-determined analysis or system. An idea that just pops into your head or hits you on the head, as is your preference.

This is the type of *intuition* that sends you a message, like a high priority email to your brain, telling you what to say or do next. It may appear to you as a thought or idea, a mental picture or vision, or a deep feeling or emotion, but it carries a special sense about it—a certain weight—that differentiates it from ordinary thoughts or feelings. *Directive intuition* is not based on any kind of analytical reasoning or experiences from the past. It is knowledge that just appears, and it may make little or no rational sense. In fact, *directive intuition* often gives a directive message that is quite opposite to what you think you should do based on your previous experiences.

2. *Analytical intuition:*

This is a type of *intuition* that will help you solve problems requiring some kind of factual analysis. It occurs at those times when you feel stuck in your thinking, when you don't know what to do next to solve the problem. Perhaps you are doing a financial plan and reach a point where you can't figure out what the next step should be. Then, like a lightning bolt, there it is. The answer just pops into your head. You say to yourself, 'I've got it.' And you do, out of nowhere, with no rhyme or reason. The solution to the problem just appears like magic.

> **Analytical Intuition**
> The great "Aha!" you get when trying to solve some kind of a problem. Often occurs after a good night's sleep (if you ever get one).

3. *Predictive intuition:*

Predictive intuition predicts the future. It may come to you in the form of an inkling, a gut feeling, an impending sense, or a message that flashes through your mind. *Predictive intuition* is the most difficult type of *intuition* to identify, because you have so many other ideas and feelings circulating about the future that are just that, ideas and feelings, not *intuition* at all. These other ideas and feelings muddy the water so much that you will find it quite difficult to determine if any of them are really *predictive intuition* at work. Once you begin to gain confidence in your other

> **Predictive Intuition**
> Intuition that predicts the future. The most difficult intuition to come to trust. You just get a sense of it. No crystal ball will help here, just your clarity and attention.

Chronicle #14

intuitive modes, this level of intuition can develop very quickly.

4. *Impulse intuition:*

This type of *intuition* is the easiest to recognize because it will drive you to do or say something before you can stop or change it. It is not, however, a *knee jerk* reaction to what your prospect does. It is an *intuition* that moves you as it wishes, without you having any hint that it is coming, or any idea as to why you may be doing what *impulse intuition* is compelling you to do. When *impulse intuition* presents itself, you will not recognize it until after you have performed the task, which this type of *intuition* literally forces you to do.

> **Impulse Intuition**
> Intuition that forces you into action that you cannot stop or take time to consider. Not based on previous experience of any kind.

"These four fundamental types of *intuition* will propel you and your prospect instantly into the *unknown zone*. Once you get used to relying on your intuition, you will begin to get comfortable about being in your discomfort zone. *Intuition* actually creates a safety net for you, helping you maintain your *balance* wherever the sales meeting takes you. It gives you the power to helpfully guide your prospect in his *unknown zone,* where the root of his problems, and the motivation to buy, are living."

Intuition at Work, My Work

"Let's take a look how *intuition* might work for you in some selling situations:"

Scenario #1

You meet the prospect for the first time. He looks like a nice guy but something about him tells you that this prospect will be difficult to deal with. You take a moment to consider whether this is *predictive intuition* or just some random thought circling in your mind. Both the strength and depth of the prediction convince you it is *predictive intuition* at work. While you are doing your routine greeting and "how are you's," your mind is constructing an ideal way to handle what your *intuition* is telling you. *Directive intuition* kicks in with an idea to address the issue right up front. In a moment you say to the prospect, using your best *good friend* personality:

> "Mr. Prospect, how about I give you a little background about me? I've been in this business blah, blah years and have blah, blah, experience to offer you if we discover you need it. And, by the way, I work with all kinds of people—some easy to work with, some difficult. Now I don't know what kind of a person you are to work with, but I can tell you this: I will always be very candid with you, and I hope you will be candid with me as well. You know, now that we are talking about it, just what kind of a person are you to work with?"

When you ask this question, you may be as nervous as you can be. But you know, although you have never been down this road with a prospect before, that it is natural when moving into the unknown to be a little nervous. More importantly, you also know that your intuition can be a trusted guide. So, although you may be nervous, you will also be confident.

Now in your caveman selling tradition, you would rarely ask a question like this, thinking it would be too bold, or would upset your prospect, or was just none of your business, or that you just had to put up with prospects who are difficult and that you had no right to talk to them about why they are difficult, all of which is a bunch of hooey.

The prospect answers:

> "No one has ever asked me that before. Well, since you asked,

Chronicle #14

> I'll be candid with you—I can be a bit difficult, and I usually get that way when I feel like someone is beating around the bush or not giving me a totally straight answer, which is the way most people are. That's all I want, and it's hard to get."

Now, instead of using your *psychic abilities* and guessing what your prospect will be like and why, your venture into the *unknown* has put it right out on the table. Now you can keep walking in your prospect's shoes and guide him further into his pain:

> "Sounds like you've been burned before by other sales people?"

And he replies:

> "That's quite true. I find most salespeople are really irritating because they just don't tell the whole truth. Why I bought this blah, blah, blah, and the representative didn't tell me a whole bunch of stuff."

Now you are getting to the core of an issue that has the potential to kill this whole sale. This prospect has a big trust issue. His distrust meter is off the charts, and it sounds like his gruffness could erupt at any time during the meeting. Now, your *directive intuition* takes him yet a step further:

> "You know, how about we do this: Let's you and I agree that today I won't act like a salesperson and today you won't behave like a prospect—no buying and no selling. Nothing can happen other than we will talk, because it sounds to me like we might have a big trust issue here and we'll need to work through that. Fair enough?"

For the first time the prospect has begun a meeting with a salesperson where the truth has come out before a product, trial close, tie-down or anything else like that. Even though he has a trust issue with salespeople, his trust level begins to soar with you. In caveman selling, this issue would have been swept under the rug to fester into a big problem for both of you. That is the power of *directive intuition* and *predictive intuition,* moving both you and your prospect into the *unknown zone.*

Scenario #2

Let's say, no matter how hard you try to keep the focus on concepts, your prospect keeps asking details about product and other technical questions. *Predictive intuition* keeps telling you that it is way too early in the meeting process to get technical and that if you do, this sale will be in trouble. Then *directive intuition* kicks in and tells you to say the following, using your *best friend personality*:

> "Bill, these are great technical questions and I'll be happy to share all that technical information with you. Before I do that, would it be okay if we spent just a few minutes helping me understand why your current advisor isn't making the grade? Once I know that and how all this affects you, I can tell you whether my product is a potential solution or not. Of course I would like it if we were a good fit, but you never know—we just might be a bad fit from the getgo."

But he doesn't take your lead!

> "Trust me, he's not getting the job done. What I need to know from you is if your blah, blah, and if you can work within the parameters of my blah, blah."

Chronicle #14

Now you're thinking that your prospect must really have a big problem that needs solving, and he wants to know if you offer a good enough solution—a perfectly reasonable request. You are about to begin blabbing out a litany of technical stuff that demonstrates the best features of your product when *impulse intuition* abruptly stops you cold from talking and literally stands you up from your chair. In a moment you find yourself a bit red faced, awkwardly looking down at your prospect with your lips virtually glued shut. You notice that the impulse that closed your mouth and stood you up did not carry any anger, fear, or any other negative type of emotion. It just happened, and there you were: still your friendly self, but in a totally different position.

You think to yourself, "What on earth do I do now?" You are in the most *unknown* of territories. But then, so is your prospect, who is thinking, "What on earth did I say to this guy that shot him up out of his seat like that? All I did," he says to himself, "was ask a few questions about how his product works!"

For a long moment you and your prospect, each in your respective surprise, look at each other. You roll your eyes in wonder and begin to laugh at yourself. To your amazement, your prospect smiles and begins to laugh too. In the next moment he's telling you about the time he started to get out of his car and then was propelled to shut the door; in the next moment a motorcyclist zipped by, amazingly too close to the car. If your prospect hadn't shut the door, the cyclist would have slammed into it. Then, he says:

> "Okay, now let me tell you what's really going on here. You see, I'm under a lot of pressure from my children to get this thing fixed yesterday. I'm really hoping you can help me out. So, here's the history. My current blah, blah, blah …."

You sit down, having, in total silence, via one intuitional move, cut through your prospect's pressure and gotten agreement from him to follow your lead in the meeting process. Had you not allowed your *impulse intuition* to move you out of your chair and into an *unknown zone*, there is nothing you could have done, using your caveman selling techniques, that could have accomplished, in so short a time, the same result.

Scenario #3

Your meeting is going well. You think that this is going to be a sale. Inwardly, your excitement rises, along with thoughts about how you are going to go for the *close*. Falling back into your caveman habits, you start to look for the right *closing* moment. The prospect asks about the rating of the insurance company whose product you are recommending, and your *closing* antennas begin to vibrate big time. You are about to pull out an app and ask for an order number when your *directive intuition* gently tells you to wait; that this is not the right time, and that you should back off. You listen and hold off on the *close*, deciding not to worry about the sale, choosing instead to believe it will take care of itself. You enter an *unknown zone*. You choose to answer the prospect's questions about the company, only to find that the ratings he is looking for are not available. Fifteen minutes later the prospect says, without any prompting from you, that he's the type of person who would never be satisfied with any company, even if the rating were very high. But, since you did not push him for the order, he is going to buy from you. You whisper to yourself, "Thank you, intuition. If I had tried to close earlier, it probably would have cost me the sale."

Scenario #4

You sit down with a new prospect. After five minutes a big red flag is raised by your *predictive intuition* that says you are wasting your time. Nothing has been said to indicate this, but you get the red flag anyway. You take heed to the warning, look at your prospect, and out of the blue you say:

> "This may sound really strange, and I hope you don't get upset, but I have a feeling—and please correct me if I'm wrong—that there is no way on earth that you will ever become a client of mine. Do you have any idea why I would feel that way?"

> The prospect, without batting an eyelash, answers:
> "Oh, you're right. There is no way. It has nothing to do with you, but I don't have any money to invest with you. I just want to keep learning so that I understand what my options are when I do get some money.

So you pack up your bags, bail out of the meeting, and prevent the wasting of a whole bunch of time—all in the flash of an intuitive moment. Interestingly enough, your current method may have reached the same conclusion, but, in all likelihood, it would have taken substantially more time.

You Can't See It, But You've Got to Trust It

"Steve, when all is said and done, there is no system that can tell you what to do in every situation in which you find yourself. Life, and prospects, are simply too creative to allow for predetermined coverage of every possibility. You need to let go of your mechanistic headset and, so to speak, go with the flow. Using a combination of new thinking, new terminology, new beliefs, and a new paradigm of selling, combined with a healthy and vibrant intuitive sense, you'll be able to negotiate virtually every situation, known and *unknown,* turn each into a business advantage, and efficiently determine if there is a possibility of creating a business transaction or not."

A few months ago I was sitting in a meeting with a prospect. It was our third meeting, and, up until that point, I had felt everything was going along fine. At the moment we met, a thought flashed through my mind that there was a problem; that the sale was in trouble. It was a thought I didn't want to hear. Yet, it kept, how shall I say it, disturbing me; made me feel uncomfortable with him and with the process. But, again, I wanted to hear the other thought that was sitting in the background, that everything would be fine and that the sale was mine to have. So I did. We worked for an hour or so and I went for the close.

"Mr. Prospect, things seem to be looking pretty good here. Would you agree?"

"Oh yes, this is looking good to me too."

"Great, I'll just get the paperwork out here and we'll be on our way."

"Oh, I don't want to do any paperwork!"

"Really, but I just thought you said things were looking good?"

"Things are looking good, but I've just been told about another problem I have, a health issue, and, well, you know, I just can't address two problems at the same time. It's too much for me to handle."

"I understand, but do you see how we can now get this one off the table so that you can focus on the other problem? It will make life easier for you."

"No, I just can't do it. I don't like making decisions when I'm not in a good place to make decisions. I'll just need to wait a bit."

"I can understand that, Mr. Prospect. But, by waiting, you'll have to deal with two problems instead of one. All I need is some information here and we can get this one out of our mind."

"No, I'm just not comfortable doing that. Anyway, I'd like to run the numbers to make sure we are on target here. Give me a couple of weeks and then we'll get together. I like what you have, I really do, but let's do it in two weeks."

"Well, okay. Let's set a time to get together."

"You know, because of what's going on, I'd rather just give you a call. I'll

Chronicle #14

call in two weeks. Okay?"

"Well, uh, okay. How about I put you in my calendar, and I'll call you too. Is that okay?"

"Sure, that's fine with me."

Man, what a waste of time that experience was. I'm thinking my intuition had been right, but I wouldn't trust it. It was almost two hours by the time this guy was in and out of my office; two wasted hours, two hours that I could have been talking to real prospects, out having fun, networking, whatever, but not wasting time. All I had to do was follow what my gut was saying, what my *predictive intuition* was delivering, like an important Fedex, to me.

Excited, I turn to him and say, "I think I'm there. I think something turned in my mind, that the world doesn't look the same to me than it did when we first met. My mind won't go back to that old world, can't go back to that old world; it's just a memory, like a past generation, that is old. So, I believe I've somehow gotten the right dose, the right number of kicks in the butt, the right medicine, the right thought provoking comments, whatever you want to call it.

"And now I'm living in a new world, different from everyone else. In a way, it's very gratifying, but it's also a little scary. I'm not sure I know my way around this world. It's like moving into a new neighborhood and not having all your old friends and a place to meet and hang out in. So what do I do now?"

He looks at me, clearly contented. There is a certain sense of peace, different from before, that he radiates. He is still thoughtful, very passive. I almost feel like he's not going to say anything.

He turns to me and says, "I think you're there, too. Steve, the door is opened, now you just need to walk through it. I am very proud of you."

It was the last thing I'd ever hear him say.

The Selling Chronicles

Chronicle #15
I Close Like a Champ But Lose Like a Chump

I wait at our appointed time and place but he doesn't come. I'm not really surprised. At the end of our last meeting he said that he'd opened the door and now the rest was up to me. I doubt if I'll ever see him again, so, I guess it is up to me.

It suddenly occurs to me how little I know about him. Not that it matters, but it would have satisfied some curiosity percolating within me from the time we met about where, why, how, and when he learned all this stuff and how it wove into his life. He said that there was much more, but that would be a matter of my own personal discovery, just as it was with him. I was, in his words, ready. I'm not certain what I was ready for, but he was certain I was ready. And that was that.

Since he said I was ready, and I'd come to believe a lot of what he said, I took a little time to reflect on our thirteen meetings. For some reason I was transported to a time I was in Little League baseball. I can still hear the cheers of my teammates and see the moment the ball and bat collided for my first hit. Time seemed to stand still as I looked proudly at my coach from the safety of first base. Then I got the sign, steal second on the next pitch. "What? Steal second? Are you kidding?"

My mind was going crazy. And then came the next pitch. I looked at second base. It looked like it was five miles away. I could see the ball leaving his hand, headed for the catcher. "Now," said my mind, "NOW." But nothing happened. As the ball thudded into the catcher's mitt, I couldn't move from first base. I was frozen. Frozen in the safety of being on base. And, I wasn't leaving. And I stayed there the rest of the inning. During the sides change, my coach put his hand on my shoulder, knelt down, and with a friendly smile said, "Steve, here's something I want you to remember for a long time. To get to second base you must leave the safety of first base."

Now at that time I thought he was talking about baseball, but he was really giving me a message that has encouraged and given me the willingness throughout my life to grow and change; to try new things, to explore the unknown and develop new ways of doing and seeing.

And now, this man has given me the same opportunity: to stay on first or to go to second, using all the things he has taught me. In looking back over our meetings, I realize that I left for second, although I wouldn't have admitted it then, right after our first conversion.

So, since he's not here and I am, and I'm ready for another lesson, I decide to give myself one. I agree with myself that a good lesson would be for me to uncover the principal thing I learned from all our conversations. What did I get out of all that? How did it move me? Am I changed? Will I get to second base?

My Self Lesson

The first thought that hits me is how susceptible I've been to what I call *other people's thinking*. By adopting and adapting thoughts, opinions, and beliefs about selling from other people, rather than developing them through my own experiences and creative processes, I've become an **automated selling machine woven together with a yarn made from the**

Chronicle #15

> **Other People's Thinking**
> Thoughts, opinions, and ideas adopted from other people rather than from personal experience or your own creative processes. Most of what you think and believe.

idea of *closing* and a fabric made from the idea of *winning*. Those two ideas, permeating every moment of my selling life, have created a false sense of security and a split with reality. I am, as he said, living in *denial*; and, I am, like he said, not sure I want to go through the pain of *waking up*.

You see, I could always *close* like a champ. I was really good at it. And, before we met, I would say to you that my career was quite successful and satisfying. But, a drug addict would tell you the same thing, that his drug life is also successful and satisfying. That's the power of *denial*; and *denial* will rule until something or someone comes along and gives you a swift kick in the butt, an opportunity to *wake up*.

Closing, that word, once standing before me like some ancient god to which I owed obedience, now appears more as a tattered and broken icon with little modern day meaning. Yet, while its power had sway over my actions, I did *close*—hard, often, and successfully. But, as with many things in life, I did not see its true cost. It turns out that I now understand that the concept of *closing* is a terribly expensive idea. It is paid for with the erosion of relationship, trust, self-esteem, integrity, respect, and life energy. I win, but I lose; I close like a champ but lose like a chump; champ and chump all rolled into one. So where do I go from here?

Where Does Steve Go from Here?

He never shows up.

I take a hard look at my reality and decide to give some structure to what I've learned from him and from using the materials and tools he gave to me.

The Selling Chronicles

I no longer will buy into the mass consciousness of selling fervor. I want to be awake, full of individualism, personally growing, more creative, more excited, and having greater life energy. And, of course, I want to make more sales than ever. That is what the rest of this book is about.

Section II
Structure

Structure Chronicle #16
The Must List

Let's take a global approach, like looking at the earth from afar.

There are two core selling templates from which you can choose:

- *Illusion based template*
- *Reality based template*

Illusion Based Template
A mechanistic model or pattern based on the illusion that the world is linear and that you can prepare for every situation that arises.

The *illusion based template* is designed for a *linear thinking* world—an ideal world where there is predictability. It is a model based on how you would like your selling world to be. It is prefabricated in a way that you believe will make it predictable, so you are able to foretell how, when, and why events will repeat themselves. It appears to be a secure and comfortable world. Of course, it doesn't exist, so it is an illusion.

The opposite of the *illusion based template* is the *reality based template*. This template is constructed as a guidig light on the selling path, neither predicting events nor giving pre-digested answers to events that might happen. It is a world that is alive and creative. It is not pre-digested. Yet the world of *reality* can become more predictable than a linear world,

> **Reality Based Template**
> A reality based model utilizing specific patterns for developing sales that are suitable for a non-linear world that takes into consideration changing situations, actions, environments, and prospects.

because it is just that, *reality*. *Reality* is the core of the template of managing change into *win-win* selling results.

The foundation of the *reality based template*—thoughts, approaches, concepts and actions—is what you will use to build your *reality chain of events* that was visited earlier in the dialogues. These core thoughts, approaches, concepts and actions are called the *Must List,* things that must be kept in mind in order to develop a *reality chain of events.*

The *Must List*

1. You *must wake up.* Become more aware of your thoughts, feelings, opinions and beliefs.
2. You *must* be gut honest with yourself and your prospect.
3. You *must* respect your prospect's intelligence, in both its initial presentation and in its potential.
4. You *must* become a *no man.*
5. You *must* learn to *walk in your prospect's shoes.*
6. You *must* develop a *good friend personality* and use it throughout your meetings to build *relationship.*
7. You *must* develop your *lethal business personality* to earn *respect* and make sure sales meetings don't turn into social gatherings.
8. You *must* address your *fear* and stop *pain dumping, double loading,* and trying to force *control* of your meetings.
9. You *must* identify your true priorities and goals when in a selling situation.
10. You *must* understand and trust that the world works in *reverse.*
11. You *must* stop forcing a *close.* Instead, spend most of your time finding the prospect's true *motivation* via the process of *disqualification.*

12. You *must* never *chase*.
13. You *must* be willing to step out of your *comfort zone* and enter, along with your prospect, into the *unknown zone*.

> **The Must List**
> The ideas that must be consciously kept in mind in order to effectively move from an illusion based selling model to a reality based selling model.

14. You *must* allow your *intuition* to lead the way.
15. You *must* become familiar with a new vocabulary.

Although I never like to say that something is a must, the *Must List* is a must! You cannot change your selling unless you take a step into a new *reality*. The 15 actions on your Must List will take you there. **They are guaranteed to give the results you want.** But they won't work if you don't have a serious drive to change, if you don't have the internal motivation to improve your selling life. In a very real sense, you need to sell yourself, find the internal *motivation* for you to change. It is only from that *motivation* and the *emotional charge* that creates it, that you will continue to grow in a new reality.

The 15-Week Debriefing Worksheet

To help you implement the *Must List,* I have created a 15-week journal in which you can enter your experiences each week for each item on the *Must List*. It is a way of debriefing yourself about yourself, solidifying how you feel about each of the *Must List* items from your real experience. The daily debrief should take no longer than 15 minutes. It should not be a drudge.

Run the *Must List* for 15 weeks, or until the list is complete. Take one *Must List* item at a time. Don't try and take any shortcuts and complete the list in a shorter time. This stuff needs time to process in order to be effective so take your time and do it right.

At the end of 15 weeks you will see a vast change in how you look at your selling world, even if this is the only exercise you do from this book.

Here is a blank *Must List* you can copy.

The *Must List* 15-Week Debriefing Worksheet

Week #	Describe What Happened	How Does That Make You Feel?	What Did You Do? What Happened Then?
This Week's Must Do:			
Monday			
Tuesday			
Wednesday			
Thursday			
Friday			
Overall Summary			

Chronicle #16

And, here is what my second-week *Must List* looked like when I was starting to learn to take charge of my selling reality:

One of My Old *Must List* Debriefings

Week #	Describe What Happened	How Does That Make You Feel?	What Did You Do? What Happened Then?
This Week's Must Do: I must be honest with myself and with my prospects.	Give a literal description of a particular situation or incident.	Describe the emotion that you discovered within you—not about other people, only yourself.	Describe what you did and then what happened after that.
Monday	Prospect was giving me a real hard time and was unwilling to talk about his issues or problems.	I felt very frustrated because there seemed to be a real barrier between me and my prospect.	I asked him if I could tell him something that might bother him. He said okay, and I told him how frustrated I was. He apologized and told me he was having a bad day. The meeting went very well after that.
Tuesday	Prospect told me they were going to think about it at the end of the meeting.	I felt deceived since they had agreed to a No or Yes decision.	I reminded them about our agreement on how the meeting could end. They said if they had to make a decision it would be No. I said okay, and we ended the process.
Wednesday	I made the sale.	I was happy about the sale but unhappy that I had fallen back into some old, bad habits, i.e., going for a trial close.	I reviewed some old notes about what I was doing incorrectly and saw how it could have easily backfired on me and how fortunate I was to have made this sale.
Thursday	My prospect kept getting phone calls from his daughter.	I felt disrespected and that I waited far too long to deal with how I felt about what the prospect was doing.	After the fifth call I asked my client if he would like to reschedule, that this sounded like too busy a time and he had other things on his mind. He turned off the phone.
Friday	No meetings today.		
Overall Summary	There are more internal things happening at my meeting than I was really aware of. Lots of feelings that I normally would let go by and neither recognize or deal with.	It makes me feel as though I've been missing a lot of opportunity to both grow as a person and grow as a salesperson.	By honoring how I felt and deciding to deal with it in a nice way, my meetings had more clarity, candor, and ease. I made two sales that I don't think I would have made had it not been for my taking the chance of dealing with what was going on with me.

The Selling Chronicles

Structure Chronicle #17
Developing Your Reality Based Chain of Events

Your *chain of events* is created to deliver specific and clear selling results. But first you must decide what those results are going to be. Most salespeople establish, at a minimum, three result possibilities for their chain of events:

1. Prospect agrees not to buy and ends the selling process.
2. Prospect agrees to buy and signs appropriate agreement, contracts or paperwork.
3. Prospect makes another specific appointment to meet.

Sometimes I will add into my *chain* some of the things that I *don't* want to happen. These are items which you may believe need special attention, as they keep coming up for you in your sales meetings. For example, if you find that you're always getting people who use "think about it" as a stall, then you might add something like this to your chain: "Mr. Jones, we're probably going to spend a bunch of time together. I would imagine, after spending that much time, if you still had to think about it, the solutions that I recommend are probably the wrong ones for you. Usually people tell me they want to think about it because they don't want to hurt my feelings. So, if we get to that point, would you be candid enough just to say 'no' instead of 'think about it?' I promise you that I'll be okay with that. Does that sound okay for you too?"

Developing Your *Reality Chain*

The next step is to develop the steps in the actual *chain*. Every business will be somewhat different, and every personality may demand a different approach. But, in all cases, the *chain* must be a series of events that have to lead to the outcome that you want. Here's what my chain looks like. From the moment I begin a meeting with prospects, I am looking to see if they have any problem with the chain that I've developed. If they do, I might end the meeting.

> **Reality Chain of Events**
> A flexible sequence of events that effectively deals with every situation as it is presented. While the Reality Chain is often learned in a specific order, the order of its use is determined by what is happening in the sales meeting.

My *reality chain* has 10 steps. I think of myself like FedEx. Each step leads me to the end goal of my meeting. Like FedEx, I know that if I follow each step, then the package—my end result—will be delivered. Here are the 10 steps:

1. Express a hearty "Thank you" for agreeing to meet.
2. Explain the purpose of the meeting.
3. Get agreement on the allotted time for the meeting.
4. Establish what will happen at the end of this meeting and address special situations such as *think about its*.
5. Determine when and how the meeting process can end, and by whom.
6. Gather emotions.
7. Adopt the Advisor Mode.
8. Perform Global Solution Matching.
9. Summarize and decide.
10. Set goals for next meeting.

Chronicle #17

Let's take a closer look at each one:

Step 1. Express a hearty "Thank you" for agreeing to meet.
I am looking to see if they are positive, enthusiastic, open minded, reserved, outgoing, or talkative. I'm looking at their body language. If they're a couple, who's doing the talking? Are they serious, joking, or appreciative? Are they the kind of people I want to work with?

Last week, a couple came to my office who claimed they had a substantial amount of money to invest, over five million dollars. It was the first thing that came out of his mouth. Then he gruffly told his wife to get him something out of their car. Then I took notice (you couldn't avoid it) of how poorly they were dressed and how unkempt they were. It seemed to me that they hadn't bathed in a few days. After that, he threw his statements on the conference table, which showed me that he was for real. There it was, five million dollars. Now I had a dilemma: five million dollars or tell him to take a bath. I didn't want to work with this person, so I disqualified him. That's what my chain of events told me to do. If I don't want to work with them, that's it. No matter what. It's over. *Finito*. The end.

If they don't pass this part of the chain, we're done. There is no more. Otherwise I'll end up cornered, working with a person I dislike, resenting every moment of it, and probably not making the sale in the end. That's where you have to have the courage of your chain, whether you believe in it or not. If you don't believe in it, follow it, use it, and implement it, what good is it? It will just make you feel good to say that you have one.

Step 2. Explain the purpose of the meeting.
For me, the first meeting is always to see if my prospects and I are a good fit. In this part of the chain I am looking to see if we have a personality issue, if they are agreeable to a specific goal for the meeting, what is in

their minds as far as what they think the goal of the meeting is. It gives me the ability to explore with them what kind of advisor would be a good fit for them; to find out their experiences with their current advisor and with other salespeople; to find their disappointments and their successes.

I recall a meeting where I asked my prospect what kind of financial professional he was looking for. He gave me a laundry list of expectations that were far beyond what I was willing to do or could do. He was high maintenance—too high for my liking, my timetable, and my personality. We were not a good fit. End of meeting. There's always another, more appetizing prospect waiting out there.

Step 3. Get agreement on the allotted time for the meeting.
Here I want my prospect to know how much time I plan on taking and whether that is okay with him. I don't want any time pressure or uncomfortable interruptions. I make it clear during the meeting how much time we have left and check in with my prospect to see if he is still okay with time.

Time seems like such a simple thing, but people generally are not very good controllers of their time. They will tell you that they are okay, but they really are not. In one meeting I had slated for an hour, I could see—it didn't take much to see—that my prospect had ants in his pants. You can't let that go. Once I checked in on the time, he admitted that he was just trying to be nice to me but he did need to be on time for a doctor's appointment and, since it had started raining, he was getting increasingly concerned about traffic. We rescheduled and out he went. He was happy, and so was I.

Step 4. Establish what will happen at the end of the meeting and address special situations such as think about its.
I am looking for three things to happen at the end of each meeting. For

example, at the end of my first meeting, either we need to decide that we are a good fit and a second meeting is called for, or I need to be told that we are not a good fit and that they would prefer to go somewhere else.

I kindly explain to my prospects that this is what I expect and that is the method by which I work. I tell them that I am a very candid person and ask if they will be candid with me too. They always say they will. I ask them if they are okay with our meeting ending this way. This is the time they need to tell me if someone else is involved and that we need to get them into the meeting to get to the results we want to achieve.

Each meeting has to have an end game that you share with your prospect. Let's say you are in the third meeting and you know it's for a decision. Then the end game for that meeting will be a "no" or a "yes," to either implement the program or terminate the relationship.

I like to also address *think about its* right at the beginning of each meeting. For example, I will tell the prospect that if, at the end of the meeting, they are still not sure that we're a good fit, and that they need to think about it, then I'm probably the wrong guy for them and that we should end the relationship right then. Remember, when making a statement like this, you must use your *best friend* personality. Otherwise it will sound too confrontational and upset the prospect.

Step 5. Determine when and how the meeting process can end, and by whom.

As part of being candid I tell them that I'm okay if at any time they want to end the meeting. It's their call; I don't want them sitting there just because they don't want to hurt my feelings. I also tell them that I might end the meeting early, too. It's just a matter of whichever of us is ready to finish first.

I really follow my intuition at my meetings. If something comes to mind that makes me feel I'm wasting my time, I put it right out on the table.

You would be amazed at the response of your prospects when you do this. Just tell them, "I'm getting the feeling that you're really not interested in what I'm telling you. How come I feel like your not liking what I'm saying? I feel like we're not going in the right direction; that you're bored; that this upsets you; that this irritates you and disappoints you; that I'm confusing you." Put it all out there, right when that intuition tells you. You will be amazed at how much information your prospects will give you, and love giving it to you, as long as you don't use it against them and go into caveman selling mode.

Step 6. Gather emotions.
What I've come to realize is that what he said about a prospect's motivation is really true. If a prospect is not moved emotionally, he won't buy, period! I used to do data gathering. Now I do emotion gathering. I use a data sheet, but I'm always asking them more details. If they tell me they own a home, I'm going to find out what emotions are attached to that home. If they have grandkids, how close are they, and how do they feel about them? If they tell me that most of their money is in CDs, I'm going to get more details on how they made that decision, what motivated them, and how owning CDs works for them, and affects them personally. I am required in my chain to make sure that I can associate, or try to associate, an emotion with each piece of data. In the end, it's not about the data, but the emotion that's attached to it. If there is no negative emotional charge, there is no reason for a prospect to make any changes at all. I am dedicated to finding the emotion, or non-emotion. It is a must.

Step 7. Adopt the Advisor Mode.
Many sales are lost because the customer will not part from their current advisor or, if they manage their own money, will not relinquish control of their assets to you. Advisor Mode is designed to test the strength of

the prospect with their current advisor or competitor.

While most financial professionals are trying to undermine the competing advisor or punch holes in the job he or she has done, I am always trying to send my prospects back to their advisor, or back to themselves if they manage their own money. **Fully 99% of the prospects leaving my office never go back to their current advisor.** I always assume that the competition did a great job and that my clients really belong in their advisor's office. In fact, the harder I try and get them to go back, the more they tell me why their advisor is not really getting the job done.

Assuming the Competition Is Doing a Great Job
The basis of Advisor Mode, whereby you test your prospect's relationship with his provider to see if there is a real motivation to do business with you. Requires you to never say what you are thinking about his provider. Think of it as a "gag order," where you can never say anything negative and must assume the provider is doing everything he can do to help your prospect. Your prospect will bring up all the negatives for you, if you follow the "gag order."

Advisor Mode requires that you also address the prospects' willingness to reposition assets with you. Once they have agreed that they don't want to go back to their advisor, the next step in Advisor Mode is to find out, if you can help them, how they are going to handle the advisor when it comes to taking assets from him or her.

Advisor Mode must be completed before any presentation of plan or product is made. It is a critical step in solidifying the decision process and your ability to consummate a business transaction.

Step 8. Perform Global Solution Matching.

With all the problems and their corresponding emotions on the table I am now prepared, without being specific, to show some general possibilities and how they might satisfy the emotional charges that we have discovered. Every conversation about a product category, idea, approach, or

> **Global Solution Matching**
> A state in which every conversation about a product, idea, approach, plan, or anything technical—data or product—is linked to the emotion that it is going to satisfy or relieve.

anything technical—data or product—must be linked to the emotion that it is going to change. I can't tell you how often during a sales meeting you must say these words: "Does using something like this, eliminate the emotion of that? Will you feel better off if we do that?" And so on. If I can't find something that will change their emotional world, I know we are probably a bad fit, tell them to stay where they are, and end the meeting.

It is here, in Global Solution Matching, that I bring up all the objections that my prospect might have about the products or plan that I might prepare and recommend to them. I do this before they bring it up. I want to see their reaction; whether it is a turn-off for them, or too much of a reach;

> **Presentation**
> Old-school delivery of recommendations for a product or service, usually using a features/benefits approach. Now called Global Solution Matching because each feature and benefit is related to the emotional charges of the problem being solved.

whether they really have their heart set on something else; whether they have another idea they heard from another advisor and how it affects their emotional charges. I believe the biggest mistake salespeople make in all professions is to talk about solutions without matching those solutions to emotions. That just becomes a mental data game: great for intellectuals, but lousy for selling.

Step 9. Summarize and decide.

In this part of my chain I give a summary of the meeting—the issues, the emotions, what we are trying to eliminate, what we are trying to enhance—each connected to a potential solution. In my business, I always ask them what it would be worth to them to have all their problems solved, their emotional life more stable, more peaceful, more whatever it might be. If there are any fees involved, this is the place to talk about them.

I then review the decisions that we agreed upon at the beginning of the meeting—either tell me I'm the wrong guy or else tell me I'm the right guy, agree to my fee (if any), and schedule the next meeting.

If they tell me that they need to think about it, I kindly take them back to our original agreement and suggest that even if, after spending this time together, they still can't see how I could add value to their lives, I am probably the wrong person for them to work with. That is *Reverse World Thinking* at work. **If they don't come fighting back, it's over.** I never agree that they will call me in two weeks or anything like that, because I know what will happen. I will end up chasing them, and I never chase. Never!

Step 10. Set goals for the next meeting.

In this part of the chain I will review goals for the next meeting, arrange to get any paperwork or statements I need and get pre-approval for what the results of that meeting might look like too.

In the beginning, when I first started using his stuff, I used to have everything written out. I would actually have, in front of my prospect, a form that would act as a double check for me, to be sure I kept to the *chain*. Sometimes I would even tell my prospect why I used that form, and the value of following the *chain of events* I use. No one ever had a problem with that. Now, it is so ingrained in my being, that I can put one step before or after another. At the end of the meeting I know that I will cover the right territory, but in a more natural order, each appearing as the meeting requires.

On the following page is a worksheet you can use to formulate your own *chain*. When you formulate your *chain of events* I am asking you to plan what you are going to do and say and what you might expect based on your experience in the past. It would be a good idea in the beginning to review your *chain* once a week, and then less often as you gain confidence in it. The trick is to always have a *chain* that **you are committed to using.** If you just make up things along the way and change it every time you run into trouble, you will never develop a *chain* that works and gets the results you want and deserve.

Your Personal Reality Based Chain of Events Worksheet

Meeting #	What I Say	What I Expect
Thank you		
Purpose of this meeting		
Time allotted or needed		
What happens at the end of the meeting		
How the meeting process can be ended		
Advisor Mode		
Emotion gathering		
Global Solution Matching		
Summary and decision		
Next meeting review		

Chronicle #17

Notes from Building My Reality Chain for a First Meeting

As you can see, my *Reality Chain* adds in a section for *think about its*.

Meeting #	What I Say	What I Expect
Thank you	Express appreciation for their choosing to come to my office to meet with me.	A sense of appreciation for my time; a degree of openness and willingness to dialogue.
Purpose of this meeting	To see if we are a fit by the end of the meeting; that I will be asking lots of questions, and that they can ask me questions too. Some of my questions will be very personal, about their finances.	A willingness to be candid; agreement that it is okay for me to ask lots of questions, some of which may be personal; an affirmation that they understand they can tell me directly that we are not a fit.
Time allotted or needed	We agreed on about one hour.	That they are still okay with one hour.
What happens at the end of the meeting	We either part ways or we set a second appointment. If still needs to think about it, I will bail out of the meeting process.	Agreement to those two choices. Understands if still needs to think about it, we are probably not a good fit and should end the process right away.
How the meeting process can be ended	I make it clear that either one of us can end the process at any time if there is no perceived value in continuing.	I want to know that will actually end the meeting if they feel like they should, and not continue "just to be nice."
Advisor Mode	Will send back to advisor to solve their problem to see if they will go. Will ask how they will handle taking assets away from advisor or self.	They must share deficiencies of their current advisor and why they won't go back to him or her. Must be willing to tell advisor that money is being moved to another area.
Emotion gathering	I must attach each financial problem to how it affects my prospects emotionally in their personal lives.	They must share deeper and deeper emotions; otherwise, I bail from the meeting.
Global Solution Matching	My presentation or proposal is only to the emotions we are trying to eliminate or satisfy. Nothing else.	They must agree that each solution satisfactorily impacts their emotional well being.
Summary and decision	Every meeting ends in a summary bringing solution and emotion together and whether that was enough to merit a next meeting, end of process, or implementation of the program. Their choice.	I expect them to talk about how the solution impacts their emotions, not just their finances. If they don't, I must go back and be certain they see the connection. Otherwise I will go negative and try to bail out of the meeting.
Next meeting review	What will specifically happen at the next meeting and the decision choices for that meeting.	They must make the appointment before leaving my office.

The Selling Chronicles

Structure Chronicle #18
Linking Your *Reality Chain* with the *Must List*

You now have two pieces of the puzzle in place: your *Must List* and your *Reality Chain of Events*. It is important to remember that your new world is not a *linear* world, a world of prediction. While you may learn your new *Reality Chain* in a certain order, eventually it should become non-sequential, reflective of actual experience, honest communication, and intuition. Those qualities are developed via your exercises and study of the *Must List*. Your world will become a world of agreed-upon results, with you and your prospect pitted as partners against the problem at hand, in a win-win environment. You will experience enhanced self-esteem, control, balance, peace of mind, and a lot more sales and fun.

In practice, the elements of a well-honed *Reality Chain* are pulled into use as the meeting progresses, giving very different forms in each and every meeting. In a sense, the *Reality Chain* could be considered the structure or chassis of the meeting, and the *Must List* could be considered the different designs you create, depending on the nature and actions of the prospect and how they link with the reality skills that you develop from the *Must List*. There is no one right way. It is only important for you to remember that at the core of the process is the goal of not having a goal. I know that sounds like a Zen statement, such as "What is the sound of one hand clapping?" But, that's what it is. There is no goal other than to get to a clear ending where everyone wins.

Your ability to move from the goal of making a sale to the goal of creating a win-win will be derived from the way you implement the 15 principles on the *Must List* into your *Reality Chain*. That's nothing more than practice, awareness, and a willingness to see and admit what is going on within you, your prospect, your communications, and your meeting. And that all begins and ends with your desire to drive yourself out of the selling illusion in which you live, into selling *reality.*

When I'm selling, I focus on exactly where I am in my *Reality Chain*. Since there are 10 links to my *chain,* I have a checklist going off in my head as to which ones I've successfully taken care of, which one I am working on, and, intuitively, which link I am headed for. Sometimes the prospect will trigger a link with something he says. Other times I just need to choose one to go to. In no event, however, will I move from one link to another, until I feel success in the link I'm in. When I debrief myself at the end of an unsuccessful sales call, I find that there is a link from within my *Reality Chain* that I have either skipped over or done a poor job with. When I skip over a link, I usually have done so because I've lost patience and focus in my meeting. Or sometimes I, like you, fall into the trap of thinking that I really have the sale locked up and I can skip a step or two. Other times I just door a poor job of using the principles on my *Must List* so I can develop the best combination of relationship and business environments.

So, let's take a look at some of the different ways (there are actually an infinite number) that you can use to link your *Reality Chain* with the *Must List.* My way is based on *five rules of the road* upon which my selling life revolves:

Chronicle #18

My Five Rules of the Road

Rule 1. No matter how grooved you think you are, review your *Must List* and *Reality Chain* prior to every meeting.

There is no difference between you and great athletes. When I was a playing tennis pro, my coaches reviewed my mechanics at every practice session. It was stuff you would think I should know. Well, I did, but still needed daily reminders to do this, follow through here, bend my knees more, rotate my arm on the serve, make sure my non-request arm was extended, and so on. Tiger Woods has a swing coach. What do you think they do by telephone after every match and together on the practice range? That's right, review basic mechanics. What do you think all those professional coaches do—in sports, music, voice, art, and martial arts? That's right again! They bring their athletes and artists down to earth by getting back to the basics, right down to the fundamentals, the foundation of the structure on which their skill was built. In my opinion, we all need to do the same thing.

Five Rules of the Road
- Before each sales meeting, review the *Must List* and your *Reality Chain*.
- Once a week, read through the 21st Century Selling Vocabulary.
- Debrief after each sales meeting.
- Create and use your Scorecard.
- Remember, you are a work in progress.

Rule 2. Once a week, read through the 21st Century Selling Vocabulary and Definitions.

You will be amazed at how easy it is to forget concepts or to think you know what they mean but you really don't; or how they may remind you of different situations at different sales meetings, teaching you how you could have handled that situation better, about different options that were available to you, or better ways you could have used the options you chose. I find the Vocabulary and Definitions the most important part of supporting my efforts of continuing to develop the *Must List* principles.

Rule 3. Debrief yourself after every meeting.

This is a quality it's taken me a long time to effectively develop. I am so busy in my practice that I think I can run from one prospect or client to another, and that I can remember what happened. That's just my big ego at work. I can't; and neither can you. Debrief yourself when it is fresh in your mind, as soon as the meeting ends. Your debriefing should cover the following:

1. Your overall summary about the meeting.
2. Where you got into trouble (even if you made the sale).
3. What you did well.
4. What you did poorly.
5. What you totally missed.
10. How you could have addressed a situation differently.

Rule 4. Create a scorecard.

When you read this, keep in mind that I am kind of a data nut. While you might not be as data oriented as I am, you need to keep some data on how you are doing. This takes the emotion of selling out of play so you can self-evaluate more objectively. After each meeting I rate myself, as part of my debrief session, from 1 to 10, one being the lowest score and 10 being the highest, on each link in my *Reality Chain*. Typically I have two to three appointments per day, so my scorecard looks like the one pictured on the next page.

Once you have a scorecard in place and keep it diligently, you will learn more about yourself and your selling than you ever imagined. In my scorecard I'm looking for certain things that help me evaluate how my process is going. Most salespeople evaluate how they're doing based on the number of sales they're making. **Unfortunately, they are evaluating the wrong item.** Remember what he taught me: The only thing you can control in the sales process is you. If that's true, then how can you use the

Chronicle #18

number of sales as the judge? You cannot control what other people do. You can only control yourself and the process. So, I'm looking for the following kinds of data:

1. What are my average scores for each meeting?
2. What are my average scores where I get a buy decision as compared to those where I get a no-buy decision?
3. What are my average scores for each link in the chain?
4. Did my averages change up or down on the things I am working on in my *Reality Chain*?
5. Have my overall averages trended up over time? (I like to keep a three month rolling record.)

What I've discovered after working with hundreds of salespeople is that we all have our own Waterloo, but the majority of the Waterloos out there are in the part of the *chain* that deals with What Happens at the End of the Meeting, *think about its*, Emotion Gathering, and Global Solution Matching. Virtually every sale I have lost has fallen to a poor job I have done in at least one of these categories at each meeting.

Now, you might be saying to yourself that keeping score like this is an awful lot of work. Well, it's not easy. We are busy people, and stopping to debrief and write down a bunch of numbers is usually the last thing on earth we want to do. All I can tell you is that all the successful business people I've met know the numbers about their business. You could ask them about any line on their expense account, amount of production per hour, sales per hour, best time of the day for business, hottest items, profit margins, expense ratios, capital costs, return on investment—virtually anything—and they know the answer. That's what business is all about: keeping score, knowing your numbers. That's the difference between treating your career as a career in sales, or a career in the business of sales. Sales, in my mind, is an art; but it is equally a business, with the same parameters, problems, and concerns as any other business, large or small. **You** must know your numbers.

In my debriefing scorecard, there is a column for each appointment in the day. My scorecard is designed in anticipation of three appointments per day. I rank myself from 1 to 10, ten being the highest score I can get.

If you look at my scorecard, it's easy to see where I am stronger or weaker. Obviously, I got the best daily scores (vertical columns) on the appointments where I did a Next Meeting Review, because my prospect

My Debriefing Scorecard

Chain	MON	TUE	WED	Thu	FRI	Chain Event Total
Thank you						
Purpose of this meeting						
Time allotted or needed						
What happens at the end of the meeting						
Advisor Mode						
Emotion gathering						
How the meeting process can be ended						
Global Solution Matching						
Summary and decision						
Next meeting review						
Meeting average						

Chronicle #18

agreed to another meeting. I always look at my worse-numbered scores and then go back to the *Reality Chain* (horizontal lines) to see where in the chain I am the weakest. So, if you look at this chart, I need more work on emotion gathering and Global Solution Matching for sure.

Keeping score is one of the elements of traditional selling that I believe is still valuable. The question is, of course, What are you keeping score of? Instead of tie-downs, closings, hot buttons etc., we are keeping score

My Debriefing Scorecard

Chain	MON			TUE			WED			Thu			FRI			Chain Event Total
Thank you	9	8	8	9	10	-	-	9	7	8	9	-	8	8	9	102
Purpose of this meeting	8	7	8	8	8	-	-	9	8	9	8	-	9	8	8	98
Time allotted or needed	10	9	10	10	10	-	-	9	9	10	10	-	10	10	10	117
What happens at the end of the meeting	7	8	6	8	8	-	-	7	7	5	8	-	8	9	9	89
Advisor Mode	6	8	9	7	7	-	-	9	9	9	7	-	5	7	8	91
Emotion gathering	6	6	4	8	5	-	-	5	2	8	5	-	9	9	8	75
How the meeting process can be ended	9	10	9	8	8	-	-	8	7	6	8	-	10	8	9	100
Global Solution Matching	5	5	3	7	7	-	-	8	4	7	7	-	8	9	9	79
Summary and decision	8	8	9	8	8	-	-	9	9	8	7	-	9	9	9	101
Next meeting review	10	8	-	9	10	-	-	10	-	10	-	-	9	10	-	76
Meeting average	7.8	7.8	6.6	8.2	8.1	-	-	8.3	6.2	8.1	6.9	-	8.5	8.7	7.9	

of events and habits that will give us what we want: reality based meetings, high levels of respect, and results we can count on.

Rule 5. Once a day, take a moment to remember that you are a work in progress.

I used to see myself as a project which, someday, was going to be finished. Once you get used to working with the *Must List*, you will find that you will soon drop the idea of being a finished product—that there is no end to your development; that you will never be finished; that you can't even see what you will be like, not only one, two or ten years from now, but right in the next moment. You are a work in progress.

To make things even more interesting, I believe that you are a work in progress where your destiny rests in your own hands. That's what he was talking about in the Dialogues: waking up, seeing the reality, and then harnessing all the energy of the past, present, and future to give yourself, and in turn your family, your community and, of course, your prospects, a better life; a better experience. So every day, one time each day—no matter how good or bad the day, no matter how you feel, no matter what you might think of yourself—take a brief moment to remember that your destiny is in your hands and that you are a work in progress.

These five rules of the road, if you use them, will help you integrate your *Reality Chain* with all the principals on the *Must List*.

Structure Chronicle #19
Establishing Priority: Uncovering My Baggage from the Past

So, where are we? These four tools are the cornerstones of making the journey from caveman to modern day selling professional:

1. The *Reality Chain of Events*
2. The *Must List*
3. The Scorecard
4. The Five Rules of the Road

Now we are going to add the last piece, a monthly assessment of your baggage from the past.

The *Reality Chain*, the *Must List*, the Scorecard, and the Five Rules of the Road will give you great insight into your sales meetings, your selling method, and you as a person. As complete as these checklists and developmental lists might sound, one more piece of valuable information is necessary to give yourself a complete and dependable feedback loop upon which you can learn and develop. And that is to be certain that you are keeping your priorities in line with your goals; that you haven't somehow, knowingly or unknowingly, changed your priorities and headed down a path that will give you less than desired results.

The Selling Chronicles

In Chronicle 8, we saw that priorities may move to the top of your priority list because of tendencies in your personality, e.g., because you were put down by your father as a youngster, or you want to impress prospects by showing how smart you are. As we saw, we often exchange the priority of making a sale with a more subtle priority such as this. In the end, you may show how smart you are, but you'll lose the sale.

All of us bring a lot of baggage from the past into a sales meeting. I do a monthly self-assessment to be sure that my baggage stays, as much as it can, in the baggage department. I have to remember that if I don't handle my baggage, and I give it to my prospects to handle instead, the sale is lost. The checklist I use—both blank and completed—are shown on the next two pages.

Now, this certainly is an extensive list and may at first be a little intimidating. But, if you review this list and rank your baggage once per month, you will find that three or four pieces of baggage really stand out. And, if you do it long enough, **you'll find that there is probably one piece of baggage that rules the day and causes a lot of upset in your sales meetings.** If you can find that core piece of baggage, that will be the first step in making sure it stays in the baggage department, or gets thrown off the train altogether.

Once you have earmarked the pieces of baggage that are of particular interest to you, or the ones that seem to cause you the most trouble, your job—following your *Reality Chain*—will become much easier. At each point in the chain, all you need to do, especially if you are feeling any pressure or discomfort, is to periodically check in with yourself to make certain that you haven't shifted your priority and taken your baggage out of the baggage department.

Also note that keeping your baggage where it belongs will cause you a great amount of discomfort during your meeting. You are going to want to take care of the baggage, to somehow satisfy it as you've done so often

Chronicle #19

in the past. This is part of walking into your own *discomfort zone*. And, remember, the more you keep your baggage in the baggage department, the quicker you will recognize the baggage that your prospect is trying to give you to carry. That recognition will give you insight into the emotional workings of your prospect and how his surface problem is emotionally cooking inside him. For you, that is the secret you are searching for. It is the place from which your prospect will buy.

Baggage from the Past: Monthly Self Assessment
Month of :_____

My Baggage	0–10	Personal Notes
Need to appear smart		
Need to please others		
Need to feel important		
Need to control		
Need to feel better		
Need to avoid confrontation		
Need to help others		
Need to look professional		
Need to feel needed		
Need to feel comfortable		
Need to be understood		
Need to appear impressive		
Need to be heard		
Need to be perfect		
Need to justify things		
Need for approval		
Need for friendship		
Need to be liked		
Need to win		

The Selling Chronicles

My Overall Baggage from the Past
My Initial Baseline Self-Assessment

My Baggage	0–10	Personal Notes
Need to appear smart	9	This is danger for me. Makes me talk too much and listen too little.
Need to please others	9	I am happy when other people are happy. Ruins communication as I don't like telling it as it is.
Need to feel important	3	I don't have this need.
Need to control	10	I am a control freak. I need to watch this and make sure I give customers the feeling they are in control.
Need to feel better	3	I don't look to prospects to make me feel better. Not an issue for me.
Need to avoid confrontation	5	I am willing to differ in opinion but don't like it when people seem to like me less. Careful here, need to deal with prospects candidly.
Need to help others	10	Big drive for me. Sometimes to the point that I don't focus on business but more on being a great helper. Bad for the bank account.
Need to look professional	9	I think it's the right thing to do. I must make sure I'm not too stuffy or professional that people are uncomfortable.
Need to feel needed	3	I'm pretty independent. My customers never feel that I'm pulling at them.
Need to feel comfortable	4	I'm OK with feeling uncomfortable and letting things take care of themselves.
Need to be understood	10	This is a big desire of mine. Causes me to offer too much explanation of things.
Need to appear impressive	3	I don't strive to impress but like to make an impression. Doesn't work against me.
Need to be heard	9	I always want to get my point across. This does work against me, especially when it's a minor point or when I'm working with more technical kinds of prospects.
Need to be perfect	10	I am a perfectionist. If I let this get out of hand, my prospects begin to see me as inflexible or very critical of them.
Need to justify things	4	It is what it is. I don't rationalize.
Need for approval	4	I don't need approval of what I do, but I do like to be liked.
Need for friendship	3	I get my friendships taken care of outside of a selling situation. Not an issue here. I don't look for friendship from prospects or customers.
Need to be liked	7	I like being liked. Took me a long time to realize you can't be liked by everyone. Sometimes I am not candid enough with prospects because of this.
Need to win	10	Ultra highly competitive. I love winning. Must remember that everyone wants and needs to feel like they are winning too. Also, need to keep in mind that a loss can be a win in disguise.

Structure Chronicle #20
The Power of Reality

What Is Reality?

I once asked him how I would know if I was in *reality*. He gave me this mystical answer that if I were really living in *reality* I wouldn't know it; that each moment would be a lifetime; that time would have no meaning; thoughts would pass like clouds, having no effect on me, neither pushing or pulling me; actions would be appropriate for every situation; I would be loving, kind, and strong at all times, in all places, and with all people. He said that if I were living in *reality,* life would flow through me, out to other people like rain falling from the sky, nourishing everything upon which it fell; I would understand, be compassionate, have great inner strength, great insight, and a simplicity that would be magnetizing to other people. When you live in *reality*, he said that *reality* and I would cease to exist. He said that if I lived in *reality,* I would be living life at its best. That's the power of *reality*.

That's what *he* said.

I asked him how all that could be? How would you know if you *couldn't* know? I told him it sounded like a place you could try to get to but would never arrive. And if you did, you wouldn't know it anyway. I remember his telling me, in a very gentle voice, that I was right and I was wrong.

I never asked him why!

Now I can't say, with certainty, that he's correct in his description—but let's just say he is. I, for one, am not living in *reality*. For sure! Absolutely! Without a doubt! Not even close! But what I've learned is that the journey we sales professionals walk gives us a rare opportunity to enter, through our selling, into this mysterious world. It allows us to draw from it and bring that power into our practice for the betterment of us and all those around us. Selling *reality* is the first journey. And if it works on you like it did on me, that will spill over into other parts of your life.

He also reminded me that *reality* is not a goal. That would make it a linear model and he said he could see me rushing to get to *reality*, like the finish line of a race, so I could get there before everyone else. The deal, as I see it, is that *reality* is just something you work on. It is the path established by the *Must List*. That's what the *Must List* does; it allows you to walk the talk. That's why I want you to look at it so often.

Use the *Must List* to Bring You into Reality

If you take each principle of the *Must List* and look at it more closely as it applies to selling, you will see the power it contains. Following, for your consideration and reflection, are my viewpoints for each principle. I hope they will help you identify their power, how they will influence you, your prospect, your meetings, your communications, and all the other aspects of your selling life.

1. **You *must* wake up, become more aware of your thoughts, feelings, opinions and beliefs.**

    Would you rather deal with someone who is half asleep or someone who is very alive, infusing you with motivation and energy? Being aware of what you're saying, thinking, and doing takes you immediately from your mechanical nature and passes life into everything around you. When you wake up, it will influence others to wake up. Awareness is like an energetic feedback loop: You move towards a greater sense of reality, and so will others. Through your selling you can become of greater meaning to the people you meet, whether you make a sale or not. You have the opportunity to impact their lives, not only through your products and solutions, but through who you are and how you bring reality into your life.

2. **You *must* be gut honest with yourself and your prospect.**
   There is nothing like the truth, however you may see it. Being kind and speaking the truth to your prospects will give you a certain power, combined with a certain humility and vulnerability. When you speak the truth about what is happening with you, you are putting yourself right out there in the open, showing yourself, undressing in public. You will develop courage you didn't know you had, candor that other people will respect, and magnetism that people will, like iron, be drawn to and will stick with. Prospects will become loyal clients. They will bring friends because they want them to have the same experience they had. You must remember that speaking the truth about you is not proselytizing or preaching; it is just being absolutely honest about what is going on in your mind and emotions about your sales meeting and communication with your prospect. (It isn't your personal life—that needs to be taken care of in another venue.) There is no telling the power of the truth and its impact on other people. It will leave you standing tall and strong, feeling better about yourself, and never disappointed. Wouldn't that be a nice thing?

3. **You *must* respect your prospect's intelligence, both in how it**

presents itself to you and in its potential.
Reality brings intelligence into focus. It delivers the best you have, and it allows your prospect to bring the best he has to the table. Your respect and truthfulness infuse your prospect with potential that he didn't know he had. It helps him see through his sleep into the riches of his own mind and heart. It gives him the freedom to dig deep, search his own treasure, and find his best solution. That solution, whether it is to your liking or not, is his destiny. Respect brings you and your prospect to the brink of improving his destiny. You and he will either clutch that opportunity or leave it on the shores to be washed away, like a sandcastle, by the next wave—or in our case, the next disrespectful thing you say to him. Respect stands as the single greatest gift you can give to your prospect; it will allow him to be propelled along his way and to reach the heights and depths of his own life.

4. **You *must* become a *no man*.**
   Reality is about setting boundaries. Boundaries can be a very powerful ally for you in your selling. A boundary sets the limit of operations, the field of the game. When properly constructed—like that of a jet motor, for example, where the boundary of exhaust reduces in size to compress air and give power—boundaries will add tremendous power to your sales meetings. The negation of the traditional positive, "go get 'em" mentality by becoming a 'no' man, is very much like that jet engine. Every time you bring your prospect back to reality by trying to get him or her to do business with someone else, or not to buy your product, he will, by himself, reduce the exhaust size of the door he is trying to go through. At the end of the meeting, he will, via the power of reality, the power of negating all other options, propel himself with great energy into the purchase of your product. Once your meeting develops established boundaries—

boundaries that your prospect participates in erecting through your 'no' man attitude—your meeting will become easier, friendlier, shorter, more candid, more honest and more successful.

5. **You *must* learn to *walk in your prospect's shoes*.**
   What is the power of knowing that someone is on your side, both for you and the other person? What is your prospect really looking for? Is it a product or an experience? Is it just a product experience, or a total experience, which includes their experience of you? Reality gives you the freedom to climb into the shoes of your prospect and to see the world from his point of view. It also gives your prospect the freedom to untie his shoes so that you can climb into them with him. Only reality has the power to do that, to overcome you and your prospect's practice of distrust, putting up barriers, hiding, telling lies, and the feeling of being just out for oneself. By walking in your prospect's shoes with the truthfulness of just walking in them, to experience your prospect's experience, you will develop a deep and respectful appreciation of other people's lives, their struggles, their celebrations, their fears, their loves, and their wants, needs, and desires. You will learn, through the power of reality, that the lives of your prospects are like jewels or crystals, each with a different and valued shimmer and color, each, important and meaningful, just as it is.

6. **You *must* develop *good friend* and *lethal business* personalities and use them throughout your meetings.**
   Reality demands reality. Life is not just one aspect or another. Your meetings with prospects must span the entire scope of human interaction. It isn't just business, it isn't just friendship, it isn't just kindness, it isn't just serving—it's all these and more. Your prospect needs your guidance so he can better discover and create his destiny, just

as you need your prospect's cooperation so you can create your own destiny. Sure, you want to make a sale; sure, you need to pay your bills; sure, you want to get to the top. These are all typical human desires. But to accomplish what you want to accomplish, to bring you to the fulfillment of the highest level of destiny open to you, you must integrate with your prospect in a healthy, full-spectrum reality of friendship and business.

7. **You *must* stop *upstaging* and focus on a true sense of *co-creating* with your prospect.**
Reality is nothing more than a great play, where the spotlight shines on one character or another, depending on the plot. It is, however, a powerful play with a wonderful plot that includes you and your prospect as major players when you're in a sales meeting together. That meeting is like a play within the play. Reality demands that you let it play out, to develop its destiny, its own plot, its own theme, its own ending. Taking the spotlight, or taking your prospect out of the spotlight, changes the nature of the play—reduces its quality, impact, and message and dilutes its power for both you and your prospect. Everyone suffers when creativity and attention are demanded by one person, like a child demands of a parent. Your sense of reality will bring your prospects along on the path of co-creativity, something they have rarely experienced. It will be one of the most powerful experiences they may have in their lives. Remember, it is not a product, but an experience that they really want.

8. **You *must* address your fear and stop *pain dumping*, *double loading*, and trying to force *control* of your meetings.**
There is no controlling reality. It is what it is. There is only the ability to dive deeper into it, like one would dive into an ocean of fath-

omless depth and breadth. The power of your reality, your willingness to create it and, at the same time, live with and appreciate what it is that you've created, will guide your prospect, giving him the courage to take a dive into that same ocean where control is not an issue. Your power and control will come from your practice and ability to guide your prospect, who will, naturally, feel lost and in new unexplored territory. He will look to you, like the passengers in a raft headed down a furious river, for guidance and to control the boat, your meeting. Reality carries no fear, because the reality of fear is that it is an illusion. The reality of your past is that it doesn't exist, except in your own mind. The reality of the future is that it is yet to come and its existence is only in your own mind as well. Reality is now. Not the moment that just passed. No, now! Not the now that you just read. Now! That is where your power to lead and guide your prospect lies, between that moment that just passed and the instant before the moment that is just coming. Now! Once you're there, your pain will have no need for dumping and you will have no need for double loading. It's all here for you in the reality of now.

9. **You *must* identify your true priorities and goals when in a selling situation.**
Reality is a clear mirror of your own making. It shows you what you're thinking, what you're doing, what your goals are, what your opinions are, how you affect people, how you relate, what you relate to, what drives you, what pushes people away from you, what draws them to you, why they buy, why they won't, why they hide, why you get angry, how you can handle your kids, how you manage your budget—every little bit and aspect of you is reflected back to you via reality. When you are sitting with a prospect, that prospect is a reality check for you, a mirror for you. Whatever you are getting from

your prospect, there is a strong chance that he is giving you a reflection of you. If he is stubborn, it is probably you; if he is kind, it is probably you; if she is unwilling to open up, so, too, are you unwilling to open up. And so it goes. So, you must be clear about your reality. What do you really want? What is your real goal? What is your real purpose? Get in touch with it. Be honest. Don't hide from yourself. Stay in the reality of *you* and watch it flourish as it is watered with its own rich and nourishing power, *reality*.

10. **You *must* understand and trust that the world works in *reverse*.** How does the world really work? Can you see it? Do you believe what you see? Did you notice that everything is turning, changing, growing, dissolving, dying, all right before your eyes? Can you identify the opposing forces, night and day, warm and cold, light and dark, love and hate, peace and war, order and chaos? Can you see your prospect moving in opposition to you? Do you see him as moving back when you move forward, moving forward when you move back? Can you play in the reality of backwards, of finding yourself by going exactly where you think you don't need to go? Can you help your prospect find himself by helping him go where he wants to go and then you can find yourself, as he is then willing to go where you want to go? It's all backwards—going is coming; leaving is staying; closing is opening; finding is losing. That's reality. It'll make your head spin, but it'll also open the hearts of you and your prospect. It will also open his pocketbook to take advantage of the experience he is getting by sitting with you.

11. **You *must* stop forcing a *close* and instead spend most of your time finding the prospect's true *motivation* via the process of *disqualification*.**

Chronicle #20

The power of reality lies in its independence. It has no desire to be one way or another. It takes what is given and gives what it believe needs to be given. Results are meaningless. The only meaning is what to do next. Reality has the power to find your prospect's true motivations by helping your prospect first discover what they are and then share those results with you. Every time you try to force reality to your own end, you deepen your illusion and create an illusive reality that you believe is reality itself. That illusive reality will fool you every time into believing that it is the way it is. It is from that place that denial arises and causes all level of distrust, disingenuous conversations, and self-serving beliefs. Illusion pushes you and your prospect further and further from you and your selves. Reality, although seemingly working often in reverse or in a shroud of mystery, does just the opposite. Reality is the most powerful magnet in the world. It draws out the motivations of you and your prospect and lays them out on the table for both of you to deal with, in an effort to reach a mutually agreeable end. Although reality is quite powerful and puts great force at your command, it will never be a force that is artificially manufactured to be imposed on a naïve prospect.

12. **You must never *chase*.**

You cannot chase reality and you cannot chase, in a reality paradigm, your prospect. Chasing will take you out of the reality of co-creating a win-win meeting. Chasing says to you that things are not going your way and that you need to grab for what you want, take the ring from the merry-go-round, cut your prospect off at the pass so that he will do business with you. This is what salespeople do when living in the illusion that they cannot get what they want from their prospect because the prospect won't give it to them. Reality creates instant results that are perfect for you and your prospect. Unfortunately, it may not be the results you dream of or hope for. If that's the case, then that is your destiny. You can work hard to change your destiny, but once something happens, once you have an experience, *that* is your destiny and it cannot be changed. Chasing creates a destiny that is far removed from the potential that reality holds for you. When you feel yourself chasing, stop. Just stop! It is not what reality is about. It is not what you are about. You don't need to chase, you need to work harder at becoming aware, becoming alive, being real.

13. **You *must* be willing to step out of your *comfort zone* and enter, along with your prospect, into the *unknown zone*.**

    The power of reality lies in its mystery, in its ability to take you on a journey where you don't know what, why, or how things will happen. Reality is a mystery in itself. Reality will always take you to the edge of your comfort zone, until, as he said, your comfort zone disappears and there is only reality, nothing else. You and your prospect need to go to that place where reality lives. In all likelihood, your prospect will not go there: He is afraid, he is in denial, he is wary; he is just like you. So, it becomes your job to lead, to lead people where they don't want to go. When the mystery of reality becomes your excitement, your desire, something that you enjoy, it will magnetically draw your prospect into the same feelings. If he won't go there, move in that direction, or reveal his reality to you, you can't be his partner. He can't work with you and you don't want to work with him. Go out and find people who vibrate on the same frequency you do; who want to explore like you do; who are enthusiastic to work with you. Enjoy them, work with them; and they will give you what is due to you by doing business with you and sending their friends and co-workers your way.

14. **You *must* allow your *intuition* to lead the way.**

Chronicle #20

Reality's undefined mystery presents an unfathomable opportunity to discover new ways to build trust, relationship, respect, consideration, and appreciation between you and your prospect. But, like anything else, you either use it or lose it. Intuition is the guiding light to those new paths, thus far untraveled by you or by your prospect, that hold unique destinations and scenery for the journey they will take you on. Intuition, in the beginning, will err. But, the more often you use it, depend on it, and trust it, the more it will deliver its fruits. Intuition is reality's guiding power, transmitted in different ways, through different means, at different times. That power is open to your harnessing if you listen for it and recognize its signal. It will give a special meaning to your meetings and help you develop special relationships with your prospects. Intuition will lead you to those places where hidden information and direction await your bidding. Use it or lose it. It is reality's calling card. Use it now.

15. **You must become familiar with a new vocabulary.**

    Reality is present when you see through the illusion in which you and your prospect are living. To see through the curtain that binds you in your mechanistic style of selling, to reach the place where creative energy fosters meaningful relationships upon which solid decisions evolve, to reach that place of reality, your new vocabulary must guide and direct your awareness to be able to distinguish between the curtain and the reality that lives behind it. Words define what you are doing. What you are doing defines your level of entanglement in the illusion that life delivers to appease your appetite. But only reality will truly appease your appetite, satisfy your desires, and deliver what you want in every sales meeting you hold. It has great power over your illusion, but only if you recognize the illusion you're in. Your new vocabulary is the vocabulary of a powerful ally, *reality*.

The Selling Chronicles

Structure Chronicle #21
Conclusion: Where Do You Go from Here?

An eight-year-old boy approached an old man in front of a wishing well, looked up into his eyes, and said, "I understand you're a very wise man. I'd like to know the secret of life."

The old man looked down at the youngster and replied, "I've thought a lot in my lifetime, and the secret can be summed up in four words. The first is think. Think about the values you wish to live your life by. The second is believe. Believe in yourself based on the thinking you've done about the values you're going to live your life by. The third is dream. Dream about the things that can be, based on your belief in yourself and the values you're going to live by. The last is dare. Dare to make your dreams become reality, based on your belief in yourself and your values."

And with that, Walter E. Disney said to the little boy, "Think, Believe, Dream, and Dare."

There are millions of stories of success, most of which we will never hear. I will, in all likelihood, never hear your story. I wish I could. How will it evolve? What will your selling life become? Will you grow, do better, become wealthier and healthier—financially, physically, mentally, and spiritually? I don't know what your story will be, but I do know this: It will be a great story. It will be a story that I would want to read.

Our craft of selling demands skills far beyond the typical profession. We have to carry within us a formidable array of tools that we can use in a formidable array of circumstances. Every day, every hour, every minute is different; but all are equally demanding in the scope of what we need to know and in our ability to execute it. In one moment we might be a psychologist; in another, a businessperson; in another, a good friend; and yet in another, a tough, hard-nosed negotiator. To reach our goals, we have to negotiate through the politics of big corporations, through the mire of different personalities, through gatekeepers, and through a host of other kinds of selling traffic. Like actors on a stage, we need to provide excellence every time the curtain goes up; but the venue is always different and the audience, in the beginning, is never rooting for us. What a life we lead. It is so embarrassingly interesting, isn't it?

So, how will your story turn out? Will you be the hero or the villain? Or, like many of us who have learned to step further into the present day, into the present moment, with a new bag of tools and a greater sense of what is real and what is not, will you start as the villain (it is the salesperson's plight to always be seen that way at first) and then end up as the hero? Whatever the details, I hope that is the story for you.

While so many things are going on in our world, we struggle to make our next sale. And, if you're like me—which I suspect you are—as many sales as we make, the next one will be just as rewarding as the first. Isn't that so? Little compares to that feeling of getting the contract, of yes, of winning. There is no problem with winning, none whatsoever! But there can be a problem with how we go about winning, the stuff we have looked at throughout this book. How will we win the next one? With what quality? At what expense? At whose expense?

How will you win the next one? Will you add to the consciousness of "me first" that pervades our lives? Is it all about the money, as many of

Chronicle #21

our leaders would proclaim; is there no room for an effort with a greater and nobler goal than making the next buck? Would more money make you happier? If you were happier, but with less money, would you accept that?

How will you play in the future? Will you start playing differently now, or will you procrastinate, creating a stall or objection in your mind, like so many of your prospects do to you?

What's going through your mind right now? Are you saying things like, "Oh, this is so lofty, too lofty for me; whatever I do won't have any impact on the world anyway; to change like that is just too hard, and it probably won't work anyway. It's a great book, and I'll make sure to read it again in the future. Hey, I've got to make a sale, and I really don't much care how it happens; you know, when it comes right down to it, I kind of like being a caveman."

What is really going on for you, right now? Can you see it? Can you feel it? Something is surging through you. What is that?

At one of the meetings I didn't report to you, he asked me if I thought it would be easy or difficult to get people to change, to look at their selling life from a different perspective, to jump into a different, more positive reality, as good as it might be for them. I told him I didn't know the answer; that all I could do was my little dance and see what happens.

But you know the answer, right now, in this instant. I'm sure you do.

I wonder what it is ....

The Selling Chronicles

Section III
My 21st Century Selling Vocabularly

Analytical Intuition *(page 226)* The great "Aha!" you get when trying to solve some kind of a problem. Often occurs after a good night's sleep (if you ever get one).

Assuming the Competition Is Doing a Great Job *(page 255)* The basis of *Advisor Mode*, whereby you test your prospect's relationship with his provider to see if there is a real motivation to do business with you. Requires you to never say what you are thinking about his provider. Think of it as a "gag order," where you can never say anything negative and must assume the provider is doing everything he can do to help your prospect. Your prospect will bring up all the negatives for you, if you follow the "gag order."

Aware *(page 36)* The state of knowing what is really happening with you, your prospect, the communication between you and your prospect, and the process of your meeting. Aware is the opposite of asleep, a disposition in which many salespeople find themselves far too often.

Balance *(page 208)* The secret of controlling a sales meeting. Out of balance equals out of control. Balance keeps you from being blindsided by your prospect.

Begging for the Sale *(page 202)* What you end up doing when you lose control over the sales process. Prospects have internal antennas that immediately pick up any form of begging, a signal that you have now given control of the meeting to them.

Blah, Blah, Blah *(page 129)* Much of what salespeople say. Can be replaced with *Yap, Yap, Yap*.

Business Meeting *(page 160)* A meeting in which all parties agree on the process that leads to the goal of exchanging money for goods or services, better known as a sale. The opposite of a social meeting, which unfortunately many salespeople prefer.

Buying Signal *(page 127)* A mythical flag or beacon raised by your prospect to let you know that he or she is ready to buy. The flag is said to contain the words, "I am ready to buy and I want you to know that."

Caveman Chain of Events *(page 175)* A series of steps, developed to be performed in specific, pre-determined situations, in a linear world, all leading to unreliable and unpredictable results. In short, a system that does not work well.

Caveman Salesperson *(page 21)* An eagle-eyed *Homo sapiens* who's looking for hot prospects. This species is specifically trained to do whatever it takes to prey on other *Homo sapiens* in order to make money.

Change *(page 199)* Here now, gone in a flash. "Look, I see my prospect. Look again, uh-oh, he's different. And now he's changed again. Is this ever going to end?" No!

Chase *(page 45)* A college-like effort to catch what you want. Often the result of teasing by the prospect, who appears irresistible to you.

Close or Closing *(page 26)* Closing is an annoying process that "pisses off" your prospect while you try to get what you want.

The Selling Chronicles

Closing Ratio *(page 25)* A number in which many salespeople take great pride. The most important element upon which you can build and maintain a big ego.

Co-Create *(page 143)* A mutually respectful effort to achieve an agreed upon goal or goals. A shared responsibility. Often thought of by caveman salespeople as a sure road to a lost sale, because they have to keep their mouths shut in the process.

The Comfort Zone *(page 205)* Thoughts, feelings, and actions that are pleasant and feel good.

Conscious *(page 51)* Alive in the moment. Not mechanical. Non-reactive. Not pre-digested. Not knee-jerk. Not robotic. Not predetermined. In other words, a state in which you have very little experience in your selling.

Control *(page 198)* The ability to maintain your balance in a sales meeting. Has nothing to do with controlling anything or anybody but yourself. A sense you would like your prospects to feel but not actually experience.

Denial *(page 48)* An unconscious defense mechanism used to reduce anxiety by denying thoughts, feelings, or facts that are consciously intolerable. Otherwise known as the elephant in the room.

Directive Intuition *(page 225)* Knowledge that arises in the moment that tells you what you should do next. Not based on any pre-determined analysis or system. An idea that just pops into your head or hits you on the head, as is your preference.

The Discomfort Zone *(page 206)* The place within the prospect where he discovers the emotional motivation why he should buy from you. A place where thoughts, feelings and actions reside that don't feel good to the prospect. A place where he doesn't want to go, because it is not an enjoyable place. It is also a place where *you* don't want to go because it is equally uncomfortable for you.

Disqualifying the Prospect *(page 189)* The process of trying to end your sales meetings as fast as you can. It is your first job as a modern sales professional and the most fun you could ever have in a sales meeting. Allows the prospect to qualify himself, sell you, and close himself.

Disrespect *(page 61)* Result of the salesperson's belief that he knows more than his prospect and has superhuman powers that can solve the prospect's problems. Often a parent-child type of thinking.

Dog and Pony Show *(page 128)* A circus with dogs and ponies. Also, a presentation given before you know you have the sale. Something you should never do unless you are in the circus or own a dog and a pony.

Double Loading *(page 117)* The unique ability to make matters worse. Adding more pressure to an already pressurized situation. Letting your own personal issues confuse matters and create more pressure.

My 21st Century Selling Vocabulary

Emotional Charges *(page 65)* The positive or negative emotions you and your prospect attaches to data or knowledge (which is always neutral). All sales are the result of a prospect's desire to change an emotional charge he or she is experiencing. All lost sales are the result of a lack of sufficient emotional energy to motivate change.

Fear *(page 44)* The root of all your selling problems, issues, hopes, concerns, fantasies, and disturbances. Typically hidden by a severe case of false bravado to the extent that the salesperson believes it is nonexistent. (See *Denial*.)

The Five Core Principles *(page 176)* The central aspects of yourself from which your selling journey is formulated:
- The Secret: Awareness
- The Key: Reality
- The Method: Letting Go
- The Excitement: The Unknown
- The Motivation: Satisfaction

The Five Elements of a Lethal Business Meeting *(page 106)* Procedures that must be agreed upon to move a meeting from a social meeting into a business meeting.
- *Purpose* for each meeting.
- *Time* allotted for the meeting.
- *Bail Outs:* How each party may end the meeting.
- *Decisions:* When decisions will be made and what those decisions can be.
- *People* who need to be present to accomplish the above.

Five Rules of the Road *(page 263)*
- Before each sales meeting, review the Must List and your Reality Chain.
- Once a week, read through the 21st Century Selling Vocabulary.
- Debrief after each sales meeting.
- Create and use your Scorecard.
- Remember, you are a work in progress.

The Four Overriding, Dominant, Unceasing Desires *(page 159)* Desires that are part of the inner nature of you and your prospects: winning, rightness, control, and dreams coming true. They are like children who want something in the toy store—they never give up.

Get Excited *(page 128)* The process of lighting up your prospect's enthusiasm for your product or service so that he will continually say "yes" to almost anything you propose. Sometimes used as a sexual term that is applied to selling.

Global Solution Matching *(page 256)* A state in which every conversation about a product, idea, approach, plan, or anything technical—data or product—is linked to the emotion that it is going to satisfy or relieve.

The God of Selling *(page 25)* That from which everything in selling comes; in this case, especially, the concept of closing, a sub-god to the God of Selling itself.

The Selling Chronicles

The Good Friend Personality *(page 104)* The part of you that creates an unfailing effort to be kind and look out for the betterment of your prospect. If one is not careful, it can lead to becoming a nice guy who makes no sales.

Hope *(page 81)* A state of mind that causes you to chase after the prospect. Often confused with goals. It is a thing that springs eternal. Good for love, bad for selling.

Hot Button *(page 74)* A mysterious hidden button that you have to find and push in order to make a sale. Somehow makes the prospect's temperature rise until he or she is hot (probably to trot).

Illusion Based Template *(page 243)* A mechanistic model or pattern based on the illusion that the world is linear and that you can prepare for every situation that arises.

Impulse Intuition *(page 227)* Intuition that forces you into action that you cannot stop or take time to consider. Not based on previous experience of any kind.

Interdependent Sales Meeting *(page 70)* A sales meeting where there is mutual respect between salesperson and prospect. Requires the unusual and rare ability to see others as human beings who are capable adults.

Intuition *(page 216)* Knowledge that is based on neither data nor experience. Comes in four flavors:
- Directive
- Analytical
- Predictive
- Impulsive

Also a quality used by psychics who are generally fakes. Be careful with intuition. A necessary quality to be handled with wisdom.

Knee-Jerk Party *(page 32)* Typical communication method between salesperson and prospect whereby one person reacts to the other without really knowing why. Often makes the knees sore.

The Lethal Business Personality *(page 105)* The part of you that creates an unfailing effort to create a solid business meeting and sales transaction. If one is not careful, it can lead to becoming a cold-hearted salesperson whose only interest is in making the sale.

Linear Thinking *(page 153)* Believing that to get from A to B you can walk in a straight line. Thinking that the world will adjust to your wishes so you can accomplish your goals. In sales, focusing on the close and going directly for it, no matter what.

Loaded Listening *(page 97)* Listening that seeks a specific objective, like a hot button or a closing opportunity. Better known as selective hearing.

Mantra *(page 75)* Something you repeat over and over again until you come to believe in it, e.g., you should always be closing.

Maybe *(page 184)* A *think about it* in disguise. A placating remark prospects use, designed to

My 21st Century Selling Vocabulary

give you hope for the future so you will give your prospects what they want now—information. Often used with children to placate them in the same way.

Mechanical Salesperson *(page 36)* An old-school salesperson who believes that a square peg fits any size hole. Akin to a bull in a china closet, or believing that if you walk a straight line in a world that is changing, you will get where you want to go.

Motivation to Buy or Do Business *(page 167)* The prospect's inner emotional drive to do business with you. Leads to a sale where the customer decides to buy based on his or her own emotional drive to change rather than your ability to 'close.' In other words, they close themselves as you sit back and relax.

The Must List *(page 245)* The ideas that must be consciously kept in mind in order to effectively move from an illusion based selling model to a reality based selling model.

No *(page 72)* A two letter word that ignites a salesperson's greatest selling fear: losing the sale. If the salesperson was spoiled as a child, this word especially rubs the wrong way. Most salespeople run from the word "no."

No Man Salesperson *(page 78)* A salesperson who has reversed his or her natural desire to get to "yes." It is akin to turning down a date with someone to whom you are really attracted.

Objection *(page 162)* Something the prospect doesn't like and that you usually get defensive about.

Off Balance *(page 209)* The state in which prospects reveal more than they want, including all problems your product or service may solve. It also could be the state in which you reveal more about your product or service than your prospect wants or should know, in which case he will thank you for the information and then give you a *think about it* stall.

Other People's Thinking *(page 240)* Thoughts, opinions, and ideas adopted from other people rather than from personal experience or your own creative processes. Most of what you think and believe.

Pain Dumping *(page 117)* Relieving your own pain, especially the fear of losing the sale, by dumping it on someone else, which, in selling, will be your prospect. Often leads to feeling better about losing the sale.

Predictive Intuition *(page 226)* Intuition that predicts the future. The most difficult intuition to come to trust. You just get a sense of it. No crystal ball will help here, just your clarity and attention.

Presentation *(page 256)* Old-school delivery of recommendations for a product or service, usually using a features/benefits approach. Now called Global Solution Matching because each feature and benefit is related to the emotional charges of the problem being solved.

Priority Killers *(page 133)* Land mines in your personality and emotions that blow up your true goals. Unconsciously switching your primary goal for a lesser goal. Leads to winning the battle but losing the war.

Probing *(page 72)* A selling game akin to "Where's Waldo?" Uses the process of poking clients with questions in hope of finding their hot buttons or tender spots. A tool also used by cowboys when they're herding cattle.

Prospect Dependency *(page 76)* When you look for help from the prospect in order to satisfy some personal emotional need, e.g., being liked, satisfying your ego, being a friend, or being appreciated.

Psychic Listening *(page 98)* The superhuman quality of hearing things that were never said. Sometimes called assuming and other times called mind reading. Most often heard are positive messages, especially buying signals.

Pull of the Future *(page 32)* Hopes, dreams, and fears that pull at you in the present moment. These condition and impact all your actions and decisions in sales meetings. Note: Your prospect is doing the same thing.

Pump Session *(page 30)* A process by which salespeople are pumped up, like balloons or tires, so they can do better at selling. Usually a lot of hot air is used. Known for momentary pain relief for selling failure.

Push of the Past *(page 31)* Past experiences, usually negative, that push you in the present moment and affect everything you do in a sales meeting. Note: Your prospect is doing the same thing.

Qualifying the Prospect *(page 179)* An undependable, old school, doctor-like examination performed on a prospect to determine if he is worthy of your selling efforts. Actually the opposite of what you should be doing: disqualifying the prospect and then letting him qualify himself. (See Disqualifying Prospects.)

Quantum Leap Thinking *(page 96)* Making a psychic jump in believing that once prospects express a desire for your product, or reveal a hot button, they are going to buy. Kind of like the smelling the aroma of good food and then believing that you already ate the meal.

Reality Based Chain of Events *(page 176)* A series of steps, linked to reality, that may occur in any order, but which lead to reliable and predictable results. Akin to great systems like FedEx, McDonald's, and Starbucks.

Reality Based Template *(page 244)* A reality based model utilizing specific patterns for developing sales that are suitable for a non-linear world that takes into consideration changing situations, actions, environments, and prospects.

Reality Chain of Events *(page 250)* A flexible sequence of events that effectively deals with every situation as it is presented. While the Reality Chain is often learned in a specific order, the order of its use is determined by what is happening in the sales meeting.

Relationship *(page 103)* Something that cannot be gained by intellectual discourse. Requires a significant and emotionally close connection between two people. Starts with the sharing of emotion.

My 21st Century Selling Vocabulary

It's the kind of connection you have with someone whom you are willing to let look into your closets.

Reverse World Thinking *(page 154)* The understanding that you often should do the opposite of what you think you should do to get where you want to go. To get the prospect to "yes," for example, you push him to "no." To get the prospect to buy your product, try to get him to buy a competitive product first.

Self-Fulfilling Prophecy *(page 56)* Something you bring upon yourself by what you do. In selling, it's stalls, objections, *think about its*, and virtually every other negative thing that happens to you in a selling situation. The common remedy to the Self-Fulfilling Prophecy is to blame someone else as the cause of your troubles. Creates a temporary feel-good moment that instantly dissipates when the problem soon reappears.

The Selling Barrier *(page 41)* A structure manually created by you and your prospect when using caveman selling techniques. Often used for a great game of hide-n-seek, whereby neither person really understands nor speaks truthfully to the other.

Selling Paradigm *(page 16)* Paradigm is a fancy word representing a set of theories, opinions and beliefs you are locked into. It's also a word that salespeople should never use with prospects.

Selling System *(page 175)* A chain of events that delivers predictable results. In selling, those results are either a buy decision, a no-buy decision, or a continuing appointment.

Silence *(page 148)* What you get to hear when your lips are not moving. That from which reality springs.

Social Meeting *(page 161)* Yap, yap yap; blah, blah, blah. All without any business meeting agreements such as those found in the *Five Elements of a Lethal Business Meeting*.

Stall *(page 94)* The prospect's developed ability to delay a decision while getting as much information from you as possible. Also a place where salespeople go to hang their heads in shame when their sales end up in the toilet.

Stalls and Objections *(page 42)* Elements within the Selling Barrier that are defensive tactics used by prospects to get information without making a decision. Often seen as a hurdle that needs to be jumped over, as if in a race. Typically creates panic and fear in the salesperson.

Stopping the World *(page 219)* The attempt to take the continuum of change and the unknown out of your life and selling situations. In other words, attempting the impossible.

Stuff *(page 146)* Your talk during a sales meeting, which doesn't improve on the silence it interrupts. (See *Blah, Blah, Blah.*)

Surface Issue *(page 69)* Any problem, issue, or concern your prospect willingly tells you about early on in the sales call.

Think About It *(page 82)* The natural result of a lousy selling system.

The Selling Chronicles

Tie-Down *(page 126)* Something usually done when capturing a criminal. In selling, it's a way of cornering the prospect. Similar to a trial close. Relies on the idea that prospects somehow need to be tied up in order to get a sale.

Trial Close *(page 126)* The act of testing your prospect's willingness to make a positive decision. Similar to polling a jury to see if they are going to convict or acquit a prisoner. In both cases, rarely will you get the truth.

Unconscious *(page 51)* The opposite of conscious. Remember what it was like to be in college?

The Unknown Zone *(page 218)* Territory with which you are unfamiliar and which is seen as a mysterious place to you. Not to be confused with a similar sounding sexual connotation.

Upstaging *(page 204)* Putting yourself in the spotlight. The process of making people dependent on you. Making yourself more important than you are. Basically, what you do most of the time, unless you're making an effort not to.

Wake Up *(page 19)* The process of becoming aware. Sometimes you will need an alarm clock or a wake-up call. In selling, it's not making sales over and over again, until one day the bell rings (usually when you go to the bank to make a withdrawal instead of a deposit).

Walking in Your Prospect's Footsteps *(page 102)* Joining your prospects on their personal journey; exploring their lives with them; taking them to places within themselves that they would not normally go; seeing life through their eyes, from their point of view.

Warm Up *(page 43)* The idea that people are somehow not warm already and need to be warmed up (like food in the microwave). Denies the fact if people are that cold they are probably dead.

Win-Win *(page 143)* Something you think you strive for as a salesperson but really don't. Face it: You're out for yourself.

Yes *(page 73)* A word old-school selling professionals try to elicit from their prospects at all times and in all ways; considered to have a rare kind of magic attached to it.

Yes Man *(page 71)* Salespeople who focus on getting yeses during their sales meetings because it makes them feel better and they think that they are getting nearer to the close. (See *Yes.*) Also a form of a selling exercise whereby the prospect's head nods up and down often enough to create a pattern that will continue when it comes time for the close.

Stay on Top of Your Selling!
Subscribe to *The Lewit Letter*

Each week you will receive step by step sales ideas that will ignite your sales calls and covers all aspects of the sales process presented in *The Selling Chronicles*. In *The Lewit Letter*, Steve will review the elements of his 21st century selling philosophy and system, and introduce new concepts that he develops in his meetings with clients. This invaluable weekly letter is available to you **FREE**.

To subscribe go to **www.stevelewitselling.com**.

Now you can get all your sales questions answered, hear Steve's latest war stories, and get insight into Steve's unique philosophy, understanding and strategies by visiting his blog at: **www.stevelewitblog.com**.